The Chancer

SHANE
LYNCH

WITH **STEVE LEGG**

The Chancer

CanaanPress

CanaanPress

ACKNOWLEDGEMENTS

A book is always something of a team effort and this one is no exception. Massive thanks to the following for all they've done to get it finished: Alexa Tewkesbury, Hugh Southon, Mark and Lynette Leitch, Andy Ashdown, Jonathan Coad at Swan Turton, Chris Gidney, Rebekah Barker, Cressida Canadas, John Aggett and Simon Day.

CONTENTS

Having It All

"HOW ON EARTH HAD THE SON OF A MECHANIC FROM THE NORTH SIDE OF DUBLIN ENDED UP HERE?"

Who would have thought it? Anyone who is anyone has played Wembley Arena: Madonna, Bruce Springsteen, Barbra Streisand, Kylie Minogue, Queen, The Who, Led Zeppelin, Status Quo, George Michael, Lionel Richie, Whitney Houston, The Rolling Stones, Eagles, Billy Joel, Diana Ross, Cher, David Bowie – the list goes on. And now it was our turn. For five incredible nights in a row – and all sold out.

It was 1999. I was living in Purley, just outside London, so I wasn't staying in the hotel with the rest of the lads for the Wembley gigs. Each afternoon, around 4.30pm, my car appeared to take me to the Arena. A gleaming silver Mercedes 500 series would draw up outside the front gates and my regular chauffeur, suited and booted, would press the intercom: 'Shane, I'm here.'

He drove up the long winding drive, parked up outside my front door and waited. Out I came in T-shirt and jeans, a skateboard tucked under my arm. This was it. The life I knew – rich, fast, magnificent. But I was missing it somewhere. I may as well have been getting the morning train to go to a regular nine to five stint. Somehow this was just another day at the office.

The Wembley complex is just off the A406 North Circular Road. The driver always took the same route and, once you saw the Conference Centre, you knew the Arena was right around the corner. That's when the nerves kicked in big time. And then there it was, the massive Boyzone banner flying over the top of the world famous venue.

Lining the streets were hordes of jostling, screaming fans, hungry for just a glimpse of a face in the car window. In amongst them were the ticket touts and guys knocking out dodgy merchandise and, as the car got closer to the drop-off point, the tension started to build amongst the crowd. You could almost see it manifest itself: all the waiting around, the shivering with cold and excitement, the eager anticipation culminating in an electrifying moment of ... *there's a car approaching!* The hysteria grew as we drove closer. I wanted to wind the window down, reach out a hand to wave and say hello to the loyal fans that had been waiting around all day long. But I daren't. I'd have been dragged clean out of the car.

You really don't know whether you're going to get through unscathed. At this moment, you don't know if anyone's going to get injured. It's actually quite intense. As we approached, our security guys were trying their best to sweep all the delirious girls out of the way so that the massive gates could be opened to let us through without any of the crowd getting in too.

I held my breath. The car was getting shaken around. There was banging on the windows. Girls were screaming. You could see the movement in the crowd, the pushing and shoving. All you hoped was that nobody got hurt. And the crowd was getting rowdier, shrieking and chanting, 'Boyzone ... Boyzone ... Boyzone!'

Once we got through the gates to the backstage area, that's when I knew I was safe. But outside, the crowd was still surging, desperately trying to get closer. As much as security hated it, me and the boys always went forward to the gates to sign autographs for as many people as possible before we got dragged away by the guards. Pretty extreme.

Barrie Knight, our head minder, always made sure every band member was safely inside. We were never very Americanised when it came to security and entourage, and liked to keep the team small. Everyone we employed we paid for ourselves. We were just a bunch of Irish lads who didn't come from a lot of money, so every penny counted. As far as we were concerned, why should we pay for a job that didn't need doing?

I was the last to arrive. I didn't tend to do the interviews. At that time I was that little bit loose-tongued and the lads preferred that I didn't speak for them, or myself. I had a reputation for being a loose cannon. I wasn't into fighting but if someone confronted me, I wouldn't back down.

Ronan, Stephen, Mikey and Keith were hanging around inside but, as the doors to backstage were always open, they'd usually pop out to have a kick around with a football. On this tour, though, the promoters had given us fancy electric scooters. Ronan was showing off in front of the fans on his. He sped around the car park and decided to pull a wheelie. What he didn't realise was that scooters don't work like that – and he landed on his arse on the ground with a great thud. Barrie Knight raced over to check he was all right, and we almost died laughing as he helped a very red-faced Ro to pick himself up and hobble meekly back inside.

Before sound checks and food, there were normally competition winners to meet. Today, there were only fifteen or so, but what they lacked in numbers they made up for in noise. They screamed the place down as we wandered into the room.

Steo was the first to approach the girls and they were genuinely awestruck to be coming face to face with him. We all had a chat, had photographs taken with them and signed CDs. A blonde girl was in tears as she hugged Ronan. He looked a bit bemused as he tried to talk to her and calm her down, but she just stared at him, tears streaming down her face. It was all par for the course. When the girls were finally ushered out of the room, we headed off to the stage for our sound checks, just a quick run through before dinner, which was always chicken. We were total chicken heads.

We sat down to eat and then we heard it: the first murmur of the fans. The doors had opened. The sound began like a little bass going. It was almost like music. You were vaguely aware of something going on. And then it got louder and you realised it wasn't music. It was the voices of the people coming through the doors, the throb of their eager footfalls, and the crash of the chairs they were pulling down to sit on.

All that noise just grew and grew. And that's when you realised you almost couldn't eat your chicken because you knew there were twelve thousand people pouring into the Arena. You wanted to eat but you knew everything going on outside was because the crowds wanted to see *you*. Then your heart would start to pound and, before you knew it, you could hear the songs playing. We used to pick out our favourites, the ones that would get us excited, like *California* by Dr Dray, or Thin Lizzy's *The Boys Are Back In Town.* Backed by the music, flashes of our individual faces were appearing on the screens for just a second, electrifying the entire stadium. You almost heaved at that moment, trying to build up your energy, trying to get your food down. You knew you had to eat before you went on stage, but at the same time you couldn't because of your belly twisting and the audience going crazy when you weren't even out there.

Then it was time to get changed. We always shared dressing rooms but we didn't sit down together before we went on. There was always something to think about – some dance routine you felt unsure of, or you'd be mulling over different scenes in the show. Everyone did their own thing. Mikey would be the one strumming away on the guitar. He was always very involved in the music, the instrumental side of things, and wrote songs with the musos from our band. Ronan might be starting or finishing an interview or doing something related to the music. Keith would be hanging around, drinking Red Bull and having the craic with the security and backstage people. He just enjoyed life, not focusing too much on anything, always living for the moment. Steo, on the other hand, would probably be away worrying somewhere. He panicked a lot before we went on stage. Out of all of us, he was always the best performer, but every night he'd get so wound up about going on. And then there'd be me, playing basketball or milling around on a skateboard, BMX or whatever I could find.

There were always two or three support acts to warm the audience up – not that it ever sounded as if they needed it. Then there was a five-minute break backstage. And this was our moment.

From the second we emerged through the floor amidst an impressive display of explosions and billowing smoke, the crowd knew it was going to be a night to remember. Our live shows could certainly deliver on spectacle. Energy and dynamism burst off the stage, beams of light flashed, twisted, changed from bright white to pink to blue in response to the mood of the music. And the dance moves – not always that sophisticated maybe, but powerful, pulsing to the beat that throbbed its way through the up tempo songs, and echoed by the movement in the audience as they swayed and waved in time, and sang enthusiastically along.

We seemed to speed through some of our better known hits, opening with *Picture Of You* and moving on to chart-toppers like *Baby Can I Hold You*, *Love Me For A Reason* and *You Needed Me*, where dancers threaded their way deftly around us carrying large, empty picture frames to frame our faces at strategic moments. Our 'disco' medley of *Celebrate*, *Blame It On The Boogie* (with Stephen singing his heart out in his absolute element) and *Grease* was a huge crowd-pleaser, as we strutted our stuff in our street gear, backed by the dance troupe full of fun and life.

The amazing array of costumes was like a show all on its own – from stylish suits to fleecy jackets to glittering extravagance. It was always me in the floor length coat, something to swirl around as I moved about the stage, while Ronan did a great line in memorable hats, including one that made it look as if a turkey had come to roost on his head.

As well as our usual hits, the show also gave us a chance to do our own thing, to reveal something of ourselves as individuals rather than always as a part of the band. But even Ro's performance of the *Notting Hill* hit, *When You Say Nothing At All*, touchingly accompanied in sign language, couldn't put Steo in the shade as he sailed over the auditorium on wires singing *Bright Eyes*.

Top it all off with a comically staged boxing match between Keith and Stephen, a moment of stunning percussion beaten out on corrugated iron sheets and inflated lilos, extraordinary pillars of flame, and a brilliant hail of sparks raining down as we belted out the final song, and I guess you have a sensational 90 minutes.

When we'd finished, we hurtled through the trap doors and backstage to the dressing room, threw on our dressing gowns and shot straight out of the back door. The tour bus was there waiting to whisk us away to the hotel and we dived on board. There was never any hanging around. We had to bolt before any of the fans got out. Our costumes were always wet with sweat by the end of the show, and it was a relief to change into our normal gear on the bus. Wardrobe would always be there to gather up the outfits ready for washing and pressing in time for the next gig.

It was 10.45pm by the time we finally got to the hotel. I said goodbye to the lads and then sat back in the silver Mercedes that would take me home again. It was the end of another hugely successful night. But I was used to that. Success seemed to follow us wherever we went. I was 22 years old, enormously wealthy with a lifestyle I could never even have dreamed of a few years ago: a £1,000,000 house, a Porsche and Ferrari parked up in the garage. I had it made.

How on earth had the son of a mechanic from the north side of Dublin ended up here?

CHAPTER 1

The Charmer

"I WASN'T A SWAT, BUT THEN I DIDN'T WANT TO BE. I
ENDED UP SOMEWHERE IN THE MIDDLE. AND THAT'S
HOW MY NEXT BLAGGING JOURNEY BEGAN."

The summer of 1976 was a scorcher. Long, lazy days melting into hot, sultry nights. The heat wave that hit went on for weeks, with temperatures soaring to 95°F. There was a drought, hosepipe bans were in force, and the heat was so intense it caused the ground to crack and even the tar melted on roads.

It was the year Ford launched their new Cortina, the Mk IV, which was to become a huge success. The Eurovision Song Contest was won by Brotherhood Of Man with *Save Your Kisses for Me*. Elton John and Kiki Dee's *Don't Go Breaking My Heart* was number one for six weeks and seemed to be playing almost everywhere. And then, of course, there was The Wurzels, with their unforgettable *Combine Harvester*.

Also in 1976, on Saturday 3 July, I was born to proud parents Noleen and Brendan in the Coombe Hospital in Dublin. They named me Shane Eamonn Lynch, and happily took me home to Grangemoor Drive,

Donaghmede in Dublin.

We lived in quite an ordinary, four-bedroomed house that just happened to have a three-car garage and a swimming pool. It was the only place with those luxuries on a fairly regular estate. I was the one boy in our family and I had two older sisters, Tara then Alison, and three younger, twins, Keavy and Edele, and little Naomi who came along five years later.

The two older girls were always getting in trouble. They stayed out too late, they went nightclubbing when they should have been studying, and their taste in boyfriends was a particular source of strife. Alison even dated a certain Mr Keith Duffy who was to become a fellow Boyzone band member years down the line. She was the one who did the most outrageous things, but for some reason it was my oldest sister Tara who tended to take the flak for it all.

I learned a lot from my two big sisters about the tricks of ducking and diving. I was able to watch them and see where they went wrong – not in what they did, necessarily, but in how they gave themselves away and ended up getting caught. That's how I discovered ways to get around my parents and avoid them finding out what I was really up to.

I used to spend a lot of time with the twins as were we growing up, although I'd have to say I was a terrible rogue. I wasn't happy unless I made them cry at least once a day. Whenever they were enjoying themselves, just having fun and playing, I'd take their dolls away and trash the clothes the twins had lovingly dressed them in. Sometimes I'd even cut the hair off those poor dollies or yank their arms and heads off, or, if I was feeling really evil, I'd pull the stuffing out of their Care Bears. I honestly was a truly horrible big brother, an absolute torment to those little girls. For some reason, I always looked at them as very much younger than I was, absolute babies compared to me, but there were actually only a few years between us.

It was Naomi who I always thought of as my little kid sister. I didn't give her a hard time. She was the one I was probably closest to because we spent a number of years sharing a bedroom when she was a baby. I suppose petty brother and sister spats are fairly harmless, all part of growing up in a family and, looking back, I did have an amazing childhood. I never wanted for anything. My Ma, Noleen, was a homemaker. She didn't go out to work but was always there looking after us, keeping everything ticking over in the house, making sure we washed behind our ears. I always remember how she loved to paint. She created the most wonderful oil paintings.

My dad, Brendan, was my hero. I guess we bonded as well as we did back then because our house was full of women – although neither of us would have dared say so at the time! His interests were my interests. He was a mechanic and not only fixed cars but raced them as well. I thrilled to watch him at the stock-car events and working on hot-rods. He owned his own garage and was up and away by 5.00am every day for the 30-minute drive to work. As he was always long gone by the time I was out of my bed and downstairs, I suppose I never really got to see that much of him. But on Friday nights he would try to come home early, and I remember I wouldn't eat my dinner until he arrived. I must have driven my ma spare just sitting there, waiting and waiting. I'd peer impatiently through the front curtains, hoping and praying he might have brought me some ball bearings from a car at the garage, or maybe even an air filter. I used to play with the air filters, dropping my toy cars inside them and using them for a loop the loop.

Yes, Friday was special. It was my dad's steak, chips and onions night and there was no way I was going to eat or get myself to bed until he was back.

That really was a highlight for me – my dad coming home with ball bearings or air filters for me to play with. We had a conservatory. I used to call it my 'porch', and nobody was allowed in there because that's where I kept my treasures: my toy cars. I had every car you could possibly imagine, and I made my own garages, houses and petrol stations out of shoeboxes and cornflakes packets until I'd built a massive town. If anyone ever wanted to find me, that's where I'd be – lost in my own world, the cardboard kingdom of my porch.

I liked to make my games as realistic as I could. So much so that, if I was setting up a road accident, I'd sometimes take my dad's hammer to the odd Dinky car. As far as I was concerned, if a car was in a crash then it should look as if it had been in a crash – and, believe me, that's just what a hammered Dinky car looks like! Then I'd bring in the police cars and line up the family cars full of onlookers. Everything had its perfect place and purpose. I loved my cars.

Every Sunday, without fail, Ma and Dad would march us the five-minute walk down to our local church. It was part of our Sunday ritual whether we liked it or not. Off we'd be dragged (usually kicking and screaming), the girls in their dresses and me in my Sunday best – a pair of slacks and a smart jumper. The service always bored us out of our minds, but my dad loved it. He's a very religious man and, no matter where in the world he is or what language is being spoken, he'll find a church on a Sunday. He never attends the whole service though, just slips in half an hour before the end. Every Sunday, wherever he happens to be. That's the routine.

As we grew up, my parents took us on the most wonderful family holidays, although I think I was sometimes a little too young to appreciate them. We went to Disney World in Florida when I was only three years old. I don't honestly recall how I felt about exploring those amazing parks, but I do remember that, after meeting Mickey Mouse, I asked, 'Can we go home now?' All I really wanted was to be able to play with my cars again. It was a case of, 'Yes, there he is, we've done Mickey Mouse. Can I get back to my porch now, please?'

I was lucky enough to go to Disney World again when I was about 14 years old and that time the wonder of it all didn't pass me by. I had an absolute ball.

One of our regular holiday haunts was a caravan park near the seaside, not far from where we lived. We made friends with another family, the Courtneys, who were also regulars there, and we quickly became very close. There were three boys, David, Brian and Colin, and two girls, Tracey and Grace. Their father was a mechanic like my dad, so they had a lot in common. Tracey and our eldest, Tara, became best pals. The two younger boys, Brian and Colin, hung around with Alison and me, while the twins had endless fun playing with their youngest, Grace. They were fantastic times. We'd stay in their caravan; they'd stay in ours. We'd have barbecues and go to the beach together.

We made friends with some of the other kids at the caravan park, too. That's where I encountered Darren Robinson. He was a couple of years older than we were, and the coolest kid we'd ever come across. Not only that but he also had the best bike in the world. I didn't have any idea what type it was, but it was like a Chopper with mirrors and aerials, all chrome with a sleek, long, black leather seat. Unbelievable. Darren wore an earring and I reckon he used to dye his hair black – and he was just a kid. But what a wild child. He was the leader of a gang called the Skulls. We were just a band of innocent, ordinary little kids who always got picked on. So we decided to form our own gang and called it the Dragons.

These were our summer holidays – endless hours of bike chases, fights at the sandpit and eating ice cream. Crazy, great days.

Then there were our family Christmases. And they were just brilliant. Our house was magical at Christmas time and Santa was a big and exciting part of our lives. My parents made setting up the tree a real occasion. It always looked magnificent, draped in tinsel from top to toe and shimmering all over with lights and baubles. And the night before Christmas, there we'd be, all ready to get to bed early, even though we knew we'd never be able to sleep. But before we went off to our bedrooms, we'd fetch a glass of milk and some cookies for Santa, not forgetting carrots for his reindeer, and then we'd gather round and each hold a bit of the plate of goodies as we slipped it under the tree.

My nana would always spend a week in our house at Christmas time and she was great fun. We used to sit down and watch *The Golden Girls* and Elvis movies together. I was mad about Elvis.

Then, as we got a bit older, each Christmas Eve my ma and dad would always go over to my ma's brother who lived just around the block. On Christmas night, the cousins came to our house. There were three of them and we'd disappear off and rehearse some sort of little play which might be about anything, from the story of the birth of Jesus to characters on children's TV. We might also act out a little tale about Santa Claus where we'd be dressed up as reindeer. Every year we'd perform something for both sets of parents, and it was hilarious. I guess it also gave me my first taste of having an audience.

Like a lot of young children, I don't suppose anything could really have prepared me for my first day at primary school. The school itself was only five minutes away from our house but, even so, both my parents drove me there with my sisters on that first morning. I had no idea what was in store as I watched the two older ones stride confidently off into some pre-fab buildings that made up the Santa Sabina schoolhouse.

Trailing meekly along behind my parents, I remember peering anxiously around at the funny wooden buildings – and that's when I came face to face with them – the nuns who were to be my teachers. They towered over me, an austere huddle of severe-looking ladies dressed from head to toe in deepest black. I didn't know what nuns were. I'd never seen them before. I didn't understand why they were here. All I knew was that I was scared.

They led us off to be introduced to the children whose class I would be joining, which I thought was all right. Having to say goodbye to my parents, on the other hand, was another matter altogether, and I broke down and bawled. I just cried my eyes out and I couldn't stop. My face was burning hot and it must have been as red as a tomato, but I didn't care. My ma and dad had gone off and left me and I was devastated. When one of the teachers finally managed to calm me down a little, I took a tentative peek at the other children in the classroom and they were all girls. Would you believe it? I was surrounded by girls at home and now, here I was, the only boy in a school full of girls.

It didn't really register straight away because, after all, it's what I was used to. But then it came to my first art lesson and, to protect my clothes, the teacher expected me to wear a pink and white check smock. That was it. Hold it right there. I was not a girl and this was *not* going to work out. I burst into tears again and refused point blank to put on this ridiculous pink 'thing'. Nothing on earth would persuade me to wear what the girls were wearing. I stood my ground and, in the end, I got a special smock all of my own. Only this one was a fetching *green* and white check.

That was the beginning, I guess. The beginning of a different approach to life for me. The beginning of survival. I was four years old and thrown, wide-eyed and clueless, into an all girls' school, with black-shrouded nuns for teachers. And I rebelled.

Things went downhill from there. As time went on, my dad was called into school a couple of times because I'd sworn at the nuns. Then came the morning he was ushered in to face the headmistress.

She sat him down, coughed delicately and said in a hushed voice, 'Now, Brendon, we have a problem.'

My dad was self-employed and didn't allow himself to get called away from work for just any old thing. This must be important.

'It's Shane,' the headmistress continued, as if she could barely believe it herself. 'He keeps swearing at the Sisters.'

My dad is a straightforward man. He sees things in black and white. For every problem, there's an obvious solution.

'Right,' he said calmly. 'When he gets home from school, I'll bounce him off every wall in the house.'

The headmistress was horrified.

'Oh, no, no, no,' she spluttered, with a nervous little shake of her head. 'Oh, no, no, it's absolutely fine. We're just letting you know that we're okay with it.'

After that, the nuns never called my dad again. From then on, they turned a blind eye to my little misdemeanours at school. So, there I was, getting away with things – and growing accustomed to getting away with things. Of course, my dad was only joking when he spoke to the headmistress. He had no intention of punishing me. In fact, he's never laid a finger on me in all my life. But that was the end of my troubles as far as school was concerned, because the nuns decided it would be better not to discipline me or report my ill doings to my parents in case I went home to a beating. I had long hair, just like my dad and my sisters too. I was something of an innocent-looking boy with that little bit of charm. But it was enough. And I got away with absolute murder.

I spent a lot of playtimes messing around on the monkey bars. I got to be quite nifty on them in the end. I'd climb right to the top to impress the girls because I was the only boy. They were a big attraction, those monkey bars. That's where you'd find me almost every day. And that's where I met Debbie. She was a beautiful girl, tanned, brown hair swinging around her face in pigtails, and soft, brown eyes. Her older sister was in the same class as my older sister and, whenever there was a birthday party going on, my sister invited Debbie too. She would come to our house and we'd hang out together. Me and Debbie Hughes. My first love and my very best friend.

But change was coming. A huge change. After I'd made my first Communion, I had to go to a different school. I found myself moving from an all girls' to an all boys' school called St Brigid's in Killester. It was a big shock to me. All of a sudden, I was walking into a place full of boys. I was no longer the king of the monkey bars. I was the same as everybody else and I didn't really like it.

I'll never forget my first day. It was horrible. At the age of six, I was quite a tall kid and I looked older than I was. I was supposed to go into the Infants but I was actually marched straight into the Juniors because of my height. Apparently, there were two Shanes due to start that day and they thought I was Shane for the Juniors.

I remember being shuffled into this classroom and, as I stared blankly around, everyone might as well have been speaking Chinese to me. I had no idea what was going on. I just huddled there, stock still on a chair that was too big for me, in what seemed to me like a massive room. I could have been in Wembley Arena, gazing round, completely silenced by the utter enormity of the place. That's how I felt in that classroom – tiny, and so very, very scared. The blackboard by itself was about the biggest thing I'd ever seen in my life. I remember having to sit there with everyone around me doing maths, and I suddenly felt as if my whole life was crashing down around me. The other kids all had their heads down getting on with something that meant nothing to me. I didn't understand a word. And then that harsh, familiar lump started to rise in my throat. I couldn't fight it and, just as on my first day with the nuns, tears got the better of me.

The teacher peered at me curiously and asked, 'What's wrong with you?' I didn't know how to explain and, even if I had, I was so choked with sobs I don't suppose I'd have been able to get the words out. But then I heard that knock at the door – the knock that rescued me. A teacher marched in with another boy and explained very calmly, as if it happened all the time, that there'd been a mix up. This other boy was the Shane for the Juniors and I was in the wrong place. I remember thinking, thanks be to God. I was saved. Somehow I'd been plucked from this monstrous situation. It was better than a miracle.

Down in the Infant classroom I could breathe again. The chairs and desks were tiny and the crayons small enough for my stubby little fingers. I was back in the world I understood and felt comfortable with. My teacher, I learned, was called Mrs Pearce. She was very tall and not too stern, but definitely not too friendly either.

That was the year I realised I had a problem. I was different from the rest of the kids. All of my classmates could write their names. I couldn't. They could all spell. I couldn't. I tried hard but somehow my brain didn't seem to work that way. I couldn't read or write and I couldn't figure out why. And one day, I came to a decision. I made up my mind that no one was ever going to find out.

St. Brigid's was a major sports school. That's why my parents sent me there. We played Irish football, did high jump, long jump, sprint, and all the main athletic events. Basketball was also important in the school, and I began to concentrate all my efforts on being the very best at every one of those sports. I certainly had academic failings, but being a top sportsman somehow gave me the opportunity to gloss them over.

In the classroom, I got to be quite an expert at copying and cheating. After spelling tests, we had to swap papers with our neighbour so we could mark each other's work. Because I was a big guy, the lad sitting next to me always played safe and corrected my mistakes in case I decided to wage war on him, which, of course, he didn't want. Gradually, I began to be seen as one of the cooler kids in the class. I wasn't cheeky so I tended not to get caught by the teachers, but I was definitely one of the lads. David Peter Peddereski became one of my best mates and we were close for a long time. He was an intelligent guy who could write well, whereas I couldn't. But then, I was big, strong and popular. So we looked after each other and, during our primary school years, went through quite a lot together in that place.

I continued to be the school sportsman. I seemed to get a gold medal in everything. From time to time we'd be taken to an international arena where all the schools in Ireland would come together. We'd compete against hundreds of great athletes and I was the one bringing home plaques, trophies and cups for my school. I was very, very athletic as a kid but, as far as I could see, that's what I had to be. I had to have something to make up for the fact that I couldn't do what the rest of the kids seemed able to do so easily. I couldn't read, write or spell.

No one knew much about dyslexia then. It wasn't recognised the way that it is now. I was always getting letters and numbers round the wrong way and leaving letters out of words. But rather than tell anybody I was struggling with reading and writing, I just did my best to avoid it. I did what I thought was writing and what I hoped made sense. If I was asked to read my work out loud, I'd just make up a story right there and then. I wasn't reading what I'd written. That's how I got by and how I managed to blag the whole thing. My teachers were forever saying to me, 'Shane, I can't read this. I can't make head or tail of what's on this paper. What is it you're saying here?' Nobody could read what I wrote. Even *I* couldn't read what I wrote. So I'd just have to make it all up as I went along. That's how I dealt with it. And I guess that's also how I got away with it for so long.

But as I approached my last few weeks at junior school, my parents were finally called in. It must have been a devastating moment for them when they were told their son could barely read or write. I know my dad went absolutely mental with the school. I was 11 years old. I'd been in that place for four or five years. How in the world could it be, then, that I couldn't read or write?

The Principal of the school was a creepy character. There was just something about him. Nobody wanted to be alone with him. He'd stroke your head and sometimes put his hand on the back of your shirt. He was an odd kind of man. I'll never forget him.

I remember what seemed at the time to be one of the worst moments of my life. In my last year before I went up to secondary school, I got taken off all the sports teams because of the Principal.

At the end of every afternoon, I'd come out of school to get the bus home. As often as not I'd be at the bus stop with my mate, Thomas Kelly. He lived close to my house, which was about half an hour's ride from our school. On this particular day, Thomas happened to get into a scrap with another kid at the bus stop, and my teacher, Mr Fox, cycled past at just the wrong moment and caught him fighting. He yelled at us, 'Right! You, Mr Kelly, and you, Mr Lynch, down to the Principal's office first thing tomorrow.'

Now on the way home, the two of us decided that this wasn't going to happen. We weren't going to go anywhere near the Principal's office because he was just such a weird guy. So we hatched a little plot together, and the next day was the very first time we ever bunked off school. We got on the bus in the morning as usual so that our parents wouldn't suspect anything but, as it drew up at the school stop, we slid down in our seats, stayed where we were, and went on in the bus into town. We spent the whole day walking around the Ilac Shopping Centre in Dublin, then caught the bus back at end of school time and went home.

All this to avoid being hauled along to the Principal's office. Of course we were left with a bit of a problem because the following day we'd have to explain why we'd been absent. I didn't know how Thomas was going to deal with it, but I persuaded my sister, Tara, to write me a letter and I forged my ma's signature. I was very good at that because I was already doing it almost every night. We had to have our homework signed so, by now, I was pretty much a master forger. I must have forged my Ma's signature for years and even my dad's at times.

The next day, I sauntered brashly into school with the letter in my pocket. I wasn't the slightest bit concerned. No-one would suspect a thing.

Later that morning, the tannoy went. It was the Principal. He was calling Thomas Kelly down to his office. Thomas dutifully went off but, after a while, he was back – and the tannoy sounded again: 'Will Shane Lynch come down to the office.' I wasn't worried. I had my letter, this little golden ticket, and I'd shown it to my teacher who had accepted it without a problem. Only, that's when I looked at Thomas Kelly. He was wearing the shiftiest, guiltiest face. He'd told on me. He'd ratted me out. He'd said to the Principal that he'd gone into town with me. And there was my carefully forged escape plan, completely blown out of the water.

It was like a film in slow motion; almost as if I was watching myself slope along the corridors to the office. All I could think was that I'd have to stand in front of this odd man who might rub my back and touch me. Part of me wanted to bolt, to get out and go home, but I knew I couldn't. I took a deep breath, knocked reluctantly on the door and went in.

'Sit down,' the Principal said.

I did as I was told. He was on the other side of the desk but I didn't really look at him. I couldn't.

'Okay,' he went on after an uncomfortable moment. 'Now, obviously

Thomas has told me his side of the story that you were in town with him yesterday. What do you want to do about it? Do you want me to phone your parents now, or do you want to take this letter home to them?'

He held out a sealed envelope. I couldn't wait to get out of that room, so I agreed to take the letter.

My ma knew something was wrong the moment I walked through the front door. I thought, if I explain it to her before my dad gets home, maybe she won't tell him about it. Maybe she'll just keep it between us. Our little secret. So I blurted it all out. I didn't give her the letter at the time, but I told her what I'd been up to.

'I bunked off school. I'm in trouble.'

Then I waited. But my Ma was actually all right about it, although she said she'd have to tell my dad. I guess that was one of the days I didn't look forward to him coming home.

When he got in, we walked slowly down the garden to the shed where the swimming pool was and had a talk. Amazingly, he was quite calm about it all, like my mum. He didn't rant or shout. It was more, 'Sit down with me, Shane, and tell me why. What happened?' At that moment, I just broke down. I told him how I'd bunked off school because the Principal was gay and I couldn't stand the thought of being alone with him in his office. My dad was as confused as hell. I tried to explain to him how the Principal was weird and felt up kids at school but, not surprisingly, he couldn't make it out and decided to pay him a visit.

I waited in the library for what seemed like an absolute age while my dad was in with him, talking. I have no idea what it must have been like for him, marching into this man's office to confront him with the things I'd said and the allegations I'd made. I couldn't even imagine the conversation. In truth, I didn't really want to.

My dad eventually came back to the library to get me and take me with him to the Principal's office. I felt sick. I'd said all these things about this man – and now I had to face him.

Dad said, 'Look, son, the Principal and I have had a chat. Do you really understand the difference between gay and straight?'

There I was, 11 years old, and he was asking, 'Do you understand this?' I stared at him. 'Yeah, I think I do.'

Then he explained that the Principal had a wife and kids of his own. And, to me, that was my dad telling me everything was all right.

I'll never forget the smug expression on the Principal's face as he sat behind his desk looking across at me. Then he got up out of his chair and came round to shake my dad's hand.

'Thanks, Brendon,' he said.

We turned to walk out of the door. My dad went first, but when I moved in front of the Principal, he patted me on my backside.

I didn't say a word. I said nothing because my dad said there was no problem. My dad said it was all right. But, even then, I knew the Principal had just said to me: 'Gotcha.'

From that moment, The Principal made sure I was taken off the basketball team, the track team, in fact every sporting team going and everything I enjoyed. He set about ruining anything good I had going for me in my last six months at that school.

Just before I broke up from there for the final time, I had to sit my secondary exam so that the new school could grade pupils for classes. With my literacy record, I don't suppose anyone expected me to pass. But, once again, I cheated my whole way through. I was brilliant at copying. I was able to write the alphabet but I couldn't put it together in words and sentences. What I could do, though, was copy what other people had written, in the same way as I could forge my ma's signature.

In that exam, I sat next to a lad called Karl Melhorn, and that was how I got graded. I sat next to him, I copied all that he had written, and I got myself put into class 1 of Sligo house in my new school. I wasn't a swat, but then I didn't want to be. I ended up somewhere in the middle. And that's how my next blagging journey began.

CHAPTER 2

Fools On Horses

"THE TIME WAS COMING WHEN I'D HAVE TO FACE MY DAD. I COULDN'T AVOID IT FOREVER. BUT HOW ON EARTH I'D FIND THE COURAGE, OR THE WORDS, I REALLY DIDN'T HAVE A CLUE."

With the shift up to secondary school came another huge adjustment for me. The Grange Community College in Dublin was a mixed school and, once again, I found myself scared witless as I tried to hide away in a corner of the unfamiliar classroom, surrounded for the first time in my academic life by boys *and* girls.

Most of my days in that school, just like in the others, were a question of survival. I had to muddle my way through the educational maze as best I could without being noticed. I wanted to impress the girls in my class but, as I still struggled badly with reading and writing and didn't want them to think I was stupid, I needed to reinvent myself. So I worked on being the charmer more than anything else. And it paid off. Even the teachers seemed to like me. In those early days, they thought of me as a polite boy, an all-round Mr Nice Guy. That was the only way I could get away with things. There was no point not putting the work in and being a troublemaker too. My life would only have got worse.

To be honest, by then I was really just living for my bikes. I got my very first when I was three, and then my first BMX when I was eight. My love for bikes came from my dad and his ardent enthusiasm for motorbikes and cars. As the new biking craze hit Ireland in the 1980s, my BMX became my passion. You could ride a BMX fast and do incredible manoeuvres and stunts. Seized as I was with a growing desire for speed and danger, that was just perfect.

Derek Kane was a mate from school. He was a year older than I was, but we had this shared interest in bikes so when we heard about a big BMX Championship, we decided we wanted to take part. Kaner's bike was hand-painted green with black bars, black rim, and one front brake. Mine was probably a little more outdated than that, but it was still heavy framed, and we made up our minds we were going racing.

When the day of the Championship came, we couldn't get anyone to give us a lift, so we cycled 12 miles to get to the competition at Balbriggan. Our lunch was stuffed into the rucksacks on our backs – sandwiches, a bottle of milk and a stick of black pudding. Whenever my friends bought Mars bars and a can of coke, I always bought milk and a black pudding!

We arrived eventually on our pretty well clapped-out bikes – and we could hardly believe our eyes. There were massive Winnebagos, caravans and trailers scattered about, and a host of BMXs were being lovingly fine-tuned by mechanics. We could have been walking down the pit lane of a Formula 1 event, gazing admiringly at all the state of the art equipment and machinery, and then glancing back at our two humble Morris Minors standing geekily in the car park. It was stunning and surreal. We just looked at each other and burst out laughing. What in the world were we doing here? We didn't have helmets, gloves or fancy outfits. It was just us and our tired, old bikes. We went to sign up and, even though we were clutching our birth certificates, as usual the admin people wouldn't believe I was the age I said because I was tall.

The guy in charge of registration asked, 'Where's your gear?'

Kaner and I looked at each other. Of course, we didn't have any gear. So we were sent along to this fella in a red van, and out came some off-cuts of old orange carpet which he wrapped around our bikes for padding. We couldn't help chuckling again. We didn't think it was possible for those bikes to look any worse than they did in amongst the glitzy new ones all around us – but that was before we saw them all wrapped up in ripped pieces of old carpet!

We eyed up the BMXs the other lads had. They were beautiful. And the riders had shiny helmets and glossy gloves. We weren't going to be put off, though. We managed to borrow a couple of crusty old helmets and up to the start we went. Derek was going to be racing first because he was in the older age group.

And there the riders were – poised, focused, adrenalin pumping, all ready to launch into the fray. As the starter snapped 'Go!', the gate dropped (something else we weren't expecting) and out the riders went. For an instant, Kaner was left standing at the start line, but not for long. As soon as he grasped what was going on, the life burst through him and he shot off like a rocket as fast as he could pedal.

Now most of the kids at that age slowed down for the hills, which were called doubles and tabletops. But not us. Kaner and me, that's what we did. We spent our lives jumping doubles and table tops and when it came to these, while the other kids held back, Kaner seized his moment and flew – straight past three of them and right over the table top. He'd done it. Kaner had finished his first race and won in spectacular fashion.

Then it was my turn. I sat astride my bike hoping that maybe I had a little bit more of an idea what was going on now. I was ready for action at the starting gate, literally trembling with fear and anticipation, my foot against the metal plate. I glanced left, then right at all the guys lined up on their amazing array of hi tech BMXs. Then I looked down at my carpeted old rust-bucket and asked myself for the second time that morning, 'What on earth do you think you're doing here?'

The announcement came: 'Pedals ready.' The gate dropped. And away I went.

All my attention was concentrated on what lay ahead. I don't even remember breathing. But I couldn't see anyone around me. Where were all the others? Should I look back? No. Just keep going. Over the table tops to the next section jumps. You can do this!

When I arrived at the finishing line, I was sweating and gasping. I couldn't speak. And there was still nobody. I'd left them all for dead.

I could see Kaner standing at the end, shaking his head in total bewilderment. Neither of us could believe what was going on. We'd cycled 12 miles to get to the Irish Championships. Our bikes were worth tuppence and looked ridiculous draped in ragged carpet. We had no gloves or helmets other than what we'd been able to scrounge. We were new lads on the circuit yet we'd torn the place up! We'd left these guys standing. We had three races each that day and won the lot of them. As we rode triumphantly home with our trophies in our rucksacks, we still couldn't really make it out.

After that day, we were officially BMX crazy. A couple of race mad kids, almost everywhere we turned up the other boys seemed to hate us. I suppose we'd become minor BMX celebrities, and they didn't like it at all. Our biking 'careers' kind of grew from there. We won prize money, we'd spend it on the bikes, and we just got better and better.

From BMX bikes, we eventually made the natural progression to motorbikes. That was when I got into engines in a really big way. My dad's garage was virtually attached to a police station and, as he'd fixed a couple of the cops' cars, he had a good relationship with them. Two off-road scramblers happened to be dumped out the back of the station. They'd never been claimed, and one of the coppers asked my dad if he wanted them. Because I was only 12 and Kaner 13, we weren't officially allowed to ride these machines on the street, but there was nothing to stop us learning everything we could about them. We spent hours stripping those bikes down, opening up the engines, putting new forks on.

Of course, in the end, the temptation to get out on them was too great. I got a part-time job mowing lawns to pay for petrol and new tyres, and we rode up and down the roads without helmets or protective gear – a BMX throwback. We'd get home from school, tinker with the bikes, and start getting into conversations with other bikers. They'd tell us, 'If you file this down and file that down, you'll get it going quicker,' and that's what we'd do. We'd come in, file a bit down, and go back out on the road to see if it made any difference. We must have spent hours on those motorbikes and the neighbours grew to hate us. Then the police would come around. We didn't really cause that much trouble but, all the same, what we were doing was illegal so, after a while, it seemed that the safest place to do our riding was at the beach.

We used to push the bikes up to a place called Donabate, my family's summer caravan hotspot when we were young children. Kaner and his family had moved from Grangemoor to Donabate because they wanted to get into the whole golf scene, but, once he was there, all Kaner wanted to do was ride motorbikes. He would get the train down to where I lived and we'd push our beloved mounts for around 12 miles to get to the beach.

It would sometimes take us six hours to do that walk, although I have to admit that if we saw the slightest patch of green and no one was about, we'd quickly jump on the bikes and hare across that field before anyone saw us. Then we'd turn the engines off and push across the road to the next stretch of grass. That's how we made it all the way to Donabate. Once we were there, we'd ride the beach all day, throwing up spray and churning the sand. We loved it. We were kings of the seashore and in biking heaven. As the tide retreated and the ocean dropped back, we'd go down to the shoreline and have the time of our lives, even though we ended up having to dig the bikes out over and over as the wheels stuck deep in the marshy sand.

My growing up was packed with fun weekends and wild days like that. My dad's garage business was booming. He was a hard-working man and never spoke about difficult times. As far as we kids were concerned, all our times were the best, and we seemed to have plenty of everything. Not that we were a generation who wanted to have it all. It wasn't like that. We had our BMXs and our motorbikes, and if our motorbikes broke down and we couldn't fix them, we rode the BMXs. And if our BMXs had punctures, we rode our skateboards. As far as I was concerned, I didn't want for anything. My only problem was that Monday morning or the start of a new term seemed to be forever just around the corner, and, for me, that was always an enormous reality check.

I would do my utmost to be late for school. Apparently if you were late, you got sent home. I had a few goes at it and it worked. If it happened more than five times, you got suspended for a week. What more could an academic no-hoper like me ask for than being sent home and suspended? Of course, I made sure my parents never knew a thing. Every morning I'd get up, put my uniform on and hide my trainers and tracksuit bottoms in my school bag. As quietly as I could, I'd push my motorbike out of the garage and hide it down the side of the house. Then off I'd go to school – or so my parents thought. My dad would get away to work, my ma would go shopping or out to see friends. And me, I'd be able to sneak back and get the bike, then ride it over the fields. That's how I spent many happy, suspended days when everyone at home thought I was at school, tearing up the cornfields (and even the occasional golf course) on my motorbike.

Over one thousand students attended The Grange Community College, the boys drably dressed in a uniform of grey slacks, grey jumper and a grey and red striped tie. The girls were identical except that their jumpers were red. As time went on, I didn't always bother with the uniform.

The school itself was a hexagonal shape. I never really saw the point. To get around, you needed to go one way along a single main corridor. That was the route you had to follow. You couldn't make your way back against the tide of oncoming bodies.

If ever I was told off in school during my first few terms, it wasn't for making trouble. Apart from my tendency to be late, it was usually because I just couldn't understand anything. I didn't feel as though I belonged. It was the same old story. Words were a complete puzzle to me and, as I found reading and writing such an impossible mountain to climb, how was I meant to make sense of it all?

I suppose maths was my favourite subject because at least numbers weren't quite such a problem for me. I wasn't by any means the best in the class, but I could probably do maths better than I could do anything else. I enjoyed art too. Perhaps some of my ma's artistic ability had rubbed off on me. Then there was woodwork. I liked it because it was a physical thing, and my practical projects always turned out pretty well. I started off making simple boxes with dovetail joints, then moved on to crafting baseball bats on the lathe. I used to make them quite square and knobbly. I loved the smell of the wood, the warmth of it between my fingers and the sense of satisfaction as I transformed it into something with definite shape and purpose. When it came to the theory, though, I just couldn't do it, so I always failed my exams.

I'll always remember school for one particular teacher. His name was Dinny Ryan. He was Irish (Gaelic) and he was totally nuts. Absolutely mental. I hated Irish and didn't understand the first thing about it until I had Mr Ryan as my teacher. He was brilliant. Kaner, my BMX pal, was taught by him before I knew that much about him, and the stories he told me about this crazy Irishman were so far-fetched I never used to believe them. But then it was my turn to be put in Mr Ryan's class. And I found it was all true. Every word of it. The man would wreck tables, break chairs, throw blackboard dusters at you, punch holes in doors. His temper was that fiery and quick. He may have been fairly ordinary-looking, with brown, wavy hair and glasses perched on his nose, but when he exploded into a fury, his face turned bright red – and that was when you got scared.

Mr Ryan was the kind of guy who got on well with the kids who weren't so clever. If you were a swat, he'd tease you and give you a hard time. As teachers go, he was completely insane, but what was amazing was that you came out of Mr Ryan's class having actually learned something. You didn't even want to go into his class and come out *without* having learned something. And I honestly enjoyed his lessons. He put me, Frank Murphy and William Henderson in a group together. We were the three mischievous ones. Then one day, another lad joined our gang. His name was Dermot O'Mara. He had a stutter and was completely hilarious. If ever we got into strife for some minor misdemeanour or other, it was always Dermot who was our spokesman. When something dodgy was going on and questions were asked, we'd all look at Dermot and wait for him to speak up for us. It wasn't really fair. He was one of the nicest guys you'd ever meet in your life and I loved him. And the stutter he had actually wasn't that bad, but under pressure the poor lad couldn't get a word out. Still, we'd just stand there and keep looking at him.

Mr Ryan would almost always be on our side. I can't imagine why. I would slouch up in a tracksuit that was a far cry from my school uniform, with no books, pens and no homework done. I had nothing to give this guy, but for some reason he didn't seem to mind. He took our part and slagged everybody else off. Dinny Ryan was one of the boys. And he was one of the only teachers I actually took the trouble to listen to.

The four of us, Frank, Dermot, William and me always stuck together. But then along came another guy who we called Nailer – most of the time, that is. If we wanted to wind him up, we'd call him Mungo, after Mungo from the cowboy movie, *Blazing Saddles*. He hated it.

'Don't call me Mungo!' he'd yell, tearing round the classroom after us, knocking chairs and tables out of the way as if he was the proverbial bull in a china shop. But Nailer was a fantastic kid and a great friend. He was given a hard time in school because he was big lad, so Frank, Dermot, William and I always took it upon ourselves to look after him. And that was the whole gang of us. Five alive.

All this time, I was still cutting grass and doing odd jobs. I used to charge my regular customers £2 for the front garden and £4 for the back. I was just about making enough to keep my motorbike topped up with petrol. Then one day, I came to a decision. There wasn't a lot of logic to it, now I come to think about it – but I made up my mind I was going to buy a horse. I'd never really thought that much about horses, until I came across a guy called Logzar from a travelling community, and his horse looked so cool I thought, I'm going to get one of those.

I wandered down to the travelling community and enquired about the horse I'd seen, and they said I could have it for £40. It was ridiculous. I knew nothing about horses. Was this one male? Or was it female? I had no idea. Either way, I couldn't have cared less. It was brown and it was a horse. That's all that mattered to me.

It took me about three weeks to earn the cash. When I handed it over, I still had no reins, no saddle, and no hat. Nothing. But the travellers just took the money and gave me the horse.

The real joke was that I'd never sat on a horse in my life, but I thought, how hard could it be? Anyway, I was proud of myself. I felt as though I'd got a really good deal, and off I marched with my new friend.

To start with, I just held onto its mane and walked it down the road. Then I spotted a wall by some houses and, without given the matter a second thought, I climbed up and was able to jump onto the horse's back. And there we stayed. For about 20 minutes. We never moved an inch. It must have been a comical sight, a 14-year-old lad perched on top of a horse standing as still as a tree because I didn't have the first clue how to make it go.

I was thinking to myself, I wonder what the trick is to getting these things started, when, as luck would have it, one of the traveller guys came along and remarked, 'You're still here, then?' I explained that I couldn't seem get it to move and, without another word, he gave that poor horse a slap hard enough to wake the dead. And it bolted! All I could do was cling onto its mane for dear life as it galloped up the middle of the road. I found myself bounced around so violently, I was convinced I'd never escape with my life. All I remember thinking was, where in the world are the brakes on this thing?

It was more by luck than judgement (much more) that I finally discovered I could get the horse to slow down if I pulled on its mane.

Eventually, we eased into a steady trot and I relaxed and felt, yes, I know what this fella's all about.

When I finally arrived at the end of my road, I managed to slow my horse down enough to slide off its back. I walked it to the patch of grass outside my house, put a rope around its neck to tie it to a tree, and spent all day petting it and letting it eat the grass. The trouble was, I didn't know anything about horses so I couldn't take proper care of it. It was just a horse, and horses eat grass. Then I'd take it down to the fields and let it drink out of the ditches. It was a simple as that to me.

For the first few days, I'd wake up in the mornings, wait for everyone to be gone, and then I'd ride on my horse to school and tie it up to the bike rack. It certainly made the journey a lot more interesting. Of course, the teachers noticed. I suppose a horse tied to a school bike rack is a little difficult to miss.

'Who owns the horse?' they'd ask. I kept quiet and never said a word. The trick was to get in to school late (which I was already an expert at) and then get out early. But it wasn't a trick I had to practise for long. One morning I got out of bed and the horse was gone. That was the end of that. I guess the travellers must have come by and taken him back.

Because of my passion for my motorbike, I never really had time for girls while I was at The Grange. They seemed to take a fair bit of interest in me, but I never dated anyone. That was the last thing I wanted. As far as I was concerned, free time was for messing around with motorbikes, not girls. I did start getting into music, though, and began to buy records. My very first was Vanilla Ice, and from there I went and bought my first two albums, N.W.A's *Straight Outta Compton* and Ice Cube's *AmeriKKKa's Most Wanted*, both late 80s/early 90s hip-hop.

At home, my bedroom was something of a disaster area. It certainly wasn't the sort of place you'd want to take a girl. The walls were layered with posters mostly to do with cars. I had one of a beautiful Lamborghini, as well as all the trade posters that my dad brought home advertising air filters, Dunlop tyres, even spark plugs. And then, of course, there were my pictures of Transvision Vamp and Wendy James. I was so in love with Wendy James.

Underneath all the artwork, my bedroom walls were painted black. I must have liked black. The ceiling was draped with black silk and the carpet was black as well. On the back of my door was a red Soviet Union flag and I had an American flag hanging up too. In amongst my posters, there were bits of bikes, a frame of a BMX and a skim board fastened to the black walls.

I also had a snake called Caesar. I kept him in a box in my cupboard and used to feed him with live goldfish when my ma wasn't about. She was terrified of reptiles. If she'd ever found him, she'd have screamed the place down.

Back then, my life was for living day by day. I had no goals, no ambition. I had even less of an idea about how I might eventually earn a living. I never thought consciously that one day I'd go and work for my dad but, somewhere in the back of my mind I suppose that's always what I imagined I'd end up doing. After all, I loved engines and I was getting to know more and more about fixing them and getting them to run better. Working for my dad made sense.

My oldest sister, Tara, couldn't have been less mechanically minded. She was turning into quite a dancer. She belonged to groups that used to enter street dance competitions. That really impressed me and I grew to look up to her a lot. I'd go along with her sometimes because she and her friends were the ghetto-blaster carriers. One press of a button and the music would throb and blare, cutting through the ordinariness of a day. Then they'd start the break dancing, and I thought they were so cool. I'd watch them doing their backspins, windmills and body popping. I even tried to copy it, practising the moves in my bedroom. I would never do it in front of my friends, though. It's not something I wanted anyone to see. I was definitely a closet break dancer.

Alison knew how to move, too, but she wasn't into break dancing. She was the gymnast in our family and won all the trophies. I went wherever my ma had to take her, and I soon discovered I was pretty flexible as I learned to do rolls and back flips and the splits.

It wasn't just the older girls who had all the style. My younger sisters were also would-be performers. They went to stage school where they learned dancing, singing and acting. But what they did there didn't interest me one bit. I didn't have the desire or the need to perform. Back then, I was just a lad who loved motorbikes and cars. And, more and more, while the girls were away with their groups and classes, I'd be out with the boys learning to drive.

We used to borrow my dad's Ford Cortina when my parents went out. I say 'borrow' but it was all a bit loose. We were only 14 years old so we never actually had his permission. Fran and me, we'd get into the car, rev it up and do wheel spins. Only they barely lasted 30 seconds because we were scared the neighbours would hear and find us out. I had a bit more confidence with Kaner and we'd really burn the thing up. Then I'd put the keys back where I found them so that my dad wouldn't suspect anything.

As time went on, we bought a Nissan Sunny, another purchase from the travellers, but I didn't need any help making this one go. It cost Kaner, Fran and me £25 and we drove it to the beach where we used to ride our bikes. That's where I learned to drive a car, on a deserted stretch of coast where we'd tear about, masters of our destiny, in our very own Nissan Sunny.

One afternoon Fran burned the clutch out. It wasn't worth fixing so we decided to give that Sunny a spectacular send-off. We revved it up, banged it in gear – and pushed it off some blocks we'd made to send it tumbling into the ocean. It was in there for many a day. We used to go past on the train and see the roof bobbing serenely around in the Irish Sea.

While my first car was being cradled by the waves on its final journey, little known to me my academic career was about to come to an abrupt and untimely end. I suppose I'd been getting into trouble for a long time for my lack of productivity, and patience with me had finally run out. Ironically, on the day in question, I was being a model pupil. I wasn't talking to anyone, I wasn't causing mischief. In fact I was just sitting quietly at the front of the class because that's where I'd been moved for getting in trouble at the back. My English teacher had to get up and leave the room briefly. Within seconds, the whole place erupted. She raced back in and tried desperately to restore order, at last bellowing at the top of her voice, 'Right! The lot of you are staying back for detention.'

I couldn't believe it. For once I was an innocent. I'd done nothing and, I guess out of frustration at finding myself getting punished for something I'd had nothing to do with, I muttered an expletive under my breath. Unfortunately, it wasn't under my breath enough, and my English teacher heard.

She turned on me. 'You, Lynch, what did you say?'

I've always wondered why teachers ask that sort of question in a situation like that. Do they really expect you to repeat it? Anyway, she threw me out of the classroom there and then and, whilst I was standing disconsolately outside the door, the Principal, Mr Robert P Savage, walked past me, then stopped. He turned his head to look at me, and then slowly swung his body round. It all looked very rehearsed. As if he was in a movie.

'Mr Lynch,' he muttered quietly. 'What are you doing out here?'

'Sir,' I answered unsuspectingly, 'I did absolutely nothing.'

He paused, then nodded and sighed, 'Yes, that is the problem. You, Mr Lynch, do absolutely nothing in this school. And I would really appreciate it if you didn't come back here next year. In fact,' he added, savouring the words, 'don't even come back tomorrow.'

That was all he said. Then he turned and disappeared down the corridor.

I was stunned. My mind started to race. How could this have happened? I was just coming up to my exams. What was I going to do? And what in the world were my parents going to say? Although I'd been through my share of the small stuff, I'd never faced a real crisis before. But I was facing one now. It was the summer of 1990. I was 14 years old and I'd just been kicked out of school.

I went home and had a long, hard think. In the end, I said nothing to my ma and dad. I didn't know how to begin to tell them. Then, the following morning, I got ready for school as usual and went in to see the Principal. I never really knew what it meant to have your heart in your mouth until that moment when I was standing in front of him.

Swallowing hard, I managed to get the words out. 'Please, Sir, can I please just stay at school until I've finished my exams.'

Mr Savage looked at me for a moment, and then sniffed dismissively. 'I must say, I don't know why you're bothering,' he said at last. 'Still, if that's the way you want to play it. But I'm warning you,' and he leaned forward across his desk, 'one more incident from you and you're out. Do I make myself clear?'

He did. He made himself as clear as a bell. And for those last few weeks, I just kept my head down.

When it came to the exams, I cheated in every single one: English, French, Geography, History, Woodwork and Art. All of them were theory-based and I copied the lot from one of my best pals, Fran. I ended up with three honours and five passes. I still find it hard to believe, and I thank Fran for it all. I always tell his mother that he copied me!

I'd done it, then. I'd somehow cheated my way through the entire system. Up until that moment, that's really what I was – a chancer in just about everything I did. For me, that's what surviving school had been all about. Taking chances.

As the summer holidays rolled in, I knew I wouldn't be going back to school the next year, but my parents were still none the wiser. The time was coming when I'd have to face my dad. I couldn't avoid it forever. But how on earth I'd find the courage, or the words, I really didn't have a clue.

CHAPTER 3

Freewheeling

"THURSDAY MORNING CAME AND WE TOOK THE BUS
INTO TOWN TO MEET A DUBLIN MUSIC PROMOTER AND
AGENT CALLED LOUIS WALSH. IT WAS A MEETING THAT
WOULD TURN MY LIFE UPSIDE DOWN."

In Ireland, there was always a three-month summer break from school.
For some years, my parents took full advantage of our time off and
whisked us away to Portugal for seemingly endless weeks of family
holiday. My dad owned a high-topped conversion camper van. It had
beds upstairs and my youngest sister and I slept at the back in the
longer area, with the twins at the front. There were the usual built-in
seats and cupboards, and a table that we'd sit around to play cards.

Come 1 July, we'd gather together our pots, pans, clothes and
sleeping bags and, with the van fully loaded and towing a speed boat,
we'd set off together for the blue skies and balmy seas of Portugal. We'd
catch the boat to Holyhead, drive on down to Dover, cross the water and
motor through France to Spain. It took us about a week, but we never
tired of it.

We got out of England as quickly as possible and didn't take long to drive through France, usually staying in a camping park with a swimming pool for one night. Once we reached Spain we'd slow down a little. We all liked it there and dad would take a couple of days motoring through. When it was time to eat, we'd pull over onto a verge and he'd get his generator going. Out would come the big pot and he'd start cooking dinner right there at the edge of the motorway. With the deep fat fryer plugged in and sizzling invitingly, he'd prepare a feast of chips, onion rings and beans, or whatever he could get his hands on. We'd sit at the roadside like gypsies, tucking into our food and watching lorries whiz past. Those were the best of times.

I remember the journey the summer my school days had run out. I fancied something different to eat. We'd stopped right next to a field of maize, so I jumped over the gate and helped myself to some corn on the cob. My dad was furious.

'I hope you realise you've stolen that corn,' he shouted.

I couldn't understand what the fuss was all about. It was just a bit of corn from a field.

'Somebody owns that field,' he ranted, 'which means that you've stolen that corn.'

The cob looked wonderful cooked and steaming on my plate, with the butter melting all over it but, as it turned out, I didn't much like the taste. My dad said I had to eat it anyway as a punishment and I only just managed it.

It must have been about 2.00am when I woke up feeling decidedly rough. Within moments, I'd started projectile vomiting. I was sick over nearly every duvet, blanket and sleeping bag in the van.

All the bedding had to be stripped off for washing in the morning. What a great job that was going to be! My parents managed to get us covered up again with all that was left of the clean bedding, and they let us have theirs as well, so we'd be warm. They ended up having to sleep in just their clothes and must have been chilled to the bone. And all because I'd eaten some stolen corn.

The other thing I remember about the journey that year was coming to positively hate Kylie Minogue and Jason Donovan. My two older sisters had had to leave their boyfriends behind, and all I seemed to hear was the Minogue/Donovan hit song, *Sealed With A Kiss*, being played again and again while the two girls wept buckets over it. It did my head in.

We had a beautiful apartment in the Algarve. Every day, I'd get up at about 6.00am and ride my BMX down to the waterside where the fishing boats and trawlers were coming in. They'd been out catching fish all night, and as the fishermen transferred them into big barrels on the shore, they'd see me watching and tip some into my shopping bag. I'd go back to the apartment feeling so clever and proud that I'd been able to get dinner. My parents never had the heart to tell me that they hated sardines and ended up throwing most of them in the bin. They had sardines coming out of their ears.

Then there was the night I got drunk with my cousin and another lad we'd teamed up with. We were messing around in a corner of a bar, having a laugh while our parents were making their own fun and barbecuing outside, when one of us came up with the idea of seeing who could drink the fastest. I reckon we each sank about four pints within 20 minutes.

But that wasn't the end of it. One of my older sisters had her own boozy party planned for later that night at the beach. She asked me to sneak a bottle of Malibu up to her, but she never even got to lay eyes on it because me and the boys decided to drink that too. I just about managed to stagger to where she was waiting for me (it's amazing I found her at all), mumbled something about her Malibu being stolen, then collapsed behind a beach hut for the rest of the night. I was so wasted I had to be dragged home. It put me off booze for years.

After getting over that hangover to end all hangovers, the summer was perfect. Away out in Portugal, with the sun beating down, my life back home seemed almost unreal. Even so, it was always there, lurking at the back of my mind. When I thought about it, my Principal's face would loom large in my head, as clearly as if I was back in that corridor at school, listening to him in a daze as he told me to get out.

I still hadn't said anything to Ma and Dad. And my time in the sun was running out. It was getting towards the end of August and our long holiday was coming to an end. We'd soon be heading off for Ireland again – and in only a week or so, I was meant to be back in school. I had no idea what I was going to do. The only thing I'd come up with during our entire time away was to ask Dad to give me a job. But I hadn't been able to find the right moment to do it. I didn't want him to know I'd been kicked out of school. I wanted him to think that not going back at the start of term was my idea; that I felt school had served its purpose and it was the right time for me to move on. I was utterly downcast as we left Portugal behind us and set out on the long journey home.

I remember the curtains in our camper van. My ma had made them and they hung down in folds to separate the front from the back. I spent ages trying to pluck up the courage to open them a little, just enough to be able to speak to my dad. But I just couldn't do it. I couldn't make the move. As we sped towards the Spanish border and the cross-over into France, the freedom and warmth of our holiday slipped further and further behind us, while the return to real life grew more and more real.

That's when it finally hit home. I couldn't put it off any longer. It was now or never.

Feeling sick to my stomach, I stuck my head through the curtains and gulped, 'Dad, I hate school. All I want to do is work for you. Can I have a job?'

That was it. The words were out in a garbled rush, but out nevertheless.

My dad never seemed to give it a second thought. 'Yes, son,' he answered. 'I'd love to have you.'

I must have spent the rest of that journey grinning from ear to ear. I couldn't believe it was that easy. All sorted. I had a job to go home to and a fresh start to enjoy. And I'd got clean away with being thrown out of school without my parents ever needing to know a thing. I'd expected the worst and ended up with the best, thanks to my dad.

That was how, in September 1990, my spectacular dad, big Brendan, became my first proper boss. His workforce consisted of Ken, in charge of parts, Joe, the head mechanic, and another apprentice like me called John. To begin with I swept the floors and made the tea, like any new boy. Joe, nicknamed Noddy, took me under his wing and showed me the ropes.

Those days in the garage were brilliant. There was no heating in the workshop and it was freezing in the winter months. Some mornings it was so bitter I'd end up with spanners sticking to my hands, but I loved it. I'd left school behind and become a man. I had no homework piling up and no teachers to wind up good and proper. I was doing a decent job of work and earning £50 a week, which I put towards new parts for my bike.

The only thing that used to get me down was the journey to and from the garage. Every day I'd travel with my dad and return with him in the evening, and every day he'd use those trips to quiz me about what I'd already learned and what I was about to learn. That's when it was like being back in school.

My dad would ask me about cooling systems and brakes, and I'd be faced with a savage onslaught of general questions about how cars worked and the complexities of their engines. I literally used to break into a sweat trying to explain. He'd freak out if I got something wrong. He was always a short-tempered man and the thought of not being able to come up with the right answer for him was enough to put the frighteners on me.

I found myself longing for the summertime because that's when he'd be off to Portugal for his two-month holiday. I wouldn't be able to go with the family for the whole time anymore because, obviously, I was a working man now. But I wasn't really bothered. My young mind couldn't grasp that all my dad was trying to do was teach me what he knew to help me become an excellent mechanic. All I could think of was that I'd be able to catch the bus into work and have almost two months of no questions. No pressure. That was better than a holiday.

It was an odd thing, I suppose, but in spite of being the only boy in amongst five sisters, I always felt quite awkward around girls. Everyone told me I was good looking, but I certainly wasn't bursting with confidence when it came to the female department. When I was in Portugal that next year for just a couple of short weeks out of my family's long summer break, I did meet a girl. Her name was Claire Stebbing. She was from England and there was something about her I couldn't help liking. When we both got home, we kept in touch and agreed to meet up if we were able to.

For all my dad's passion for his cars, he also loved to be around boats. One day I heard him talking about going over to the Birmingham NEC boat show with his mate, Tom Ridgeway, and it sounded like the perfect opportunity for me to get across to England. I figured that, once I was on the mainland, I could easily get the train down to Kent where Claire lived, so I asked if could catch a lift to Birmingham in Tom Ridgeway's jeep. He was more than happy to give me the ride, and he and my dad dropped me off at New Street Station where I caught the train down to King's Cross, made the change, then journeyed on to Kent.

As I'd not seen Claire for a while, I was more than a bit nervous by the time I arrived. But she was just as I remembered her, and her family was such fun that, after a while, I found myself relaxing into it. Claire was 17, so I told her parents I was a year older than that. Of course, I wasn't, I was only 15, but because of my height I thought I'd stand a pretty good chance of getting away with it. I did.

I only stayed with them the one night, and went out to the pub with Claire to meet some of her friends and have a drink with them. I wasn't drinking at the time because I still couldn't forget the horror of that boozy night in Portugal. I made some lame excuse about being in training. I didn't want to look like some stupid, fresh-faced kid.

My dad and Tom Ridgeway were leaving Birmingham to head back to Ireland on Sunday at midday. That meant I needed to be away from Claire's by 7.00am. Her dad drove me to London and dropped me off at King's Cross where I took the train direct to Birmingham. I got to the New Street station with time to spare and just hung around waiting for my ride home. I was wearing my jeans, a t-shirt and an olive-green suit jacket. The jacket was actually too small for me, so my ma had folded the sleeves back and stitched them down to turn them into half-sleeves. I felt good in it. It was the kind of thing Don Johnson might have worn in *Miami Vice* – or so I liked to think.

I was actually feeling pretty confident in myself all round. I still had a bit of a sun tan from my break in Portugal, and my hair was incredibly short. It was just beginning to grow back. Not long before, my pal from the BMXs, Kaner, and I had decided that having a shaved head might be an interesting look for me, so we'd razored the lot of it. Then I'd presented my ma with my bald head. She wasn't impressed. I was more or less grounded until my hair grew back.

I'd been waiting on my own for my dad and Tom for about 20 minutes when two guys sauntered over. To begin with, I didn't pay a lot of attention, although they were quite a striking pair. One of them was white and must have been well over six foot tall, pale and skinny, while the other was a black man, tiny, short and stocky. They seemed to be hovering around me, which I suppose I thought was a bit weird because there was no reason for them to be there. It wasn't a bus stop or a taxi bay. I decided they were most probably waiting for a lift like me.

After a while, I needed the toilet, so I just left them standing there and wandered away to the gents. But the black guy must have followed me in, because when I went to wash my hands, I glanced up in the mirror and saw him. He was hiding in one of the cubicles, his face pushed up against the gap between the wall and the door. And he was staring right at me.

I felt my stomach lurch. I couldn't get outside without passing that cubicle and there was no one else in the toilets. How was I going to get out?

For a moment, I just stood there, frozen. But then, a businessman carrying a briefcase strode in. I'd never been so glad to see a man in a suit in all my life. I thought, nice one, waited until after he'd washed his hands, then walked with him out of those toilets.

Breathing a huge sigh of relief, I stepped into the fresh air, but the tall, white man was standing outside as if he was waiting for me and, suddenly, there was the black guy right next to him.

It was all so odd, I began to wonder if my mind was playing tricks. I needed to check I wasn't just being paranoid so I moved across to look at a wall stuck all over with posters and advertisements. I had no idea what they were all about, I couldn't really read them. But as I started looking at the pictures, sure enough, the two men wandered over too.

This wasn't good. I'd have to get back inside the terminal concourse, but doing that meant walking past them again. They eyeballed me the entire time. There were still other people around and I almost ran to get by, but those two guys weren't going to be put off. As I disappeared inside the terminal, the tall, skinny man was right behind me.

Where was my dad? I was getting seriously scared by now. I rushed past KFC and the car rental booths to get to the spot where my dad should have been meeting me. It had to be midday by now. Why wasn't he there? There was a woman by the passport photo booths. I went over and stood there with her for a moment while she was waiting for her snaps. Anything to keep those guys away from me until my dad turned up. When her photos were processed, she reached out quickly, grabbed them, and then hurried away. You never want anyone to see your photos when they come out of a passport booth, do you?

What was I going to do next? I looked back towards my pick-up point, but there was still no sign of my dad, and the two strangers were closing in on me again. In the end I shot off in a different direction. It wasn't a good move. I found myself trapped down a semi-circular walkway.

There was a wall on one side and a spiked railing ran along the other – and I had the tall, skinny guy behind me and the black man in front. My only way out was over the railing. And it must have been seven foot high.

I could see lots of black cabs parked up on the other side, but there was nobody in them. My bag went over first. I lobbed it as hard as I could, and then, powered by adrenalin and sheer terror, I managed to clear the railing without so much as a scratch. I landed on the bonnet of one of the cabs and then ran.

Just around the corner was a bus stop with a lot of people waiting. I stood there all out of breath and couldn't stop trembling. I must have drawn some very odd looks, but I really didn't care. All that mattered was to hide in this crowd and hope I'd shaken the two men from my tail. The trouble was, midday had come and gone and I had to make my way back to the station or I'd miss my dad altogether.

After about ten minutes of trying to calm myself down, I reluctantly left the safety of the bus queue, put my head down and headed swiftly back to the station – only not swiftly enough.

All of a sudden, a dirty white Ford Escort estate pulled hard up next to me. The black man was driving and the tall white man flung open the back door and tried to grab me and drag me inside. He was strong for a skinny guy, but I was strong too. I fought and struggled, and he couldn't get a proper grip on my Don Johnson jacket.

When I finally managed to tear myself away from him, I hurtled back to the station and could hardly believe my eyes when there in front of me was a policeman. I never thought coming face to face with a copper could be such an ecstatic moment in my life! I was gasping for breath and probably not making a lot of sense, but in the end I got him to understand that two strange men had tried to abduct me only, of course, by now they were long gone.

When Tom Ridgeway and my dad pulled up in the jeep, I shook the copper's hand and climbed gratefully into the back seat. And I never breathed a word. I didn't want to make a big fuss so I didn't tell my dad a thing.

* * * * *

When I turned seventeen in July 1993, I'd been working with dad for three years. I passed my driving test first time and found a new freedom. I'd been driving illegally with the lads for ages and had to move motors around at the garage, on and off the forecourt and into bays for repairs, so I pretty much knew what I was doing behind the wheel. But I felt as if I'd been waiting forever to get out on the roads with my own full licence, and now I was going to make the most of it. I drove everywhere as fast as I could and got up to all sorts of madness that would have made my ma's hair fall out had she'd known. My mates and I would race down narrow country lanes, in the dark with our lights off, and the driver who turned his lights back on first was the chicken. We were crazy.

That summer, my dad had gone away to Portugal as usual and I was driving a red pick-up truck. I'd bought it with £1500 he loaned me, and all because of the American TV show I was heavily into at the time. It was called *The Fall Guy* and starred Lee Majors of *Six Million Dollar Man* fame as cool Colt Seavers, a stunt man and part-time bounty hunter. Colt Seavers had a pick-up truck, and I wanted one too. I landed this 1979 Hi-Lux Mark 1 pick-up with a bent chassis. It was a piece of junk but that's what I loved about it.

One morning at the garage, something happened while I was working on a car. I'd been watching Joe, the head mechanic, who was showing me how to change the bearings. He was chipping a bearing case off a front hub with a hammer and chisel. I wasn't very health and safety conscious and hadn't bothered to put on goggles or any protective gear, and suddenly a metal shard shot up and buried itself my eye. It hurt quite a bit but I didn't pay too much attention and just carried on working on the car. I began to change the spark plugs, but my eye seemed to be watering a lot and I had to keep wiping at it.

It wasn't until I came out from under the darkness of the bonnet that I realised. They weren't tears I'd been wiping away at all. I was covered in the blood that was seeping out from my eyeball.

I went to the garage cloakroom and washed my eye out as best I could and then went off home to see my sister about it. Alison took one horrified look and said I should get some medical help right away. My eye was bulging out. So I got into my pick-up and headed off for the hospital. The doctor sat me down and filled my wounded eye with some kind of liquid that turned everything orange. Then he got out a scalpel and started scraping away at my eyeball until he'd got all the metal filings out. It was a weird sensation. I could feel my eye rolling without me rolling it. When he'd finished and cleaned it up, he covered it with a patch and sent me off to the specialist eye hospital in town.

I wasn't earning a fortune in those days, and anyway I'd had to get to the hospital in such a hurry I hadn't really thought about having to pay for the car park. I'd left the pick-up, a doctor had taken care of me, and now I had to get out again and off to the specialist eye place. The only problem was I didn't have any money for the machine. But what I did have was a pick-up truck. And I'd seen the Fall Guy break his way out a hundred times.

There was a big bank and a fence barring my way. I put the pick-up in forward drive, went up over the bank and smashed right through that wooden fence. In my mind's eye I was a Hollywood stuntman making a wild break for freedom just like Colt Seavers. When I arrived at the eye hospital, they told me I'd have to have an operation the next morning.

A few days later, while I was recovering at home with stitches in my eye, I got a knock on the door. It was Mark Walton. I'd known him in school and we used to BMX together but I hadn't seen him properly for a while. I invited him in and we were just catching up and swapping stories when, out of the blue, he said, 'Shane, I was wondering. Do you want to be in a band?'

A band? Was Mark really asking me to join a band? It was the last thing on earth I'd ever considered. Not that I didn't like music, I did. But of all the things that had ever crossed my mind, joining a band was definitely not up there with the front-runners. I was a car mechanic. That's what I was and that's what I wanted to be. And now Mark was asking if I wanted to be in a band.

He started banging on to me about a group called Take That. Mark was a sportsman like me and had been representing Ireland in Gaelic football. In one game recently he'd broken his ankle and, while he was stuck at home resting up, he'd been given a Take That video by some friends because they reckoned he looked like Mark Owen. He wasn't that much interested in the music. What blew him away was the lifestyles five ordinary lads from the north of England had carved out for themselves, and he wanted a piece of it. If they could do it, he thought, why couldn't we? And the idea of an Irish boy band had begun to take shape in his head.

I didn't know anything about Take That, but I did remember the massive success that New Kids On The Block had had worldwide for about five years. They'd just started out as ordinary blokes too. Then, one day, they'd hit the big time. When the New Kids era came to an end in 1994, Take That more or less took over.

Round about this time, I was going out with a girl called Catherine. Her youngest sister had magnets of the lads from Take That stuck all over the fridge in the kitchen. Because we weren't allowed to use the front room, when I went round to Catherine's we used to sit around the kitchen table, and the faces of these guys would be smirking at me from the fridge. It really annoyed me because Catherine used to go on about how much she fancied them and how handsome they were. I'd always respond in the same tight-lipped and charming way: 'They're all gay.'

That's male ego for you. My woman was saying somebody else was good-looking, and I really didn't like it.

So, there I was, with less than no regard for this group called Take That who were plastered all over my girlfriend's fridge, and my pal, Mark, was asking, 'Do you want to be in a band?' I thought about it. An Irish boy band sounded fair enough so I said yes.

Bearing in mind I had no idea if I could hold a tune, on top of which I'd barely done any dancing (other than a few private break dance moves on my own in my bedroom), and I couldn't even play an instrument, it was a pretty bizarre situation. But my total lack of musical expertise did nothing to dampen Mark's enthusiasm.

'You see, Shane, you have the look,' he explained excitedly. 'You're one of the fellas round here the girls really like. Now that's gotta be a good starting point.'

Right, I thought. And that was it.

Within a couple of days, Mark came back to me with the name of a manager. He was certainly a fast worker. He'd already set up a meeting with him that Thursday. The problem was I'd have to ask my dad for the morning off from the garage – and that wasn't going to be easy. The business wasn't a big affair and we were only a small team. Come rain or shine, sickness or health, my dad needed everyone to be there, working hard and pulling their weight. Suddenly springing a request for time off wasn't guaranteed to put him in a good mood. But with the meeting only two days away, I couldn't afford to hang about. So I picked my moment and went for it.

'Dad,' I said as casually as I could, 'I need to take Thursday morning off.'

'Really?' he replied. 'What for?'

'Well, Dad, I'm going to be in a band.'

What went through his head at that moment I can't honestly imagine, but after a pause he said, 'Right. Can you sing?'

'I don't really know,' I answered.

He asked, 'Can you play a musical instrument?'

I stammered back, 'Not that I know of.'

'So,' my dad went on, 'what is it that you're going to do in this band?'

'I haven't a clue,' I replied.

My dad was quiet for a second then, 'OK,' he said. 'Be back by two o'clock.'

It was as simple as that. Probably he was just humouring me, having a chuckle and thinking it was yet another one of my hair-brained schemes that, like as not, would come to nothing.

I had no idea what I was getting myself into, but Mark was bubbling over with excitement. He kept saying how amazing it was going to be and how we'd do massive gigs and earn loads of money. I'm not sure I was really getting into the spirit of it. It all sounded a bit far-fetched. But I'd smile at him and nod my head and go, 'Really, Mark? That all sounds cool.'

Thursday morning came and we took the bus into town to meet a Dublin music promoter and agent called Louis Walsh. It was a meeting that would turn my life upside down.

CHAPTER 4

Dream Chasers

"IN SHORT, THE FUN AND GAMES WERE OVER. THIS
WAS GETTING SERIOUS."

Louis Walsh started out in the music business as a record plugger hustling
radio stations to play new releases. He had charm and the gift of the gab.
It was a perfect job for him. It also allowed him to make plenty of contacts
within the music industry, contacts that would become very useful to him
when he branched off into the world of artiste management. He soon had
a few Irish club acts on his books, together with singer/songwriter Johnny
Logan who won the Eurovision Song Contest for Ireland. Mark Walton had
heard about him through a dancer he'd become friendly with at an
audition, and he was convinced that this was the man to bring his musical
dream to life.

Our meeting with Louis was to be in a pub just off Grafton Street. We
were both keen to make the right impression so we'd dressed up in our
best gear. I wore blue jeans, a dark green and black striped rugby shirt
and Fila trainers, while Mark wore a light blue shirt, black leather
waistcoat, blue jeans and Levi boots. Then, feeling that, if nothing else,

at least we looked the part, we strode with all the confidence we could muster through the pub doors. And there he was. Louis Walsh, in jeans and a blue, pin-striped shirt, was sitting there waiting for us, his silver briefcase lying in front of him on a low coffee table. We sank down into the deep blue chairs and started talking.

Knowing very little about music, other than what I liked to listen to, I suppose it was no surprise that I'd never heard of Louis Walsh. I had no idea what to expect, what kind of a reception we'd get but, by the end of that meeting, he'd totally blown me away. We were bringing the idea of a boy band to him, but he was the one who, all of a sudden, was selling the concept to us. He didn't laugh or sneer. He didn't brush us off as a couple of wannabe no-hopers. He believed in us. He listened as we told him the plans we had for a New Kids On The Block or Take That-like band, the difference being that this would be an Irish boy band. The point we wanted to make was that plenty of great rock bands had come out of Ireland, but never a pop act like we were describing.

Louis thought about it. He nodded. Then he leaned forward in his chair and said, 'Lads, I love this idea. This is fantastic. This is going to be big.'

Opening up his silver briefcase, he took out bundles of magazine interviews, tour schedules, and lists of aeroplane times and television show bookings, all to do with Johnny Logan and the other acts he managed.

'Take a look,' he smiled. 'This is what I could be doing for you.'

It was daft really. We didn't have a band. All we had was an idea. Yet here was Louis Walsh telling us he could change our lives. He promised us the sun, moon and stars that day. He insisted, 'Lads, I'm telling you, it's going to be massive.' He made it all sound so plausible. And, as we sat there in the pub, nestling in the warmth of those soft, blue chairs, we believed him.

I went back to work that afternoon and my dad asked me how the meeting had gone. I told him, but it must have all sounded so crazy I'm sure he never really thought anything would come of it. And why should he? Deep down, I don't suppose I honestly thought anything would come of it myself. I was excited, but was it real? I didn't play an instrument, or sing, or write music or lyrics. I was a mechanic. I mean, what were the chances?

It was only two days after our meeting that Mark and I got a call from Louis Walsh. He'd set right to work on filling out the bones of our less than flimsy project, and our first interview was already arranged on Ireland's top radio station, 2FM, the equivalent of Radio 1 in the UK. With the bit well and truly between his teeth, Louis's first step was to publicise open auditions to uncover the best new male talent Ireland had to offer to join our band. It was all a little hard to grasp. Suddenly, there we were, Mark Walton and me, without a clue what we were getting ourselves into, heading off to 2FM for our first media appearance.

Never one to miss a PR opportunity, Louis had booked a photographer and, when we arrived, we did a photo shoot by a tree for the local and national newspapers. Then, posing over, we wandered wide-eyed into the radio station to sell the idea of an Irish Take That, using the moment to plug the auditions Louis had already set up in a rehearsal studio at the Ormond Centre in Dublin.

It was all quite surreal. Live on air, we sat there and chatted on about boy bands as if we were experts on the subject. The presenter started going on about the Beatles, Bros, New Kids and all the boy bands that were currently on the scene, and wanted to know how we were going to be different. We didn't have a plan. To tell the truth, we didn't have a clue. All we kept saying was, 'We're Irish. There are no Irish boy bands out there. It's going to be brilliant. It's really going to work.'

Then, just when it all seemed to be going so well, we had a little surprise sprung on us. We were asked to sing. I looked at Mark, horrified. Sing? I thought we were there to talk not sing. What were we going to do? How were we going to get out of this? I found myself picturing Louis Walsh trying desperately to bury himself in a very deep hole at that moment. But somehow Mark managed to keep a cool head and, after a frantic and extremely short consultation, we ended up doing a rendition of *Daydream Believer* live on national radio. Me, I didn't sing a note because I couldn't. In any case, I didn't know the words. I just added 'oohs' and 'aahs' in what I hoped were all the right places and, miraculously, the presenter seemed happy with that.

The next day, we opened the papers – and there we were. We looked scared out of our minds in the photos as we stood under that tree, and the reports went, 'New boy band with Shane Lynch and Mark Walton. Ireland's answer to Take That. Auditions down at Ormond Quay. Manager Louis Walsh.' The story was splashed everywhere. And within hours of the word being out, Louis's office was inundated with enquiries from young hopefuls all across the country.

The day of the auditions finally dawned: Thursday 18 November 1993. I sat behind a desk in the audition room at the Ormond Centre with Mark, Louis and a musical director friend of Louis's, Paul Little, notebook and pen at the ready, all set to discover the pop stars of the future. It was one of the oddest days of my life.

There must have been over 300 lads queuing up to show us what they could do. They came with CVs, guitars, tap shoes, the lot. There were all sorts walking through that door: good-looking, bad-looking, tall, short, black, white. There were some lads with incredible talent and others with no talent at all. Not that I really had much of a clue at the time, but even I could pick out the ones that were pretty dire.

At one point, Colin Farrell waltzed in to show us what he could do. Strange to think it now he's scaled the heady heights of Hollywood, but back then he made his money modelling and demonstrating line dancing around local clubs. He certainly looked the part in his leathers, denim jacket and bandana, and the girls were flocking round him, but when it came to the singing, he couldn't really hold a note. It was sheer charisma that got him through to the final ten.

I remember one guy coming through who, at around 20, was slightly older than the others. He was blonde and good-looking. He obviously worked out. He stood in front of us, played his guitar and sang his heart out. As I watched him, it hit me. How on earth was I ever going to compete with performers like that? There was real talent out there. What did I think I was doing? Louis Walsh had never even heard me sing. Other than our slightly desperate radio debut, he didn't know if Mark and I had voices at all. I suppose he just assumed that we did. After all, we'd come to him with the idea of putting a band together. What kind of crazy people would do that if they couldn't sing? I sat behind that desk, bold as brass, scribbling down notes and making judgements but, actually, I had no right. All I had was the front to go through with it. As far as talent was concerned, I shouldn't have even been there.

A fresh-faced, 15-year-old Ronan Keating came in and sang the Cat Stevens classic, *Father and Son*. We were all impressed. He showed Louis a cutting from the paper about the modelling he was doing. Then he danced to *I'm Too Sexy* by Right Said Fred, and instantly made it through to the next round of auditions. I suppose Ronan had to go through the process like all the others, but Louis had already made up his mind to have him in the band. It was obvious. In fact, Ronan was so good with his audition song that it became the 'B' side to our first Irish single, *Working My Way Back To You*.

Stephen Gately and Mikey Graham sang George Michael's *Careless Whisper*, and it was no surprise that they also made it through to the second round of auditions to be held a week later. Stephen's dancing was sensational.

As much as I believed our new band was going to be the next massive thing to hit the pop world, I also couldn't really see how I was going to be a part of it. I suppose I was getting so caught up in all the hype that I bought into the dream. I kind of forgot that I didn't know how to sing or, at least, I pushed it to the back of my mind. I thought I'd just try and look good and that would be enough.

Around the time of the auditions, Take That happened to be performing in Ireland so I went with Mark to see them in concert. It was weird. Only a month before, it's the last place on earth I'd have wanted to be. But all of a sudden, it was relevant. It was important to go. We stood there in the middle of the crowd, watching, soaking it all in. There were thousands of girls, lost in the music, screaming. And I was totally blown away.

As we came out, we bumped into one of my past teachers in the car park. Mrs Armstrong had taught me history, and she greeted us like old friends. I was stunned. I'd never felt special or important. I'd been kicked out of school and hadn't really amounted to anything. I was just a messer. But suddenly, there was one of my teachers saying she'd read about us in the papers and how great it was to see us. She was even shaking my hand. We stood in that freezing car park that night signing dozens of autographs because some other girls had recognised us too. It was our first real taste of being known, our first taste of being 'somebody'. Bizarre and extraordinary, but out of this world.

Keith Duffy joined us for the second round of auditions. Louis had seen him dancing on stage at the POD nightclub, liked his look and the way he moved and had invited him along. I'd known Keith for years. We used to see each other at the gym and he'd dated one of my sisters. We never used to like each other. His dad was in the rag trade and his mum was a hairdresser. It was his mum who put the blond streaks into his shoulder length hair, and he was always clad in denim, smart as could be, from head to toe. I, on the other hand, was always head to toe in muck and grease, a sorry sight in tatty overalls, pushing motorbikes up and down the road. I suppose we were rivals because we were the two good-looking lads in town. We were chalk and cheese but the girls seemed to like us. I couldn't help myself. I envied the guy. I hated him because he looked so amazing with his cool gear and perfect hair. And he always had a suntan. Years later I found out that he'd envied me, too.

Second time around, the short listed guys had to perform again. It was Ronan's turn to choose *Careless Whisper* and Mikey came up with Meat Loaf's *Two Out Of Three Ain't Bad*. Keith did *I'm Too Sexy* which gave him a chance to show what he could really do on the dance floor.

As the auditions rolled on, the task of picking the absolute best became harder, but Louis knew he had to whittle the boys down again and, at the end of the night, there were just ten left: Colin Farrell, Karl Power, Jason Farrell, Richie Rock, Ronan Keating, Keith Duffy, Stephen Gately, Mikey Graham and, of course, Mark Walton and myself.

Then Louis had one final test. It was time for Mark and me to push back our chairs and get up there with the rest of the lads. We had to perform. Together.

I thought to myself, that's it, then. It's over. It's barely begun and it's over already. I was about to be uncovered for the no-talent chancer I really was. All the others, including Mark, seemed confident enough. There was plenty of banter bouncing back and forth. Or perhaps it was just bravado. Then a track was played and we had to dance. I guess Louis was looking for who would get the girls going and who would gel well together. He had an expression he used to come out with: 'If you gel well, you sell well.' I didn't think I had a hope in hell, but I danced my little heart out that day.

When we'd finished, Louis announced, 'We'll let you know, lads.' And we just had to wait. For what seemed like forever.

Finally he called us in.

'Ok, guys,' he said, 'I've made my decision.'

The room went silent. There was finality in his voice. No room for negotiation. No going back.

Then – 'I'd like Ronan Keating, Stephen Gately, Keith Duffy, Richard Rock, Mark Walton and Shane Lynch.'

And, just like that, we were the band.

I can't possibly even begin to describe what that moment was like. We were ecstatic. As Louis reeled off our names, we were suddenly lifted out of the ordinary, the everyday, and launched into something fantastical, something breathtaking. And it was already beginning. We headed off for a celebration, and found ourselves whisked past the queue outside the POD nightclub and escorted into the VIP area. There was a fashion show being staged that night so the place was full of gorgeous ladies and the eager press. People bought us drinks and photographers snapped away. All Louis's hype about the search for a new band had paid off in a remarkable way. Everyone seemed to know about us. We were celebrities already.

Things were happening incredibly fast, and Louis wasn't about to let the pace drop. Never mind that we'd never sung a note together, people were talking about us. And Louis wanted to make sure that they went on talking about us. Within 24 hours, he'd secured us a spot on the country's biggest TV chat show, *The Late, Late Show*. It was so unreal. We'd been together for a day. We hardly knew each other's names let alone if we could sing and dance together. I still wasn't sure I could sing at all. But Louis wasn't bothered. The act could develop over time. For now, what he wanted was as much publicity for his boys as he could get.

We were at the TV studios all day long. The researcher looking after us ran through the technicalities, where we would come on and go off, and where the presenter, Gay Byrne, would stand during the interview. We knew exactly what we had to do and it all seemed pretty straightforward. It wasn't until we were getting our gear on for the live show that the nerves started to take hold of us. But that wasn't the worst of it.

We'd just come out of make-up when the producer of the show marched into our dressing room and said, 'Right, lads, this is what's going to happen. Gay Byrne isn't happy with you boys just going on and introducing yourselves. He wants you to do something – to perform.'

Reality couldn't have hit home any harder. It wasn't just the rug that had been pulled from under us. Gay Byrne had just demolished the whole floor. We looked at each other and back at the producer. We tried to explain that we'd only been together for a day. We hadn't put together any songs or routines yet. At that precise moment, we didn't actually *do* anything.

'I know that,' the producer continued, alarmingly unruffled by our confession, 'but Gay wants you to do something.' And with that he left the room.

We had a frantic band conference and decided the best thing we could do was dance. We had no experience of proper choreography and only two hours to rehearse, but in the end we managed to come up with a routine that we all thought was pretty good. Anyway, there was no going back now and no more time. We had a line-up, some moves together and plenty of free styling. It would just have to do. And as the live show got under way, we waited our turn, then burst out in front of the cameras, full of energy and enthusiasm, and blagged our way cockily through the interview.

Eventually the big moment arrived. Our first TV performance. Our triumphant entrance into the world of pop, screaming girls and endless adulation. We did our routine to *Burn Baby Burn*. We gave it everything. And it was utterly diabolical. Not that we realised it at the time. We thought it was fantastic. Ronan was wearing his cap backwards and a striped t-shirt. Keith was in jeans and Budweiser braces. Steo sported a white, unbuttoned shirt and a brown waistcoat. Richie was all in black, Mark in jeans, t-shirt and waistcoat and I wore my blue dungarees. We moved, gyrated. We felt like the hottest thing on the airwaves – and we looked like a bunch of total eejits. I kept grabbing my crotch. I'm not sure what message that was supposed to send out but I suppose I must have had something in mind at the time. The audience was in stitches but we didn't really notice. We were too busy concentrating on 'working it'. This was our time. We were in the zone. Or so we thought.

To say the host wasn't exactly on our side would be a massive understatement. Gay Byrne was condescending and sarcastic. Horrible, to be honest. He kept making snide remarks to the audience about how we couldn't play instruments, how we couldn't sing or write music. He told them that, basically, we had no talent whatsoever. But this was our television debut. As far as we were concerned, that's what counted, and we weren't going to let him get us down. We'd done what we'd been asked to do. We'd performed for the cameras and in front of a live audience. We were now officially pop stars.

Strange as it seems, we weren't in the mood to rush right out afterwards and celebrate. All we wanted that night was to get home. Our parents had videoed the show and we were desperate to see ourselves. And when we watched it, we were so proud.

It wasn't until the following day that we woke up to the truth: we'd actually made complete fools out of ourselves. The local newspapers took enormous pleasure in slaughtering us all weekend. They tore us to shreds. We were written off as a bunch of useless, untalented nobodies. Everywhere we went, people sniggered, pointed and laughed. The game was up, and we came crashing down off our cloud.

On the Saturday night, Mark Walton and myself went for a quiet drink at Smith's bar in Malahide. Mikey Graham happened to be there with a bunch of his mates. He'd got down to the last ten at the auditions but hadn't made the final six which, in a way, he was now delighted about. We'd just spent the day being universally panned because of the previous night's TV fiasco. He must have felt he'd had a lucky escape.

Everyone seemed to think they could have a go at us, and when one of Mikey's friends decided to stir things up by making a sarcastic comment, we'd just about had enough. There wasn't a full-blown fight but there was certainly a scuffle with some pushing and shoving. We'd never prepared ourselves for this. Everyone hated us. They barely knew the first thing about us and they hated us. We felt completely crushed, under fire from a barrage of negativity from all directions – all except one, that is. Louis Walsh wasn't worried in the least. To him, we were still brilliant. To him, we were superstars destined for fame and fortune. In his ambitious eyes there was no such thing as bad publicity. He just kept saying, 'Lads, don't mind that. All press is good press. They're talking about you. What more could you want?' And he went on saying it until all we could do was believe him. It was his faith in us that kept us going. No-one else would give us the time of day. But Louis Walsh had plans and nothing was going to get in their way.

What we needed now was an act. For the next couple of months, we got together each night in a dance studio in Dublin for band rehearsals. We were more or less left to our own devices so there was little or no structure to what we did. We just turned up and got used to singing together by working on some music. We had no voice coaches or dance teachers at that stage. We just had to make it up as we went along. Steo was the best dancer so he did what he could to teach us some moves. But we weren't taking things all that seriously. More often than not we'd end up in the pub after only half an hour, and then the rest of the night would be spent talking and dreaming about our future rather than actually working towards it. It wasn't long before we became good friends but, at the same time, we were starting to realise that there was a problem with the make up of the band.

Richard Rock was the son of a well-known Irish singer, Dickie Rock, and I'm sure his father hoped he would follow him into the music business. Richard was certainly talented. At his audition, he played the piano as well as singing. He was tall and dark. He had everything going for him – except real commitment.

Financially it was tough. None of us were getting paid yet for the time we were putting in, rehearsing or performing, and we nearly all had to rely on our day jobs to earn money. Ronan was working part time in Korky's shoe shop; Steo had a job in Makullas clothes shop; Mark was a student; Keith had given up on his architecture course and was getting dole money, and I was back at my dad's, tinkering away on cars. Richie was DJ-ing and often wouldn't turn up to rehearsals, either because he'd rather be earning cash working in nightclubs, or because he just couldn't be bothered. Louis always noticed, though. And then one night Richie pushed his luck a bit too far.

We were making an important appearance at the Rock Garden Nightclub and, for whatever reason, he didn't show up. He claimed he'd fallen asleep in front of the TV, but this time Louis had had enough. He'd already warned Richie about his lack of commitment, and now here he was missing another critical event. It was the final straw and, sadly, Richie had to go.

With Mark it was different. When he went, it was his choice. Since the whole thing had started out as his idea, I'm not really sure what was in his head, what he was expecting, but in the end he found the reality of trying to be a pop star difficult to cope with. It wasn't just the physical hard graft of rehearsing every night. It was all the attention from female fans. Even at that early stage in our careers, there were times when they'd camp outside our houses. It was too much pressure and Mark found he couldn't deal with it. So he left.

It was at our next rehearsal that the final Boyzone line-up got together for the first time. Mark and Richie weren't there. I don't think anyone asked any questions. They were out of the band. That was all we needed to know. Louis was in charge and we were scared to say anything in case we were shown the door too.

He told us he'd organised a new member, and when the guy walked in, we recognized him as the lad who'd come to the auditions wearing a red bandana. Unfortunately, he was also the lad Mark and I had bumped into in Smith's bar a couple of months before, after our disastrous TV appearance. It was Mikey Graham.

I wasn't sure how to react at first. He'd been slagging us off. How could he be one of us? But as he came through the door, he walked straight up to me, shook my hand, apologised and explained that the situation in the pub that night was nothing to do with him. It was one of his mates who was stirring things up. He'd actually been the one trying to calm it all down.

From then on, things moved up a gear. Louis would sometimes drop in to watch us rehearsing, and he found an amazing lady to give us dance lessons. Mavis Ascot looked about 100 years old and was a ballet teacher. Her heart must have sunk like a stone when she saw the motley crew she was going to have to mould into a dance troupe. However, she clearly had one of those indomitable spirits and quickly set to work on showing us how to move with poise. To begin with, we all fell about laughing, but that didn't seem to put her off. Of course, Steo stood out a mile. He was fantastic. But, as the weeks passed, I guess we all gradually got better.

While we were working on our moves, Louis was hard at it, desperately trying to get record companies to take an interest in us. We'd had some publicity pictures taken and he travelled all across Ireland armed with our photographs and a short demo tape we'd put together. He was a tenacious character and used his charm and contacts to arrange meeting after meeting, but all he seemed to be met with was rejection. Maybe this was going to be harder than he thought.

One night after a practice session, I gave some of the lads a ride home. I dropped Steo off first before driving over to Ronan's place in Swords. Then I headed my black Golf MK1 GTi down the back roads to Donaghmede with Keith. Earlier that week I'd pinched a set of wheels lying out in a garden near where I lived. There was hardly any tread on them but they looked good and I stuck them on my car anyway. It was the middle of the night, no one was about and as usual I was driving too fast. It had been raining and the wet road, coupled with the speed I was doing and a set of tyres with no tread was a recipe for disaster.

We were hitting speeds of over 110mph down tiny country lanes but I never gave it a thought. As I approached one particular bend, I slowed down to 90mph. And that's when I lost control. I started skidding and the back end just went. Keith was next to me in the passenger seat and I yelled at him, 'Are you ready for this?' We braced ourselves and, as a wheel clipped the kerb we thought, this is it, we're going to die.

It seemed to happen in slow motion. We were thrown into the air and the car rolled over twice. The crunching, splintering sound was deadly. I could see each window smashing. Glass flew everywhere. The pillars in the car were being literally crushed as we smacked the road and finished upside down on the roof. Then there was silence.

We were hanging from the seatbelts, heads down.

'Duffy?' I remember mumbling. 'Duffy, are you all right?'

He was so relieved to hear my voice. He'd been too scared to open his eyes or speak to me in case I didn't answer him.

The whole front of the car was smashed in and the only way out was to scramble through a back window. Keith was shaking. He was clearly in shock and was taken off to a nearby house for a cup of tea. As he was helped away, he kept looking back in a daze at the shattered remains of the Golf. It was a total write-off. I knew it was only worth around £1500 so, from a financial point of view, it wasn't the end of the world. But we still could have died that night, and I don't think he could quite take it in.

I sat outside waiting for the fire brigade to arrive. I had a baseball bat in the car and passed the time knocking stones up into the air. I suppose it focused my mind while Keith was trying to calm himself down before getting on the phone to his mum and dad to ask them to come and pick us up. What a mess. Every so often I'd glance at the wreckage upside down beside me. It was all pretty well pulverized and the roof over where we'd been sitting was completely crushed. If we hadn't been wearing seatbelts, we'd never have got out alive.

When the fire brigade arrived, it was about 2.00am. They checked in the hedges and around the car to make sure no one else had been hit or injured.

Then one of the firemen came up to us and said, 'You're the boys from that group out of the papers.'

'That's us,' grinned Duffy. We might have just nearly died and then been stranded in a lane that felt like the middle of nowhere, but he was still quite pleased to be recognised.

'Can't sing, can't dance,' the fireman went on. 'Can't drive either, can you, lads.'

And we all burst out laughing.

Keith's parents turned up in their Volvo and stared horrified at the remains of my motor. They were both in tears. So was Keith. All I wanted by now was to get home. I still had to go to work the next day. They dropped me off finally and I sneaked inside without saying a word. There was hardly any of the night left, but I managed to sleep for a couple of hours. Then suddenly it was morning and I knew I'd have to tell my parents what had happened.

My ma was talking on the phone so I said to my dad casually, 'I don't suppose there's any chance of getting a lift into work this morning is there?'

'Where's your car?' Dad asked.

'Ah,' I said. 'I had a little accident last night.'

He looked up from his mug of tea. 'Is everyone okay?'

'Yeah,' I replied. 'Everyone's grand.'

He nodded. 'Sure. No problem.'

And that was it. Until my ma got off the phone. She'd been talking to Pat Duffy, Keith's mum.

'Did you boys have an accident last night?' she asked quizzically. Poor Keith was apparently huddled up at home with a blanket wrapped around him, and his mum had phoned to see how I was.

My dad went with me to see what was left of the car later that week. He gazed silently at the mangled heap of metal for a moment. Then he turned and shook my hand.

'Good job, son,' he declared. 'If you're going to do it, do it right.'

And he never said another word about it.

Louis, however, wasn't so cool. He went ballistic when he found out what had happened. He was putting thousands of pounds and an enormous amount of effort into getting our band off the ground, and here we were, dicing with death just for the hell of it. He sat us all down and gave us a serious talking-to. Then, shortly afterwards, he came up with a contract that would put an end to any more messing around and taking risks. It wouldn't allow us to participate in any dangerous sports or take drugs. Louis wanted us fit, healthy, clean-cut and ready for anything. We even had to keep our girlfriends a secret.

In short, the fun and games were over. This was getting serious.

CHAPTER 5

Shake, Rattle And Roll

"WE KNEW WE'D STARTED TO MAKE IT REALLY BIG WHEN THE HARD MEN OF DUBLIN BEGAN COMING UP TO US ON THE STREET, SHAKING US BY THE HAND AND SAYING, 'GOOD ON YER, LADS. HOPE YOU MAKE A MILLION.'"

Louis was a tireless worker. Nothing was going to stand in the way of him and his belief in us. He kept banging on record company doors and, despite having them slammed in his face time and again, he carried on until he eventually managed to get an appointment with Paul Keogh, the Managing Director of PolyGram Records in Ireland. Paul had been the boss of Polydor for ten years, working with the likes of U2, The Cranberries and Van Morrison. Before that, he was employed at Anheuser Busch and brought Budweiser to Europe, so he knew a thing or two about marketing and promotion. He was interested in Boyzone, but still cautious about investing in us, although he was prepared to offer a distribution deal if we funded the record ourselves. In other words, if we supplied him with the finished singles, he would get them into stores.

Picking the right song for our first release would have been a daunting task for us, but Louis's knowledge of music is phenomenal. After a lot of thought, he finally came up with the disco classic, *Working My Way Back To You*, a hit for The Four Seasons and The Detroit Spinners. Next he had to find a producer. He decided on Ian Levine in London, but there was a snag. Ian wanted £10,000 to produce the track for us and Louis was out of cash. He'd already invested a lot of his own money into Boyzone and unless he could find a backer, it looked as if there was no way forward.

Still confident that we could be the next big pop act to storm the music scene, Louis turned to his friend, John Reynolds, owner of the well-known POD nightclub in Dublin. John was a shrewd and wealthy entrepreneur and it didn't take much selling from Louis for him to stump up the vital £10,000 to get our first recording off the ground. It also didn't hurt that John's uncle was Albert Reynolds, who just happened to be Ireland's Prime Minister at the time. As contacts go, that was another useful one for Louis.

If it hadn't been for John's crucial backing, everything might well have ground to a halt, but in March 1994, John and Louis shook hands as equal partners. WAR Management – Walsh and Reynolds – became Boyzone's new management company. The two of them made a good team. John took care of the business side of things while Louis looked after us boys and, with that classy double act behind us, we set off to London to record our debut single.

Apart from passing through train stations, it was my first time in London, as it was for the other lads. In fact I'm pretty sure it was the first time out of Ireland for most of them. They were like little boys, so excited and full of it all, and nothing could wipe the grin from Ro's face as he kept on about us finally being international jet setters. I was always the laid back one, shaking my head and telling them to get a grip. Of course, my insides were leaping about full throttle, but I wasn't going to let on.

It was a magical few days away. We wandered around London, awe-struck, mouths open, taking in the sights and gazing at the elegant landmarks we'd only ever seen on TV or read about in books. The huge shops, the big red buses, the constant parade of black cabs and the general hustle and bustle of the capital had our hearts pumping. It was a memorable first day in the 'big smoke' and, as it drew to a close, we checked into the hotel that Louis had booked for us in Russell Square, above a branch of Barclays Bank.

The following morning we took a taxi to Ian Levine's Tropicana studio in Chiswick. Levine was a well-known producer with great credentials. He'd worked with the Pet Shop Boys, Erasure, Kim Wilde, The Pasadenas, Bad Boys Inc and Bronski Beat, as well as writing and producing for Take That. And, let's face it, if he was good enough for Take That, then he was definitely the man for us.

We'd never been in a recording studio before. It was fascinating, if a little nerve-wracking, setting foot inside to meet Ian Levine, a huge man weighing at least 20 stone, with a reputation to match. We sat down on a big, black leather couch, Levine's white husky dog lying under his desk, eyeing us balefully, and, as the man himself leaned back in his chair, he set about explaining the record-making process to us new boys. He'd already laid down the backing track to *Working My Way Back To You* and, one by one, we had a go at singing the song to see whose voice would suit the lead best. We took turns traipsing into the vocal booth to perform, but I guess we all assumed that Ronan would be the star singer. Levine, however, thought differently. He listened closely to each of us. Then he announced that he wanted Stephen Gately and Mikey Graham. He thought they had the best voices. We were all taken aback. Later we discovered he'd actually told Louis to get rid of Ronan because he couldn't sing! But we weren't going to argue with someone like Ian Levine and, with Steo and Mikey taking the lead, the rest of us picked up the backing vocals. I'm not really sure how we managed to sing at all. We were pretty much overwhelmed as we watched the engineer at the control panel, and Ian flicking the switch on the talkback to speak to us in the studio. We were so green. I didn't even know why I needed headphones and none of us understood much about microphone technique. In the end, we managed to record the song in two days.

As we left the studio, we were ecstatic. Our first single was finished – and it felt like nothing on earth! We were messing around, shaking hands and punching each other, and I got a playful shove which is when I felt my neck creak. I still had bad whiplash from my car accident with Duffy just a short while before, and I ended up wandering around like an old man for the rest of the day. Nothing could spoil the moment, though. We walked along those London streets in a state of absolute euphoria, hoping desperately that someone would recognise us as the new Irish boy band and we'd get followed and asked for autographs. We felt famous even though no one in England had the faintest idea who we were.

That incredible trip was our first time away from families and girlfriends. It was a remarkable three days but even the best of times without the ones you love can seem to drag on a bit. None of us had mobiles back then so, to keep in touch, we used the telephones in our rooms. No problem, we thought, that's what they're there for.

When it was time to check out, we went downstairs to pay the bill. Louis had already settled the bed and breakfast each day, but the extras were down to us. And what extras they turned out to be. The phone bill was a whopping £90. It might as well have been £900. We still didn't have the money to pay it.

Back upstairs, we sat down and tried, as calmly as we could, to come up with some kind of mature and sensible solution. After a lot of careful discussion, we were eventually all agreed: we'd do a runner.

I took charge.

'Lads,' I said, 'let's pack up our stuff, then I'll go downstairs and out front with Keith and Mikey. Steo and Ro can throw the bags to us out of the window. That way it won't look as if we're checking out.'

I was quite pleased. It was a good plan. What could possibly go wrong?

Keith, Mikey and me, we sauntered casually outside, smiling warmly at the girl behind reception as we went. Then we waited out in the street.

The window opened and, as arranged, Steo and Ro lobbed the bags out of the third floor bedroom and we caught them. It all went like clockwork. Nobody noticed a thing. At least, they shouldn't have done. But what I hadn't taken account of was Barclays Bank. Its massive glass frontage stood directly below the window giving an entire line of queuing customers a stunning view of our less than covert activities. They must have thought we were robbing the place. Well, we were.

The last bag through the window, Steo and Ro, heads down, shuffled as quickly as they could through the front door and we scarpered away up Oxford Street. Then we heard the sirens – and that was when we really panicked. Of course, the police probably weren't after us at all, but we weren't to know that. We were a bunch of Irish lads hitting London for the first time and we felt as if we'd just pulled off the crime of the century. We sprinted into Burger King and through to the toilets where all five of us crammed into a single cubicle until we felt the coast should be clear. All we wanted after that was to get home.

The finished *Working My Way Back To You* mix came through a couple of weeks later and Louis and John called us all in to have a listen. We were astounded. To us it sounded fabulous. What we needed now was a top rate video to go with it. These days, pop videos cost hundreds of thousands of pounds to make, but back then you could get away with a lot less and, as things were still very tight money wise, ours cost just a few thousand. We had no fancy locations or demanding script, and the whole thing was filmed in a workshop space and on rooftops in Dublin, with us boys hammering out a dance routine in the freezing cold.

As ever, Louis used his contacts to the full and pulled some very elite strings. His pal, Bill Hughes, was the director, designer, runner, driver, and actually did just about everything, including making the tea. Then Louis managed to twist yet another arm and brought in Kylie Minogue's and Madonna's choreographer, Vennel Jones. Vennel flew over from London to teach us the routine. He even ended up on the video taking us through the moves and opening with: 'Look! Stop! What is that? You gotta work hard for this, okay? This is for you. C'mon, cue that music.' Then away we went. There were no pretty girls. No special effects. It really was all about us and we knew we had to make it look good.

Black and white shots of us dancing and singing as a band were cut snappily together with colour individual performance sequences – and a few moody takes of us running our hands through our hair! The video had drive and energy, and Mikey and Steo worked their starring roles with freshness and enthusiasm. Hard work it most certainly was (concentration went into overdrive getting those moves exactly in unison), but it was an exhilarating shoot and we loved every minute of it. Other people were getting the best out of us because they knew exactly what they were doing. In those early days of Boyzone, we were always being told what to wear and what to do, and we were perfectly happy with that. As far as we were concerned, Louis Walsh and his entourage were the ones who knew what they were talking about and we had everything to learn.

As well as performing the dance routine for the video, we had a live booking. *The Late Late Show*, where not that long before we'd made such a huge splash for all the wrong reasons, was giving us a re-trial. But this time we were ready. And this time we blew them away.

Although our first single and pop video were now all set for marketing, apart from low key personal appearances and a few club performances of the odd song, we still hadn't done our first proper gig. That was what we needed next. We already had fans because of all the hype surrounding us, but we had to get out there and be seen if more people were going to hear about us and start taking an interest. We needed a bigger fan base for the single really to sell when it reached the shops. So out we went. We put together a backing track for a set of about seven songs and hit the roads of Ireland for a solid ten months around the time of the release of *Working My Way Back To You.*

The first gig we ever played was in a truckers' café called Toghers in Naas, County Kildare. We had a team of three supporting us and we called them the '3D': Duncan, Dennis and Dobs. They were our sound guys, technicians and truck driver. They brought our gear in, set it up for us and made sure everything was sounding good.

The audience consisted pretty much of our families and friends, with just a handful of fans. There must have been 50 or so there, and while they were sitting out front, we were backstage, itching not so much with nerves as with excitement. The stage was tiny and we only had two live microphones so we had to pass them around for links. I don't think we even sang live vocals. The mikes were just there to say hello to the crowd and introduce the songs. Then it was press play, and away we went.

It was a small show and effects weren't high on the agenda, but we were very proud to have our own smoke machine. The idea was that, as the first track played, it would send atmospheric clouds billowing across the stage, then switch itself off so that about 12 to 15 seconds into the song, the smoke would clear and we'd be sensationally revealed, all-singing, all-dancing. All very professional. And that first gig, we were so up for it all. Our parents were out there and we were going to rock the place. The music played, the smoke started pumping out – and it didn't stop. The track was blasting away and we were giving the routine everything we had. But nobody could see a thing. For almost all of the first three songs, we were lost in a fog.

Unable to fix it, Duncan simply unplugged the machine, and finally the smoke began to clear. Not the best start in the world, but when the misty swathes had rolled away enough for us to be seen, the rest of the gig went brilliantly. It looked as if there were people everywhere, standing on tables and chairs, cheering and drinking. No one just sat still and listened. It was more like a big party than anything else.

As the final song played out, we made our exit. Not down into the audience, oh no, even though we knew almost everyone in the crowd. We felt so famous, we thought we were superstars. There was a window at the back behind where we'd been performing and we jumped right through it, making the getaway to our cars. We were walking on air. Even Wembley wouldn't have been a patch on Toghers Café that night.

One of the hardest things for me was getting up in front of people I was close to. But I guess it didn't show, and my parents loved it. They had their own fan club going right from the start and were bursting with pride. I don't think they could really believe it. Their son was in a band – their only son, who was never interested in music and didn't seem to have any ambitions or want to do much with his life. Sure, I'd brought home dozens of trophies as I was growing up, from running, long jump and high jump, motor-biking and BMX meets. But they never watched me competing. I didn't want them there. I just wanted to go to an event, focus, do what I had to do and get the job done. So I suppose they'd never actually *seen* me achieve anything until now.

That was the start of months of slogging the length and breadth of Ireland. We had a different game plan to Take That. We didn't target schools and gay clubs. We went for youth clubs and scout dens, and nightclubs if they'd let us in.

The nightclubs were always the rowdy ones. They were the really tough gigs, the ones we hated doing. There weren't generally many fans in the audience. And there was usually trouble. Fighting would break out and things would get thrown. We frequently had to dodge flying glasses, cigarette butts, ice cubes and 2p coins. Those nights were a real baptism of fire, and we came to dread them. We always had to perform right in the middle of the disco, and the young clubbers hotly resented our being there getting in the way of the music they really wanted to listen to.

Trevor was our driver then. He would meet us outside the Royal

Dublin Hotel on O'Connell Street and from there we'd head off for our gigs in his white Transit van. There were always a few fans hanging around as we left and, when word began to get around that this was our regular rendezvous point, the numbers swelled and some nights up to 100 girls would be waiting to see us off.

We played gig after gig in those first months on the road, but most of them were pretty small and insignificant. Often we'd have an audience of as many as 30 people, which we thought was amazing, but sometimes the numbers were dismal, maybe only 12 or 13. Sometimes we'd do two gigs a day and, after sharing the cash out, probably made around £50 a show. It was all very haphazard. We didn't have a carefully drawn-up tour schedule. There was no strategy, nothing marked out for us. In Boyzone's early days, touring literally consisted of a Transit van, a map – and a dart. We'd travel from up in the north near Belfast down to Cork in the south. It was gruelling but we loved it, Trevor chauffeuring us around in the trusty old van, well stocked with beer, and a comforting supply of sausage sandwiches courtesy of Ronan's ma.

That tour was christened *The Window Ledge Tour* because some of the stages we had to try and dance on were barely bigger than a window ledge. We did one memorable show at a tiny country club where the access was so poor, part of the fencing round a neighbouring house had to be taken down so that we could get our van in and the equipment unloaded! Even then the lads had to hump the gear up through the house where the people were having their tea. We followed apologetically along behind to get into the venue next door, but then found we had to climb over the side of a DJ box in order to get onto a stage that was no bigger than a table top. It was crazy.

We also had endless trouble with the van, but fortunately I wasn't the only trained mechanic in the band. Mikey Graham was a grease monkey too, and we both got used to making repairs as the Transit wheezed and groaned its way grudgingly around the highways and byways of Ireland.

I think the secret to Boyzone's eventual success lay in all that groundwork. There was a hell of a lot of it – and it was exhausting. We would do anything for publicity, to get our faces seen and our names on people's lips. We might be charging up and down the country to gigs, but we'd still be stopping off to do official openings for supermarkets, takeaways, even corner shops. That was often how we got our lunch when we were travelling. We'd stop, say a few words, cut a ribbon, and then get back in the van with free burgers. It was pretty relentless. Louis would find a way to book us in for anything and everything. No matter what it was, the lads from Boyzone would be there.

One night, when we'd been established in our small way for quite some time, and Duncan, Dennis, Dobbs and, of course, Trevor were a real part of the team, we got a call to do a show at the Carydale Hotel in the north of Ireland. It was a brilliant offer. We were invited to stay overnight so, rather than crawling all the way there in our clapped-out van, performing, and then having to trawl our way straight back again, we got some relaxation time. We arrived, booked into our rooms, had a swim, basked in the Jacuzzi, and ordered up room service. We felt like proper royalty.

It wasn't until we were in our rooms preparing to go on stage that John Pickering, the promoter, came upstairs and said awkwardly, 'Look, lads, they'll give you half the money to go home.'

We didn't understand what the problem was.

'You see, it's like this,' he went on. 'There are just four girls downstairs to see you and ... we'd really rather you went home.'

We had one of our brief band meetings and Ro spoke for all of us when he said, 'You know what? Four girls have come out in the freezing cold. They've bothered to come down here just to see us. So we're going to play for them. That's what we're going to do. We're going to play for them.'

Downstairs we went. An audience of four was still an audience. It was show time.

With the re-vamped smoke machine cranked up, we launched into our routines, and the girls seemed to like us. Then, because of the informality of the situation, three or four songs into the gig we decided to have a banter with them. That was when we realised they hadn't come out to see us at all. They weren't even supposed to be there. They were going to a hen do, had turned up at the wrong hotel, heard we were playing and decided to stay for a quick drink. We were so pleased they had, otherwise there would have been no one to play to that night. So I guess technically speaking that means we did once play for an audience of zero.

After what seemed like an age of dragging around the countryside, the months of slogging finally paid off. Our single hit the streets – and people started to buy it. Because of Polygram's doubts about us, we still weren't signed so, in the end, we released it ourselves. Louis Walsh set up the publicity. We did masses of radio promotion and were interviewed in all the newspapers. Louis also arranged signings of the single in stores. We would often arrive at shops with a pile of them in the back of the car. To begin with, we found ourselves greeted by maybe only ten or so girls but, as time went on and more and more people got to hear the song because of its airplay, the signings got bigger. In the end, there might be up to 60 excited fans turning up to get us to scribble on their records, cassettes, even the odd CD. It was quite a frenetic time, although at this point still only in Ireland.

I'll never forget the first time we actually heard our song being played on the radio. It was unbelievable. We were driving into town when it came on. Of course, we knew all about the airplay because people were telling us. But, hearing it for ourselves, 2FM playing Boyzone, that was something else.

I remember going home one night to find 40 copies of *Working My Way Back To You* sitting in my ma's kitchen. Everybody we knew seemed to be getting caught up in the hype, spreading the word, buying the single and making sure we got into the charts. It is a brilliant song, although I don't know about our version!

But at that point, I still didn't realise what I was getting into. I didn't grasp that I was about to be famous – properly famous. To me, I was still plain old Shane Lynch, the mechanic from Donaghmede. I didn't feel any different and I couldn't honestly say I knew much more about the music industry than I had done before everything had started. We were rehearsing and performing regularly so I must have been beginning to learn my craft, working out how to sing backing vocals and getting some tunes going. But there was still this huge part of me that didn't feel as though I should be there. I didn't deserve it. I was a chancer, just like that kid back in school. Only, this time, it was different. Things were beginning to take off. Our first single went to number three in the Irish charts.

That was when Polygram finally sat up, took notice and decided they wanted to sign us. Louis was the one who broke the good news to us and he could hardly hold back his excitement. We went wild.

The next step was an important meeting with the Managing Director of Polygram, Paul Keogh, at his office in Dublin's Aungier Street. He led us into a room where, for the first time in my life, I saw a CD player.

We sat nervously behind a huge conference table and watched a video recording from the Saturday morning show, *Live and Kicking*, hosted by Andi Peters and Emma Forbes. The programme had got the careers of a lot of famous bands off the ground, and Paul started to explain to us the importance of appearing on shows like that. The public relations would be invaluable.

'The first thing you have to do, lads, is to learn to be interviewed,' Paul said. 'You need to think about what to say and what not to say.'

That was a bit like speaking to me in Chinese. What was he talking about? How can you 'learn to be interviewed'? If somebody asked you a question, you answered the question. That was the way I saw it back then.

We sat there watching this tape of bands and artists being interviewed, after which presumably everything was supposed to be crystal clear. To be honest, I was still none the wiser. But we went ahead and signed on the dotted line, and, interview technique or no interview technique, suddenly it was official. We had a record deal. Boyzone was finally on the map and things kicked off in spectacular fashion. Our workload increased straightaway, with dozens of TV spots, road show events and personal appearances in record stores. Then came our first major show.

That summer, Jack Charlton's Republic of Ireland football team made the 1994 World Cup finals in America for the second time running. This time they went further than ever before and through to the second round, even though they were in the toughest group of all competing against Mexico, Italy and Norway. The squad didn't win but they certainly did us proud and were treated like heroes when they arrived back home. Dublin city ground to a halt as thousands made their way to a massive welcome reception in Phoenix Park. And Boyzone? We were invited to be part of the entertainment. It was the most amazing and terrifying experience of my life so far, singing and dancing in front of some 70,000 madly ecstatic Irish football fans.

In the meantime, Louis had decided it was time to bring out our second single. He picked The Osmonds' *Love Me For A Reason* which had been a number one hit for the American group nearly 20 years earlier. We liked the song and flew over to London to record a cover version with Ray 'Madman' Hedges at his Mothership Studios.

Ray couldn't have been more different from Ian Levine: tall and thin, not cold or rude or full of himself. He was a great guy with a cracking sense of humour, a real breath of fresh air. He gave me a lot of confidence and was a source of true inspiration. I was far from the best singer in the group, but he would never say so. He kept making positive comments like, 'Brilliant, Shano, nearly there, really close.' He was always an encouragement, a truly brilliant producer who got the very best out of all of us. Unlike Ian, Ray really rated Ronan's voice, and this time it was his turn to sing lead vocals with Stephen.

The recording finished, we went back home to Ireland to film the video to go alongside it. But that *Love Me For A Reason* shoot turned out to be one of the worst experiences of my life. Not because I tripped over my own feet or kept singing the wrong words, though. It was the candles. I had a phobia of candles and small flames – and the whole set was covered with the burning, flickering things. I don't think I mentioned it to anyone but it was a nightmare of a day for me. I still don't know how I managed to concentrate enough to get through it and not come out on film looking scared witless.

The budget for the video was £4000 and was shot in our co-manager, John Reynolds', POD nightclub. Some of the more arty images were actually filmed in the very posh gents' toilets. But that's show business, one long, heady round of glitz and glamour.

Bill Hughes, the director of our first video, was back in charge. I think he must have been taking lessons from Louis in subtle arm-twisting, because he managed to get away with borrowing Lainey Keogh designer sweaters and dark blue, pin-stripe John Rocha suits for us so that we could appear with two completely different and pretty sophisticated looks. He even blagged those candles, horrible things.

I guess Bill hit just the right note, though. The Irish public loved it, and in the autumn of 1994, *Love Me For A Reason* became our first number one.

By now, our perception in Ireland was beginning to change. Since the early days, with a lot of hard graft we'd been able to build up a fan base quite fast, but things were now intensifying at a rapid rate. There was a real buzz going on. Hormonally-charged girls were following us everywhere as well as still camping outside our homes. It was strange and hard to cope with at first, but I guess you get used to things.

My neighbours weren't quite so laid back. They got sick to death of all the empty McDonalds wrappings left lying around by the young ladies waiting outside my parents' house for hours in the hope of catching a quick glimpse of me. As the fast food restaurant was only just up the road, it was easy for the girls to nip off to stock up on supplies and then get back to their stakeout. We were being mobbed wherever we went. Even walking down the street or just attempting to go shopping became quite a chore.

Louis always taught us to treat the fans with respect and appreciation, and we tried to make a real effort with them, taking time to chat, sign autographs and pose for pictures. What was surprising was that they always seemed to know our whereabouts better than we did. Every time we arrived for a photo shoot, TV or radio show, personal appearance or whatever event it was, there would always be a handful of die-hard fans waiting to greet us. As it turned out, the girls were calling up Louis at his office asking for our schedule, and he was only too happy to give it to them – on the proviso that they passed the information around.

We knew we'd started to make it really big when the hard men of Dublin began coming up to us on the street, shaking us by the hand and saying, 'Good on yer, lads. Hope you make a million.'

Just a throwaway comment, no doubt. But those casual hopes were on the verge of becoming reality.

CHAPTER 6

Seeing Stars

"...THE SCREAMS OF APPRECIATION FROM THOSE ADORING FANS SAID IT ALL. THEY LOVED IT."

Boyzone may now have been bigger than Take That in our home country of Ireland but, just over the water in the UK, Polydor still weren't interested. There seemed to be no way of getting them excited over *Love Me For A Reason*. We'd hit a dead end. We needed them to release that single. If they didn't, we couldn't move forward and it was probably only a matter of time until we were finished. However, unknown to us, things were about to take a rather remarkable turn.

During the 1980s and 1990s, *Smash Hits* magazine was essential reading for music-minded teenagers. Published every fortnight, it regularly sold 500,000 copies. The big bosses also put on a huge music tour in the weeks leading up to Christmas, featuring readers' favourite bands and a few newcomers. A kids' version of the Brit Awards, *The Poll Winners Party* wasn't weighed down with music industry big wigs and boring, drawn-out speeches and, on the first Sunday of December in 1994, the final was due to be broadcast live on BBC1, with an anticipated audience of millions.

Michelle Hockley was in charge of the concerts and road show events that led up to that televised final. She'd been given a copy of *Love Me For A Reason* and, luckily for us, she loved it. A quick call to Louis asking if we were interested was all it took – and we were on the tour! It was a massive break. We'd be playing to tens of thousands every night, and be up for the best newcomer award voted for nightly by the audience. The exposure would be sensational and was the biggest chance we had of making it in the UK. This could be the big time for Boyzone.

We went out celebrating that night, and the following day, somewhat bleary-eyed and definitely not looking our best, we flew in to Heathrow Airport to meet our tour manager. We'd heard incredible things about this guy so our expectations were high and, as he rolled up to meet us, we weren't disappointed. Mark Plunkett with his long, shaggy hair, skin-tight black jeans and leather jacket, was a right greaser, a rocker through and through. We got on fantastically well, so much so in fact that, in the end, he continued as our tour manager for the rest of our Boyzone days.

Mark knew the business inside and out, but not just from a management point of view. He'd been a performer too, playing bass in a very American-style rock band called Little Angels who hailed from Scarborough. At the height of their fame, they were touring with acts like Guns 'n' Roses, Aerosmith, Van Halen and Bon Jovi.

The one thing we hadn't quite anticipated from Mark was our transport. He collected us from the airport and drove us to the venue in a rented white van (yes, another Ford Transit) only this one was rather garishly embellished – with a big pink elephant down the side. It was a bit embarrassing, to be honest. All the other acts were arriving for the *Smash Hits* tour in elegant, shiny limousines, blacked out people carriers and coaches. They all looked very glamorous. Very showbiz. This was it, our introduction to the big time. Six days that would make us famous. Still there we were, in yet another bashed up Transit, with the added indignity of a huge pink elephant.

Each night of the tour, three acts would perform their socks off to battle it out for the newcomer award and, since we wanted it pretty badly, the first thing we had to do was suss out the opposition. I have to say it looked pretty stiff. We were up against a young solo artist, Nick Howard, and a brilliant girl/boy band called Deuce, a predecessor to Steps. Tom Watkins, the man behind Bros and East 17, was Deuce's manager, and that band could and should have been huge.

Voting forms were placed on all the thousands of seats and, every evening, the eager, young spectators would each choose their favourite new act of the night, put a tick in the right box and post that all-important form into a big barrel. At the end of the week, the votes would be counted and the act with the most ticks would win the award. More importantly, the winners would land the coveted slot in the live *Smash Hits Poll Winners Party* to be televised on BBC1. That was the big break.

The tour was the most sensational event to be a part of. It was magnificent. Right from the moment we pulled up at that first venue in Newcastle, the buzz was phenomenal. We walked in and our jaws just hit the floor. There were famous faces everywhere. We spotted the East 17 boys first, then Take That and the gorgeous girls from Eternal. And I'll never forget the moment when we caught sight of Ant and Dec (or PJ and Duncan as they were known back then). The duo who'd found fame and not an insignificant number of fans on the BBC show, *Byker Grove*, had a hit single, *Let's Get Ready To Rumble*. Now, here they were, just milling casually around with the rest of the guys on the tour – and this year, the rest of the guys on the tour included us. All we could think was, wow! There's PJ and Duncan. Look how far we've come.

After a few days of rehearsals and technical bits and pieces, the 1994 *Smash Hits* Road Show kicked off in Newcastle. For us five teenage lads, still fresh from Ireland, that opening night was a sensation. We'd met up with all the rest of the acts before the show, and most of them were terrific people, but we still couldn't really get our heads around what was happening to us. We were five scared little boys, lost somewhere in the far reaches of northern England and feeling bewilderingly out of our depth. As we burst on to stage that night, fit and as ready for action as we could possibly syke ourselves up to be, all we hoped was that no one would notice how desperately nervous we really were. We launched into *Love Me For A Reason* and, to our enormous relief, the crowd seemed to love us. Definitely something to celebrate when we went back to the hotel that night.

On day two, the show hit Sheffield. We were starting to feel just a little more at home, relaxing into things and getting to know the famous faces around us. We hit it off superbly with the lads from Optymistic, Bryn, Stuart and Ian, and Deuce and the East 17 boys were also getting to be pals. I remember how much I enjoyed the pre-show meal that night – hot chicken wings and potatoes followed by lollipops. Not that anything felt any less surreal. After all, we were still in the midst of celebrity city, sharing hotels with people we'd only ever seen on TV or listened to on the radio.

As the audience piled into their seats and the second show took to the stage, the nerves kicked wildly in again. EYC were superb. One of the hottest international boy bands of the 1990s, they were a multi-racial combination with a massive following – and were a really hard act to follow. But we gave it our best shot and, at the end of the night it still looked as though we had the biggest pile of voting slips in our barrel. The crowd seemed mad for us and, as if we hadn't done enough warbling for one day, we threw ourselves into a good old sing-song back in the hotel bar later on.

It wasn't just the audience who warmed to Boyzone. We were good, easy-going, Catholic lads and just about everybody seemed to like us. Between shows we travelled round the country in the *Smash Hits* coach, sharing the space with acts like girl group, Shampoo, house-music duo, Reel 2 Real and EastEnders heartthrob, Sean Maguire. Sean, like many soap stars before him, had decided to try his hand at the music business. These were the people we were watching on TV and now we were sitting next to them on a tour bus. It was an incredible feeling.

Even so, the best part had to be the fans. There we were, out of Ireland on mainland UK, and the girls there were screaming our names wherever we went and getting the Boyzone banners flying.

I think we probably spent the majority of the time walking round with our mouths open. It was all so new to us and so much larger and grander than the life we'd been used to. We stayed in a different hotel every night and there would be Mikey and Ronan, sitting down at the piano in the bar, writing songs, singing, drinking and eating, just enjoying themselves. That tour was a truly magical episode in our lives, although there were actually some moments I found quite hard to take.

I came down one night and found the girls from Shampoo drunk out of their minds. Shampoo were what you might describe as 'pop with attitude', and the two-piece girl group had been hitting the vodka for hours. They'd just finished eating their way through a pile of sandwiches, and seemed to think it would be a hell of a laugh to pick up the empty plates and start throwing them at the hotel windows. These were big, picture windows stretching from ceiling to floor. The plates were smashing, the place was a mess – and the girls were just rolling around laughing.

It hit me at that moment just what a bizarre world I'd been launched into. To be honest, I was quite scared. These two young women in their trendy Snorkel Parkas and skinny jeans seemed intent on wrecking the place and they just didn't care. It was the middle of the night in a smart hotel and they were acting like crazy people. That was weird to me.

Weirder still, I'd come across someone having a crap in a corridor, then knocking on bedroom doors as if this was some manic version of *Knock Down Ginger*. It was the wildest way of leading your life I'd ever experienced. What was it all about? Kids having a good time, I guess. But it wasn't for me. No way was I going to end up out of control (and out of my head) like that.

Halfway through the tour, we hit Manchester. We reached the Arena early and got rid of some adrenalin charging around playing footie with Sean Maguire, and the guys from Ultimate Kaos and Optymistic. Steo, on the other hand, opted for a wind down and took a session on the sunbed back at the hotel. Even though we were getting used to performing for crowds of 10,000 a night, we never got blasé and the nerves kept on coming. With the gig in Manchester, we were even more apprehensive. This was Take That's hometown and, for all we knew, that might have been enough to turn the locals against Boyzone before they'd even heard us. As it turned out, we needn't have worried. We seemed to go down a treat.

After that, the tour reached our beloved Ireland. Home, sweet home. It was a little strange, landing back on familiar turf but, this time, checking in at the airport among some of the most famous names currently heading up the pop industry. But what a great feeling to play to an ecstatic home crowd in Belfast that night, before heading down south for day five of the tour back in Dublin.

My whole family turned out for the Dublin gig and had the time of their lives. They were so proud of me. There I was, their Shane, up there on stage with the best of them. All the stars came on for the finale that night to wave goodbye, and it was our song that was played. Can you imagine? All those pop heavyweights singing along to our single. It doesn't get much better than that.

Then, when that party was over, we all headed off for another bash laid on at our co-manager, John Reynolds', POD nightclub. It was quite a homecoming.

As we flew back to the UK ready for the London final, we tried to stay calm but couldn't help the feeling that we might be in with a real chance of winning that best newcomer award. The crowd seemed to love us wherever we performed, and the votes just piled up in our barrel every night.

But there was a moment when we thought that dream might still slip through our fingers. It had nothing to do with the public's voice and everything to do with Tom Watkins, the controversial manager of East 17, who also looked after Deuce, one of our rivals for the best newcomer category.

Watkins had a real affinity with Deuce. He'd been the one to discover the lead vocalist. Earlier that year, Kelly O'Keefe was doing work experience in his office and he'd heard her sing. He loved her distinctive voice and original style and, with his encouragement, she decided to put together a girl/boy band with herself as the lead signer. She set out to create something fun and colourful which she did by mixing pop music and art in a loud and bold way. The band's catchphrase was 'kitsch goes classic', and Tom Watkins made no bones about the fact that he was desperate for Deuce to win best new act.

When we first began to hear the backstage whispers, we were devastated. Apparently Watkins was threatening to pull East 17 off the tour if Deuce didn't take the newcomer crown and make it to the live television show. This man was a big name in the industry. He had power and a lever to get what he wanted, which was a lot more than we had. If he fixed the contest, there'd be nothing we could do – even though it was obvious to anyone with half a brain that our vote barrels were always the fullest at the end of each night.

Day six dawned but, with the Watkins rumours still doing the rounds, we really had no idea how we were going to fare. It had been an unforgettable week. The best of our lives. But, having come this far, we wanted more. We wanted it all.

Then it was time. The endless travelling around, the sleeping in a different bed every night, the rampant nerves before a performance followed by that overwhelming euphoria as the crowds went wild for us, all culminating in this: *The Smash Hits Poll Winners Party* in London.

And that's where we found out. When all the nightly votes had been counted, and the extra ones from the *Live And Kicking* viewers added in and verified, it was suddenly official. We'd made it. We were the winners.

You should have seen us, screaming and jumping up and down in a state of such utter jubilation you'd think we'd been handed the world on a plate. And that day, it felt as though we had. We were the ones the public wanted. Their favourite. Their ultimate choice. We were the best new act. We stood on that stage on the Sunday afternoon performing *Love Me For*

A Reason live in front of a sell-out crowd of 20,000 hysterical pop fans, and an audience of 11,000,000 watching at home on TV. It was like nothing on earth.

When we were called up to get our award, we thought the screaming would never stop. The Boyzone banners were flying everywhere and we were basking in the glory. We couldn't help it. We were at the top of the tree. East 17 had won the award before and so had Take That. Now it was our turn and our time. When the screams subsided enough for him to be heard, Keith took the microphone and spoke for all of us: 'Everybody at home – WE'VE MADE IT!'

It had all paid off: Louis's dogged determination, the slogging around Ireland, the tough days without a penny to our name. Even that dire appearance on *The Late, Late Show* way back when Boyzone was barely a day old must have played its part. That night, we were famous in the UK and, as we left the stage clutching the first music medal of our career, I so hoped that, somewhere, Gay Byrne was watching. I'd love to have seen his face!

Smash Hits hosted a big party after the show and laid on free beer and unlimited ice cream. All the stars were there: Ant and Dec, EYC, BBI, Jarvis Cocker, Deuce, Terrorvision, Elastica, Ultimate Kaos – and Boyzone. Everyone was dancing and drinking and having the most wonderful time. It was almost too much to take in. Even pop starlet, Dannii Minogue, was there making her way to the dance floor in a tiny, baby doll dress.

The following morning, we were due to make an appearance on *GMTV* at the crack of dawn, so we headed back to our hotel before midnight to try and snatch a few hours' shut-eye. But I guess thinking we'd be able to nod off wasn't very realistic. Adrenalin isn't conducive to sleep – and we had it by the bucketful.

We'd done heaps of press interviews, radio shows, personal appearances and photo shoots leading up to the tour. Now, there we were plastered all over the front of *Smash Hits* magazine, five fresh-faced lads from north Dublin in our brightly coloured shirts. Hordes of fans were gathering everywhere we went, screaming at us and waving scraps of paper for autographs under our noses. Everyone wanted to know where they could buy our single – which was great news. It meant Polydor UK couldn't ignore us any longer.

When *Love Me For A Reason* was finally released, it went straight into the charts at number 10, shooting up to number 2 and selling over 700,000 copies. East 17's *Stay Another Day*, which stuck at number 1 for five weeks, might have kept us from the top spot, but being number 2 at Christmas was still phenomenal bearing in mind we'd started that year as unknowns in the UK. We'd even managed to beat Cliff Richard and, more importantly, we were the first Irish band to chart in the UK with a debut single. The song sold further afield too, and we managed to make the Top 10 in most European countries. It was all way beyond anything we could ever have dreamed of. We were on top of the world.

We found ourselves at the centre of a whirlwind of media activity. Our faces seemed to be everywhere. The lovely Sam Wright was head of promotion at Polydor and she was the one who got us our television slots. It wasn't an easy job by any means and, in the end, pretty much came down to a case of whoever had the best plugger got the best show. Sam worked fantastically hard on our behalf. She was absolutely key to our success in the UK and we can never thank her enough for everything she did. So that's how it was that, very early on a chilly Saturday morning, we drove through the gates of the BBC building in Wood Lane to make our first appearance on the kids' show, *Live And Kicking*. Most people were probably still in bed, but not the Boyzone fans. There they were, a whole host of them camping out excitedly on the pavement, waiting.

Live And Kicking was such a popular programme, it was the perfect place to engage with hundreds of thousands of fans up and down the country, and we couldn't have asked for a better platform. The presenters, Andi Peters and Emma Forbes, put us right at our ease, and we had such a laugh. Kids got the chance to speak to us by phoning in with questions they particularly wanted to ask, we got hauled into daft sketches with Trev and Simon, and, of course, we performed the single.

The following Thursday, we were invited onto *Top of the Pops*. We were still in London on a promotional tour for the record and were picked up in a van and driven to Elstree Studios in Borehamwood, Hertfordshire, where the show was filmed. We were so excited. It felt like such a privilege to be asked – although if I'm completely honest, that first time we appeared was a bit of an anti-climax. We'd got used to playing to such huge audiences on the *Smash Hits* tour and, deep down, I think we were all a little disappointed. When you watched *Top Of The Pops* on TV, it looked as though a proper concert was going on, with a constant procession of well-known acts hitting the screen. But when we actually got there, we found ourselves in a dark, square room with four different stages and nothing at all like we were expecting. It was all very tiny. And although on television there seemed to be hundreds of spectators, dancing and having a good time, there was only room for maybe forty people. With the cameras turning and the technical guys barking out, 'Roll', 'Cut', 'Now go again', there was absolutely no buzz, no atmosphere. The audience was herded from one small stage to another, within spitting distance of us and the other acts on the show that night. They were told when to clap and cheer. They even had to scream on cue and there was a lot of waiting around while the shots were lined up so that everything would look perfect in the final cut. Basically this was just a no-frills TV show. It was all the clever, technical stuff that made it seem like the party it always appeared to be.

When it was our turn to sing, though, I'd be lying if I said it didn't feel special, because it did. After all, it was our moment, and there was still that aura of unreality about the fact that there we were, Boyzone, doing our first stint on *Top Of The Pops*.

It may seem odd, I don't know, but maybe that was when it started to change for me. That was when the long hours spent travelling, the hustle and bustle, the endless posing for photographs and the constant stream of interviews somehow began to lose their edge. There was a kind of monotony to it all. It was becoming the norm. We still hadn't finally made it to the top, and there was much more to come, but I began to realise that this was actually what the music industry was all about. No one would leave us alone and it was a constant round of hard, hard graft every day. Not that I was ungrateful for the success, but I couldn't help being aware that there was something beginning to eat away at the back of my mind. We'd come such a long way from our simple, Irish roots. Where was it all heading? More importantly, where was *I* heading?

These were still very early days in the business and we knew we had a huge amount to learn. We were being marketed quite specifically and had to maintain a fresh, clean-cut image. Any mention in interviews that we had girlfriends was a strict no-no. Louis used to sit us down and go over the kind of personal details we could let out to the media, but he was adamant about relationships: 'If you're asked, make sure you say no.' And we did as we were told. At least we did as far as the media was concerned. But it didn't stop us sometimes sneaking our girlfriends onto the tour buses. Fortunately Louis never found out.

While we were in London and not out doing promotions on the road, we stayed in a downstairs basement flat in a house just off Baker Street. This was our base for three weeks. Over the months of being together, we'd become great mates and, just like the kids we still were at heart, we got up to all sorts of daft things like playing hide and seek in the dark. I don't know how our mums must have felt because, really, five teenage boys living together away from home for the first time was hardly a recipe for a healthy, ordered lifestyle.

We were given a lump sum of money to buy food. It worked out at about £15.00 a day but it would have been a bit much for anyone to expect us to spend it on anything decent. I don't think any of us even did any cooking. We'd never had to be responsible for ourselves like that before because our mums had always been there looking after us. Within those four basement walls, we lived like complete slobs, stuffing ourselves with takeaways and never even bothering to take out the rubbish. The place was a perpetual tip, piled up with empty pizza boxes, plastic fast food containers and beer cans. If the press had managed to snap any photos of Boyzone 'at home', I don't think we'd ever have lived it down.

It was while we were in London that, shock, horror, I bought my first porn mag. I remember crossing the road to the newsagents to get a chocolate bar and a can of Coke, and I happened to glance up at the top shelf and think, do people really buy this stuff? I wanted to give it a go but I was dead scared. I must have looked so suspicious, peering around to make sure I wasn't being watched before I hurriedly snatched a mag from the display and sauntered as casually as I could to the counter to pay. I was pretty paranoid at the time, thinking that the whole world knew who I was, and all I hoped was that the Indian man serving me didn't recognise me as one of the geezers from Boyzone. That really wouldn't have done a lot for the clean-cut image thing.

The end of a roller coaster year was rapidly approaching and it was time to head back to Ireland for Christmas. Back in Dublin, we were invited along to the National Entertainment Awards where we arrived in flashy, white tuxedos (as per our instructions from Louis) to be presented with the coveted Best Irish Newcomers Award, our second prize of the year.

More and more girls started to hang around our houses after that. They were very well behaved. There was no real screaming or hysteria and they didn't seem the kind to do anything wild or extreme. They just wanted to be there, to be close to us, to see us go in or come out, and they looked absolutely made up if they got a wave or a hello. Sometimes I'd get woken up by the sound of girls chanting my name which, I must admit, was something of a strange alarm call. I'd get given presents – bracelets and chains. Those girls were so lovely and generous to us, and we always remembered Louis's words about treating them well, taking a little time to chat and sign a few autographs.

Now we were really getting noticed in the streets of Dublin, too. From being a little awkward a couple of months before, shopping in places like Grafton Street was now becoming near impossible. All it took was for a couple of girls to recognise one of us and we'd be mobbed. I found it hard to get to grips with, this massive change in my life. I think I was still pretty down-to-earth. I certainly didn't see myself as pop idol material and, at that time, we hadn't really made any money from being in the band so it was difficult to picture ourselves as the superstars the public seemed to think we were.

1994 ended with a flourish: our first proper concert. The Point Depot was Ireland's premier music venue. It was an awesome location down there on the North Wall Quay of the River Liffey, in the heart of the Dublin Docklands. One of Ireland's largest indoor concert arenas, it had a seating capacity of up to 8500. It wasn't only used for concerts. Over the years it had taken on a string of different identities, becoming an ice rink, a boxing arena, a conference hall, an exhibition centre, a wrestling ring, a theatre, an opera house and a three ring circus. And now The Point Depot was to host the Boyzone gig for Christmas 1994. The only slight down side to the night was that all the tickets didn't sell, so the organisers had to pull the curtain across half the auditorium to make it look full. But we didn't really care. All the big stars had played The Point and, to us, our concert there was a sign that we'd made it – sold out or not.

The usual crush of screaming fans welcomed us as we arrived, and we tried to sign as many autographs as we could on the way in. Then inside, Louis and John Pickering, had arranged a massive meet and greet event before the show, and it seemed as if there were hundreds of people milling around backstage waiting to be introduced to us.

As the throng of spectators in the auditorium began chanting the Boyzone name, I felt a tingle shiver its way down my spine, and we bounded on stage in front of our own home crowd to give them the show they'd been waiting for. It may not have been especially high tech in terms of lighting and effects, but the screams of appreciation from those adoring fans said it all. They loved it.

And that was 1994, all wrapped spectacularly up.

CHAPTER 7

Moolah!

"BUT MAYBE, JUST MAYBE, SOMEWHERE DEEP DOWN
INSIDE MYSELF, SO DEEP EVEN I COULDN'T HEAR IT
MOST OF THE TIME, THERE WAS A LITTLE VOICE
SAYING, 'YOU'RE GOING TO MAKE IT.'"

Seeing the old year out with such a bang, we almost didn't dare think ahead to what 1995 might hold. Could it even begin to match up? But, as January dawned, we were still number two in the UK charts and Boyzone fever seemed to be gathering momentum daily – although that did turn out to have its down side.

We'd all managed to grab a few days' break after Christmas; Ronan and Mikey in Lanzarote, Steo in Morocco. Keith had headed for Tenerife but, with the press ever eager to sniff out the slightest whiff of scandal, paparazzi had followed him just about everywhere. It certainly wasn't the best holiday Keith had ever had. That made quite a splash in the Irish *News Of The World*, slicing savagely through the good little boy band image we were working so hard to project. It certainly wasn't the best holiday Keith had ever had.

As well as being big news in Ireland and the UK, we were also starting to make inroads into Europe. *Love Me For A Reason* had done well there over Christmas, and when we visited Rome, Brussels, Amsterdam and Munich, the locals seemed to love us, although I'm not sure they always knew what to make of us. There we'd be, joking around, while they were probably thinking, Ireland must be pretty strange. Even so, we turned out to be such a hit that we weren't able to do much in the way of sightseeing because it wasn't safe. There were girls everywhere waiting for a glimpse of us, and we were kept shut up in our hotel rooms a lot of the time because of fears we'd be mobbed.

Back home, the executives at Polydor were planning our next move. They were convinced that the best way to build on our success was to release another cover version for our third single. We disagreed. Very strongly. It wasn't what we wanted to do, so we said no. The music industry is always rife with jealousy and negativity and we'd been hearing murmurs of a general consensus that we were just two-hit wonders, a flimsy concoction built purely on hype with no real substance. Certain people were apparently even taking bets on whether we sung live or just lip-synched when we performed. We wanted our next release to give us the chance to prove ourselves.

Louis was right behind us and agreed that we should shut our critics up the best way we knew how – by producing some of our own material for the first album that was to be released later in the year. It wasn't as if composing was unfamiliar territory. Ronan, Steo and Mikey had been writing songs for years, and Keith and I were keen to get involved in that side of the band's work. A lot hung on the quality of this next song and we were determined it was going to wipe the smile off the smug faces of all those Boyzone sceptics.

We recorded the album back in London at Ray Hedges' home-based studio, and *Key To My Life* became that pivotal third single release. It was something of a heartfelt ballad based on a 'thing' Steo had had for one of his teachers. He, Ro and Mikey had been playing around with the idea for over a year, and when the bosses at Polydor heard the final song, they thought it had enough potential to risk a gamble.

The video that accompanied the single was a blast to film, but I'd have to say that our ballooning success and influence wasn't reflected in any kind of glamorous location. No exotic beaches or spectacular landscape backdrops for us. We turned up for the shoot at an ancient stone church in Sandymount, Dublin. And it was freezing.

The film was to be set in a schoolhouse in the 1930s and the area at the back of that tiny building became a bare, old-fashioned classroom. We played a motley collection of schoolboys, sitting behind some rickety, wooden desks and wearing period costume of heavy wool trousers, collarless shirts, waistcoats and flat caps. As the camera panned across the room, we were told to look 'thoughtful'. We all wore our caps different ways round, backwards and sideways, and when Ro had his on front ways, he honestly looked like a right old farmer.

The video was shot in sepia and the storyline was simple: Steo was in love with his teacher, played by beautiful blonde model, Laura Bermingham. She had a cane and metal-rimmed spectacles but, for all her peering and pointing, there couldn't have been many 1930s schoolteachers who actually looked that good!

The idea was that, while we were singing, we had to play up in her class, passing notes to each other, with Steo left to himself and mooning hopelessly about. He was the outcast in the story and, at break time, while we were messing about on old bicycles, he was supposed to be there on his own, looking lost and moody. We all got together by the end, though, even managing to drag a smile out of the poor, lovesick lad.

For the two days of the shoot, there were groups of girls surrounding that old church. When there was a break in filming, we'd wander outside to chat to them as they huddled together, trying to keep warm. That love and devotion from the fans was an amazing thing to experience. They were so excited that we were there, and it was good to have the opportunity to get in amongst them, sign autographs and pose for pictures.

This latest release and video were a big risk. Five months earlier, *Love Me For A Reason* had been one of the top 20 best-selling singles of 1994. It was going to be a tough act to follow, but follow it we somehow did. When *Key To My Life* was released in April, it was a massive hit, soaring to number one in Ireland and number three in the UK charts.

That summer we took on Ireland. Kicking off on 2 July at the Rialto in Derry, we blitzed every major city and town, performing at a grand total of 33 different venues in 30 days. We played music festivals, nightclubs, road shows and arenas, and appeared for signings at record stores everywhere we went. The *Coming Home* tour, sponsored by Virgin Cola, was a sell-out, and the biggest nationwide tour Ireland had ever seen. It finally finished on 31 July at the National Basketball Arena in Tallaght just outside Dublin.

Unofficially, we christened it the *Unreal* tour. There was no other way to describe it. Our reception was phenomenal and this time as we trailed across Ireland, we weren't condemned to bouncing around in a rusty old Transit. We had our own small bus as recompense for all the hard work, and somehow survived the rigours of touring on adrenalin and cola.

If there's one thing you can't avoid when you're together 24 hours a day, it's getting to know each other. We were already pretty close but that tour certainly put the seal on it. When we did overnight hotel stops I always shared with Ronan. He was the youngest member of the band and had actually quit school at the age of 15 to join Boyzone. Like me, he was well into his sport and excelled at athletics. He'd won 200m, 400m and 800m competitions, and had even represented Ireland. When he auditioned for Louis, he'd already been offered an athletics scholarship in New York, so choosing to take up a place in the band was a major decision for him and his family and, to start off with, his mother was very against it. But there was something about Ronan. I had the feeling he was going to be a star from the first moment I saw him.

We nicknamed Steo, 'Homeboy', because he always got homesick so quickly when we were away. Although he wasn't the youngest, we treated him as if he was because he seemed to need us to look after him. While he was at school, he was an all-Ireland disco dance champion, so it wasn't surprising that he went on to become a dance teacher. He'd also done some acting and even ended up with tiny parts in a couple of movies, *The Commitments* and *In The Name Of The Father*. Steo was a gentle, sensitive guy who loved poetry, writing, art and drama and, on rare nights off, slouching in front of the TV with a Chinese takeaway. He became a very close friend of mine. Living so much in each other's pockets, we grew to be able to tell each other just about anything and everything.

Like me, Mikey had come a long way from his days as a car mechanic. He appeared as the strong, silent type, but he was the one who would always be the most nervous before we went on stage. He'd get almost uncontrollable jitters and be disappearing into the toilet constantly. It was odd in a way, I suppose, because, out of all of us, he was the oldest and most experienced. He'd already performed with a few bands, not to mention penning dozens of songs before joining Boyzone. It was his dad and his mates who had encouraged him to go along to the audition, and I guess he must have been a bit disheartened when Louis initially turned him down. The departure of Richie and Mark turned out to be his lucky break.

Mikey was always very close to his family and friends. The band was clearly important to him but I always got the feeling it was just a job and something to be kept separate from his private life. Not that that got in the way of our getting on well together, because it didn't. But it was definitely a working relationship and we were never going to be close mates.

Keith had found school tough, which was something we had in common. He was always getting into trouble with both the teachers and the other kids. Then, in his final year, he discovered a talent for technical drawing. He began a City and Guilds course in architecture at college, but his heart obviously wasn't totally in it because he left when the opportunity to be a band member came up for him. We were close but at times needed a break from each other. I think underneath we were very alike which is probably why we clashed so often.

When we did get time off, it was wonderful to get a bit of space at home in Ireland. I missed my family, obviously, but I also missed driving, especially when I was in the UK. I was such a petrol head I could never wait to get back into my car. I had a Toyota Corolla GT twin-cam back then. It was my pride and joy and being away from it was really quite tough for me. When Ronan, Steo and Mikey were working on their music, I'd be off wasting some petrol. For me, driving meant getting back to some sense of normality.

It was pretty much the same old gang of us from my pre-Boyzone days – me, Kaner, Franco and Simon. We all had GT Corollas and off we'd go, tearing up the tarmac. Everyone in the neighbourhood hated us. A few even put posters in their windows protesting against what we were doing. I don't know if it was worse because of Boyzone. Some people really do seem to resent others' success. But it was obvious we were famous. I was getting attention everywhere I went whether I wanted it or not. And the reception was so mixed. I didn't mind being recognised, but at times I'd get called all sorts of names or someone might come up and be very aggressive. It was hard just to go out with the lads because I seemed to end up in awkward situations or getting into rows with complete strangers.

The Ireland *Coming Home* tour certainly got us primed for our UK tour debut which was to follow in September. The shows weren't going to be anything grand, no special effects or backing dancers in dramatic costume. We hadn't reached that point yet. It was literally the five of us boys and a backing track. But this tour was a key point in our career. It could be the making of us and we knew we needed to be spot on. We had to make sure we were fit, got in plenty of rehearsal time and knew the routines inside out. Straightforward enough, you'd think. Until disaster struck.

It was July, just a couple of months before the tour. We were out in Amsterdam doing some television shows and general promotion and, one free afternoon, I got the chance to play basketball. The ball happened to get lobbed out of the court so I ran round to fetch it back, jumping over a fence, leaping across a stream and scrambling down a bank to reach it. I never even saw the rabbit hole. I must have just slipped into it and twisted over on my ankle. Before I knew it, it was broken. Of all the things that could have happened to me, this was so ironic. I'd crawled out of high-speed car crashes with little more than a scratch yet, here I was playing a harmless game of basketball, and I ended up in hospital in Holland having my ankle set in plaster. I was devastated.

Only a week later, it was Mikey's turn to do himself some damage. He was out horse riding with the rest of the lads when he had to swerve suddenly to avoid a little girl who was standing right in front of him. The girl was safe but Mikey fell and landed on his head. Apparently the crack as he hit the ground was so loud, the others were certain he must have broken his neck. He was rushed to hospital with concussion, too scared to fall asleep in case he lost consciousness. It really shook him up, but it turned out he was lucky. The worst he'd done was jar some vertebrae in his neck and he had to spend a few days in bed. Even so, Louis must have started wondering which one of us was going to be next! We kept going, though. While Mikey was laid up, the rest of us, with me on my crutches, carried on with the relentless PR that still had to be done.

Single number four (and our third UK release), a funky song about a young couple in love, *So Good*, reached number three in the UK that July. It was another one of our own compositions, with a real up-tempo vibe, which had been written in a little studio in Temple Bar. For the video, once again we didn't get the pick of luxurious locations. The whole thing was shot at a derelict power station in Dublin. Maybe it was all supposed to be a part of our image – gritty and down-to-earth! There we were, dancing out a lively routine in an assortment of dark coloured jackets, t-shirts and big boots, while all around us the set was dressed with large, burning oil drums. The flames looked hot and hungry. And to think that when we filmed *Love Me For a Reason*, I'd been scared of a few candles.

What we didn't bank on was the fire brigade turning up because passers-by had mistaken the clouds of smoke for a dangerous chemical incident and dialled 999. Fortunately the firemen saw the funny side. The air was thick with black soot and by the end of filming; our noses were just full of the stuff.

A month later we released our first album, *Said and Done*. We were so proud of it because, as well as featuring six cover versions, it showcased seven of our own songs: *Coming Home Now, When All Is Said And Done, Believe In Me, Key To My Life, Together, So Good* and *Can't Stop Me*. The album did something that none of our singles had done. It went straight to number one. Our career was in overdrive.

At long last, some money was starting to make its way into our bank accounts. It sounds crazy, I know, for a band that had had three top ten hits in the UK and appeared on *Top Of The Pops* but, until then, we'd all been stony broke. We might have been a famous boy band but we were living on PD's ('Per Days'), small amounts to cover our food each day plus a few other bits and pieces. Fortunately the record company covered the big bills, so it wasn't too bad. But Polydor had spent such a massive amount of money on travel and recordings that they had several £100,000 to recoup before we'd start to see anything much.

When our official fan club started up, I don't think any of us were prepared for the staggering 5000 letters we received in its first week of opening. Huge numbers of fans were turning up to signings and personal appearances and they followed us just about everywhere. The scenes outside the Virgin Megastore in London said it all. It was 21 August, 1995 and the day of our album launch. At one point, Oxford Street had to be shut down. In the end, we hardly got to meet anybody because the crowds were so massive the police had to clear everyone away for their own safety. The shop doors were shut and everybody was told to go home.

At the end of that same day, we headed off to Chessington World Of Adventures for our official press launch. It was a beautiful sunny evening and an area of the park had been specially cordoned off for the event. VIP guests included our music mates Gemini, EYC and Ultimate Kaos, and Sean Maguire turned up later to cheer us on as we took to the stage in our black suits and sunglasses for a performance of *Key To My Life*. Ro, Steo, Mikey and Keith got stuck into all the moves, but I still had my ankle in plaster. I must have looked really comical, only just managing to stay upright on those crutches.

To end the night, a crowd of us decided to try one of Chessington's scariest rides – the white-knuckle Rameses Revenge. We clung feverishly to the lap bar and, as Rameses spun into action, we were pinned to our seats and the breath was pretty well knocked out of us. It was exhilarating and spectacular, that monster of a machine whirling us round and round before holding us in a deadlock upside down, and lowering us head first over a water fountain. For a speed and adrenalin junkie like me it was the perfect way to end an incredible party. I just wanted more. But for some of the lads it was a bit much. They felt pretty queasy as they stumbled out onto firm ground, and Sean Maguire looked sick and ashen-faced – so much so that I wondered if I ought to offer him my crutches to support himself as he walked away!

We had three top three hits in the UK and a number one album, and were about to play to around 50,000 fans over 27 gigs in September and October. Another eight shows were also scheduled for the run-up to Christmas. We were feeling good. We'd proved ourselves and it was a smack in the eye for the Boyzone critics. We certainly weren't just a flash in the pan.

Melinda McKenna, a former dancer, was our choreographer. She'd already worked with artists like Mark Morrison and Ant and Dec. We'd spent hours learning routines, dancing and sweating in the studio. If we weren't fit before, we certainly were after that. We had to be. The problem was that, after my accident, I was going to have to perform on crutches, so a lot of re-working needed to be done with the choreography to make allowances for my injury. Nevertheless, when the time came, the show still went on. I pranced awkwardly about, gradually getting more and more confident. I could even just about manage a one-legged dance, balancing my bad leg over the handle of the crutches so I could gyrate my hips and then wave my hands in the air. I'm sure I looked a bizarre sight, but the fans loved it and I always got a big cheer when I hobbled onto stage.

Like *Coming Home* in Ireland, our first UK tour was pretty low-key as far as production was concerned, although this time we did have a support act. Damon Butler, Dave Loeffler and Trey Parker of the three-piece pop/R&B group, EYC (Express Yourself Clearly), our mates from the 1994 *Smash Hits* tour, were there to get the crowd going at the start of the night. But there was no convoy of articulated lorries packed full of expensive staging and sound equipment, no top-notch band thrashing out our music. We had one truck, a DAT machine that played our tracks, and a skeleton crew of nine people. Even that was still so much more than we'd been used to from our early days of slogging around Ireland in a Transit van. And we were determined that, small though we were in numbers with minimum technical back-up, nothing was going to stop us putting on one hell of a show. The fans wanted a sensational night out and that's exactly what we were going to give them.

We played venues throughout the UK, opening in the less than salubrious Rhyl Pavilion. Those first two nights in the north coast seaside town of Rhyl were a great warm-up for the rest of the tour. Our tour agent, Louis Parker, had grown up there, and he'd arranged them as a good starting point for us.

A real highlight had to be performing at The Royal Albert Hall on Thursday 5 October. Who'd have believed that five young lads from

Dublin could sell out somewhere as prestigious as that? Flamboyantly dressed in our stylist's choice of baggy, fluorescent orange trousers, matching jackets and plain white t-shirts, we opened each evening with laser lights flashing and sweeping around the different theatres, catching our shadows as we stood, ready for action, behind massive curtains. Then, one by one, with the screams from the crowd growing louder and louder, we'd step out onto the open stage before pulling down the whole curtain to the floor.

I had to hobble off and sing from the side as the boys launched into *Here To Eternity*, joining them again for the less active songs, and just about managing to keep out of the way when they burst into the more energetic routines. It was actually quite frustrating having to hold myself back.

When we sang *Daydream Believer*, The Monkees' hit song, the audience would jump up and down in unison, but it was during *When All Is Said And Done* that the screaming always seemed to reach fever pitch. We sat on tall bar stools with our backs to the audience (at last I got to rest my plaster-laden leg) and, as we each turned around to face them, the shrieking got louder and louder. When we all finally got up from our seats, it was absolute mayhem out there. An hour later, our first hit, *Love Me For A Reason*, closed the show. Then, with the screaming and cheering still ringing in our ears, we legged it (well, I one-legged it) back to the hotel.

Barrie Knight was now responsible for our personal security. He was a big, black guy, but certainly not the great bruiser type you might associate with a tough job like that. In the 1980s, he had looked after Matt and Luke Goss during their megastar Bros days, so he was no stranger to the insanity and hysteria that surrounded the boy band phenomenon. He'd make sure we reached the hotel each night after the gig, and shout at the ranks of eagerly waiting girls to move out of the way so that we could get safely inside. I don't know how he did it, but Barrie somehow always managed to keep us *and* the fans happy. No easy feat.

Barrie's right-hand man, Steve Alderton, was in charge of tour security. He would deal with the advance preparations, like checking that we were all booked onto the same floor of a hotel whilst making sure none of the fans had managed to sneak a room there.

Together, Barrie and Steve were such a supportive team. They were always there for us, explaining things so we knew exactly what was going on, encouraging us, and lifting us when we were down. It was like having a couple of upbeat big brothers.

* * * * *

One of the drawbacks to being famous is that the media won't leave you alone — as we discovered. Their intrusion into our lives was relentless and very hard to take at times, especially as all the reporters were really interested in doing was digging the dirt. We weren't into drugs or sleeping with groupies, so they must have drawn a blank there, but we did enjoy a few drinks. And we still weren't 'officially' supposed to have girlfriends. Louis was very clear about that. So when a story about Keith moving in with his long-term girlfriend, Lisa, suddenly broke in Ireland, it was a bitter blow. Up until then, Keith had done a pretty good job at keeping Lisa out of the public eye and, apart from those topless pictures in Tenerife earlier in the year, he'd largely succeeded in holding the scandal-mongers at bay.

But overnight, things were taken out of his hands and he had to make the difficult decision to be honest about their relationship. He must have wondered if that would be it, the end of his Boyzone career, with Louis turfing him out on the spot and lining up an unattached and uncomplicated replacement. But he needn't have worried. When it finally all came out, the fans still loved him, attached or not.

Father And Son was the final track on our album and became our fourth single release in the UK where, in November 1995, it went to number two in the charts. It was a great song for us, especially Ronan, who'd sung it at his original Boyzone audition just 18 months earlier. It had already been the 'B' side on *Working My Way Back To You* but now, re-released for the UK audience, it became one of our biggest ever singles.

The *Father And Son* video shoot was probably the strangest so far. We were subjected to all the glamour of an industrial estate in Dublin (no change there then) and there were a few mean and moody sequences of us in sweaters and jackets. But for the majority of the film, we all had to wear white underwear of the long john and button-up granddad top variety – not an immediately sexy look I wouldn't have thought, but in those days we just did as we were told. The stylists also pushed the boat out and got us to have our hair cut. Steo's and mine was clipped short, Keith looked like a well hardened convict after having his head shaved, Mikey somehow reminded us of a scarecrow, and Ronan's usually immaculate locks were twisted up into spikes. But perhaps the weirdest side of that shoot was the staging. Most of our time was spent lying on top of a huge light box – and it got really warm. So much so that we had to have protective foil inside our long johns to stop us from getting burned. Even then, poor old Steo still ended up with a burnt arse.

The song itself was a ballad originally penned in 1969 by Cat Stevens (or Yusuf Islam as he became known when he converted to Islam). He heard our version being played on the radio one day as he sat down with his son, Muhammad, to eat a kebab at a Turkish restaurant. Louis invited them both to come and meet us at the *Top Of The Pops* studios, and we all had quite an in-depth chat in the Elstree cafeteria about life, music and faith. He loved our arrangement of the song, the harmonies and the string accompaniment, and told us he'd originally written it for a musical about the Russian Revolution. We had a photo taken with him before he left. He was a very interesting man and I'm so glad I got the chance to meet him.

That was the day Keith found out that his long-term girlfriend, Lisa, was pregnant. He was putting on a brave face, but inside he was panicking. We all were. What was Louis going to say? What was this going to mean for Boyzone? And, for Keith, it wasn't just Louis he had to face. How were Lisa's mum and dad going to feel? There was certainly an irony about the timing. All day long we'd been focusing on our performance of *Father And Son* for *Top Of The Pops*. Now, here was Keith, in the early stages of becoming the father to, as it turned out, a son.

The news of Keith's impending fatherhood finally out in the open, and everything resolved on the home front with Louis, with Lisa's parents and, thankfully, with the fans, we were back on the road doing promotion. We visited Germany, France, Holland, Italy and Spain, and even ventured further afield to the Far East for a three week tour. Outside of Thailand, at that point no one had heard of us, so we crammed in trips there as well as hitting Japan, Singapore, Hong Kong and Korea. It was exhausting, hanging around in airports, forever on the move, relentlessly on show.

During *Father And Son*'s 14-week stint in the UK top ten, we were invited along to London's Piccadilly where, at the Madame Tussaud's Rock Circus, we were to make our mark on the prestigious Wall Of Hands. The Rock Circus is a remarkable exhibition that takes visitors on a lavish and extensive behind-the-scenes tour of the pop music world. On The Wall Of Hands, there is an intriguing display of palm casts of the cream of the music industry. Now, unbelievable as it seemed to us, it was our turn to join legends like Eric Clapton and Michael Jackson.

With our album now selling at an astonishing rate, at last we received our first advance: £20,000 each. We had a letter telling us the money was being paid into our bank accounts. It's the kind of news you could just kiss a postman for delivering. We were far from millionaires but we knew this was only the beginning.

Boyzone had the potential to make each of us a fortune so we saw no reason to be careful and hang onto the cash, convinced there'd be plenty more where that came from. Steo hadn't passed his driving test so he went out and spent more than a fair bit on designer clothes. The rest of us bought cars – Ronan a black BMW, Keith a white Sierra Cosworth, Mikey picked up the keys to a silver Mazda, and I went out and found a 911 Porsche.

Back home, my parents had a photo of me when I was about 14 years old, taken just before I was kicked out of school. I was standing beside a 911 Porsche because my dad used to take care of one at his garage. I loved that car. I always wanted to own one just like it one day. And suddenly, here I was, 19 with my first proper band earnings, buying my fantasy. I got it from an Arab guy, a gorgeous midnight blue 911 Porsche complete with super car tricks and gadgetry. It was like something out of an action movie, lowered, turbo body tail, and I felt sick with excitement knowing I was actually in a position to say, 'Yeah, I'll have it.'

I remember flying home to Dublin, picking my dad up and flying back to London with him so he could give it the once over and, hopefully, his approval. We met up with the owner at a Ferrari garage. Out came the car, gliding effortlessly through gleaming steel shutters like an absolute dream. I'd brought my dad with me to get his advice but, as I stood there, feeling as though I'd been magically transported onto the set of a James Bond film, I didn't care whether he liked it or not. He could have told me not to touch it with a twenty-foot barge pole, it wouldn't have made any difference. I was bringing that car home.

As it happened, my dad said, 'Fair play,' and I handed over the money and we headed for the ferry. He was driving because of my ankle. How do you describe that feeling – 19 and sitting in the lap of luxury in your own Porsche 911? You just can't.

Towards the end of the year, me and the boys were back out touring again with the *Smash Hits* Roadshow that had changed our lives 12 months earlier. We knew we owed a massive debt of thanks to the *Smash Hits* readers, and we gave every one of those performances our absolute all, coming home at the end with a couple more awards for our mantelpieces.

That Christmas, as I settled down for a well-earned break with my family, I decided to take a trip in my Porsche to the Grange Community College where I'd been a none-too-successful schoolboy. I had no ambitions for fame and fortune back then. It certainly never occurred to me that I'd ever be a famous pop star. How I thought I was going to get my hands on a car like that, I have no idea, but I always said to my mates in school, 'You know what, lads? I'm going to have a Porsche before I'm 21.'

As goals go, that was pretty steep, especially as I was something of a failure in the classroom and had nothing whatsoever mapped out for my life. But maybe, just maybe, somewhere deep down inside myself, so deep even I couldn't hear it most of the time, there was a little voice saying, 'You're going to make it.'

CHAPTER 8

Full On

"BUT IT WASN'T A LAUGH. IT WASN'T FUNNY AT ALL.
AND THOUGH I DIDN'T KNOW IT AT THE TIME, THOSE
FEW HOURS IN THAT TINY, DARK ROOM WERE GOING
TO SCREW ME UP FOR YEARS."

Louis Walsh had a plan – world domination for Boyzone. As we launched into 1996, still reeling from the frantic pace of 1995, he had his sights set on America and getting a firmer grip on the Far East. And, of course, we still had to continue making our presence felt in the UK and Europe. There could be no let up. We were on an extraordinary roll and Louis wasn't about to let it ease off.

Being nominated for Best International Newcomer at the annual Brit Awards was yet another leg on our rocket trip to superstardom. The Brits celebrates the best of British pop music. Winners are decided by a panel of record industry judges, while some categories are voted for by members of the public. The ceremony that year was held at Earls Court and hosted by TV's Chris Evans. We didn't come away with a trophy in the end – in our category, the award went to Canadian singer/songwriter, Alanis Morissette – but it was such a buzz just to be there, and a great honour to rub shoulders with the likes of Prince, David Bowie, Oasis and Bon Jovi. It was a night full of fun and celebration – although not without controversy.

Michael Jackson won a special award for Artist Of A Generation, and children from London stage schools joined him as he performed his single, *Earth Song*. But in the middle, a very drunk Jarvis Cocker of rock band Pulp jumped onto the stage to try to ruin Jacko's performance. Apparently Cocker was furious with him for adopting what he saw to be a Jesus Christ-type role during the song, and the incident ended up the subject of a huge amount of national publicity.

After The Brits, we were back to recording our next single, the first of three that year. *Coming Home Now* peaked at number three. We still didn't quite manage to bag that elusive number one. That would come later.

Coming Home Now was a very relevant song to us, bearing in mind how much time we spent away, so the lyrics had real poignancy. There was a kind of rap quality and rhythm to that single, with Keith and me having moments of speaking through the music.

I loved the video which seemed to have real attitude. It was filmed around various Dublin city beauty spots and in a street in Ringsend, and there were shots of local children running and playing, all a part of the cityscape. Dressed in black, we had to strut meaningfully around as if we owned the place. The whole thing had a definite earthy feel, the Boyzone lads getting back to their roots.

People were very friendly towards us through the shoot – which was just as well because, not being studio-based, as the day went on we ended up having to make use of residents' bathrooms. And we were also very grateful to the local Garda who stepped in to control the growing crowds of fans as word spread that Boyzone were in town.

A few weeks later, we performed *Coming Home Now* at a big charity fashion bash at The Point Depot, which was where I was first properly introduced to Eternal star, Easther Bennett, who was to become my wife a couple of years later. That was the night the world's hottest jet set converged on Dublin, and Eva Herzigova, Christy Turlington, Naomi Campbell and Jasmine Le Bon took to the catwalk, looking nothing less than sensational in Irish designer gear.

Then it was our turn – although I think we were a little wide of the sensational mark. Daubed in body paint, we had to model some designer knitwear and, at a particular moment, were supposed to rip our tops off in front of the crowd. When the time came, I took my jumper off and then thought, what the hell, and decided to drop my trousers too. I'd say it was a spur of the moment thing but it certainly got us plenty of publicity.

However, it wasn't just Boyzone making the news. There was that ever present *other* boy band, Take That. We'd first met at the *Smash Hits Poll Winners Party* back in 1994, and they'd seemed like great guys. We didn't get to speak to all of them then, but Mark and Gary were both very happy to shake hands with us. I don't know if they looked at us as rivals, but there was certainly rivalry among the fans. There were Take That fans who hated Boyzone, and Boyzone fans who had it in for Take That. It was crazy really because we never had a problem with each other personally, although of course we were aware of the competition between us, but all the press and media hype made out that we were sworn enemies.

There had been rumours for months about Take That finishing, and the lads and I were all away together when we heard the news that they were officially breaking up.

I suppose maybe Robbie Williams was always going to be the off the wall one with his own agenda. Towards the end, apparently tiring of the clean-cut boy band image, he'd begun hanging out with pop-rock group, Oasis. Those guys were notorious for drunken and drug-fuelled partying. By late 1995, Robbie had walked out on Take That. He went off on a different tangent for a while, and he and Keith actually became good friends, even living together for a couple of months. Then, at our concert at the RDS in Dublin at the end of 1996, Robbie came on and sang with us.

But his exit from Take That marked the beginning of the end for the band. The four remaining members soldiered on for a while and did produce some amazing music, but somehow there was nowhere else for them to go.

On 13 February, there was a major press conference. Gary, Mark, Howard and Jason walked into a large room at the Manchester Airport Hilton and sat in front of a long table with literally hundreds of microphones all around.

Mark began, 'Well, first …we do care very much about all our fans … We've done all that we can as Take That. We took it well beyond our wildest expectations and, I suppose, beyond many of *your* expectations. For now,' he continued, 'it's the end of Take That, but we'll still be around. Our mugs will turn up on the TV and doing things for a number of years to come. We've taken it as far as we can go at the moment, but there will be more …'

It certainly was the end of an era and a big, big press moment, with the news being beamed all over the world for days. Girls were calling in crying, and some of the group's fans were so distraught at the break-up that the Samaritans were forced to set up telephone hotlines to make support available to deal with the trauma.

We couldn't help being quietly pleased when the news finally broke. It was nothing personal. If it hadn't been for Take That, we wouldn't even have begun as a boy band. Take That was the reason Boyzone existed. On the other hand, those lads were a threat to us professionally. It's like rival supermarkets, I guess. If you own Tesco and Sainsbury's is suddenly no longer around, you're going to feel good – the competition is gone. We were the biggest thing out there now and, with Take That out of the way, we might even win over a few of their fans.

Right after the Take That disbandment, we headed off to Australia for a short promotional visit, and then, of course, came the launch of the

Boyzone dolls! They'd been a few months in production and now they were finally unveiled to the fans. The modellers had taken photographs of us from every angle so all the details could be copied exactly, right down to the earrings I was wearing at the time and the way my trademark right eyebrow was shaved. The 12-inch plastic figures arrived in their individual orange boxes and were snapped up by an excited public – with, of course, mine being the most popular!

We were also very busy with the usual round of TV programmes: *Live and Kicking*, *Top Of The Pops*, *The Chart Show*, *Ant and Dec's Sm:tv*, *Blue Peter* and a host of chat shows. On top of that, Louis Walsh managed to do a deal to get us on the box *between* programmes appearing with the Honey Monster to advertise Sugar Puffs breakfast cereal. Louis wanted us in everyone's face as near to every minute of the day as he could logistically grab. I'll never forget that surreal shoot at a Middlesex branch of KFC, where the director got us juggling burgers and mayonnaise for an advert that was to be shown in Thailand.

We even did a stint on *The Big Breakfast*, Channel 4's hugely popular light entertainment show that went out every weekday morning. The programme was broadcast live from a set of former lock keepers' cottages in Bow in east London, and was a crazy mixed format of news, weather, interviews, audience phone-ins and features. We were to join Zoe Ball as guest presenters for a week, and it really was as mental as it looked on the TV. We were up before 4.00am to get to the studios in Hackney Wick in the heart of London, in time to stroll over the towpath to 2 Lock Keepers' Cottages. Like everything on television, the *Big Breakfast* house seemed a lot different in real life – much smaller and scruffier, and there was graffiti on the white picket fence surrounding it.

Even at the crack of dawn, TV researcher turned presenter, Zoe Ball, looked stunning, and we sat in her dressing room, a portacabin next to the house/studio, and were talked through the various items coming up on the show – One Lump Or Two, Egg On Your Face, More Tea Vicar, Beat The Banger. Insane, or what?

Our *Coming Home Now* signing at Dublin's HMV store was close to anarchy. We were supposed to be there for an hour to sign copies of the single, which was shooting up the charts, and we expected it to be busy, but nothing could have prepared us (or Dublin come to that) for the near hysteria that greeted us. The city centre was almost brought to a halt by over 5000 screaming fans. In the end, the Garda had to be called in to organise the crowds and stop a potentially dangerous stampede. It was five hours later when we'd finally signed the last single.

I think we had the best fans ever. Their support was phenomenal. Every time we arrived at an airport almost anywhere in the world, they'd be there waiting for us. Every time we appeared on a TV show, there they'd be. It seemed that no matter what we did or where we went, they were always there to wave the Boyzone flag and boost our morale. A lot of them used to travel all over Europe to see us in concerts. I don't know where they got their money from, but that rank of diehards would always turn up.

There was one girl who, in the end, we nicknamed Lift. I think she was mostly a fan of Steo, but we'd be in and out of hotels and every time the doors to a lift opened, she'd be inside. She wasn't scary or obsessive, just fun. Our fans were all like that – very cool, and I like to think that I built up a good rapport with them and gave them enough time.

They were very generous to us too. I got some terrific presents. All I had to do was mention on a TV show that I liked something, gold rings, gold chains, a certain aftershave or Georgetown hats, and that particular show would be inundated with anything I'd talked about. I always wore Georgetown hats. They were my particular thing, and I ended up with hundreds of them. As well as presents, the girls would send us pictures of themselves. We never got raunchy, adult women or girls our own age coming onto us. These were just regular, girl-next-door-type kids.

Back home in Dublin, there was still nearly always a bunch of fans staking out my parents' house. In any week, there might be 20 to 30 girls outside the front door. They'd spend the night even though I wasn't home.

I know for a fact that my ma brought three or four girls inside once because it was freezing and she wasn't going to let them stay out there.

We used to worry about them too. Once, when we were gigging in Amsterdam, we were staying at the American Hotel. It was a bitterly cold night and still there were fans sleeping outside on the streets. I remember me and the lads throwing duvets and pillows down to them. It wasn't nice seeing them shivering out there on the pavement and we had to do our best to look after them where we could.

As well as being loved by the fans, it was always good to be recognised by our peers in the industry, especially in Ireland. On 29 March, we arrived at the Irish Music Awards (IRMAs) to scoop another couple of trophies – the best Irish Band Award and the Best Single Award for *Key To My Life*. TV host, Dani Behr, made the presentations, and we got the chance to chat with ex-Eternal star, Louise Nurding, and Michelle Gayle, the popular EastEnders actress. And, as the champagne flowed inside the Burlington Hilton, scores of fans set up camp to greet us on the outside.

The first few months of 1996 had blasted by in a whirl of press interviews, PA's, photo shoots and television appearances. Now it was time to knuckle down to some serious hard graft in the rehearsal studios. Our first major arena tour was coming up. We'd waited a long time to have the budget for a sensational, stage show, and with the money finally coming in, we were determined to give it the works.

We normally rehearsed in London, which we preferred. Working near home held too many distractions for us and it was always harder to concentrate on the job in hand. But both Keith's and Mikey's better halves were expecting their babies in the spring, and they obviously wanted to be nearby when something happened. So, Dublin it had to be, and The Factory on Barlow Street became our training camp for two weeks while we got down to learning the new routines. Whilst we were sweating it out in one studio, The Corrs were working away next door, and Clannad were down the corridor putting the finishing touches to their show before hitting the road. Over the years, other top Irish musicians, including U2 and Chris de Burgh, had made use of those purpose-built studios, so it wasn't unusual for the locals to see fans, armed with cameras and autograph books, hanging around outside the building.

Melinda McKenna was our choreographer and she'd work with us from about 11.00am every day, with a break for lunch, and then again in the afternoon from 2.00 until 4.00. We would sweat buckets, arriving home pretty drained and with every muscle in our bodies screaming for mercy. Melinda didn't hold back, she put us through hell. But it was worth it.

Whilst touring probably brought us closer together, it often felt as if the promotional work all but tore us apart. Promotional expeditions meant long, long hours and unbelievable schedules. At one point, we were visiting three countries in a day, which was an absolute killer. We could be up at 5.00am to catch a plane in time to get off to a morning TV show at 9.00, get back on a plane at midday, do an afternoon show by 3.00, then catch another plane and do a night gig somewhere else. I know one year we caught something like 126 flights. Definitely mental.

Touring, on the other hand, was fantastic and my time to shine. I still didn't have much of a voice for solo spots, and mostly filled in with the 'oohs' and 'aahs', but at least on tour I could perform. I could move and connect with the crowd. There would be some shots of me in our videos, but generally it was the lead singers that the camera focused on. Touring was when I really had to concentrate and apply myself to the routines. And I loved being on stage. It was sheer fun. We could laugh and joke with each other as well as with the crowds. There were no worries to speak of, no stresses – other than the responsibility to perform and put on a top-notch show. It was all about entertainment.

Then there were the regular after-show parties. We were constantly socialising with each other, not always the stage crew necessarily, but the performers – us, the 'musos' and the five boy and five girl dancers – so we were bound to get close.

Our manager, Mark Plunkett, was everything we could have wished for. He could have a laugh and a joke but was very serious when he had to be, and he somehow got to understand each one of us individually. He seemed to know who was going to be late and who was going to be early and, to make allowances for that, he'd give us different times to be ready. He knew who he'd have to wake up and how many times he'd have to call us, so it all varied and he handled it with almost military precision. I guess it must have been like looking after five kids, still in their late teens, and at times trying to kick against the system. Mark was the one who had to get us out and onto that bus to head off at the right time for the right venue.

From our lean Ford Transit days, we'd finally graduated to a proper tour bus. It was a double-decker and, as we sped up and down the motorway from venue to venue, it became very much a home from home. On the ground floor up the front was a seating area – not quite a lounge, but any guests we had travelling with us could make themselves quite comfortable there. There was a second lounge-type area at the back, and that's where the 'musos' always were. Upstairs were ranks of bunk beds for us all when we drove overnight. There was a seating area at the very front, where I used to spend a lot of my time, and another space to relax in at the back, complete with TV and video, which is where the rest of the lads would tend to hang out. A motley assortment of videos helped to pass the time as we trawled from gig to gig, anything from *Sister Act 2* to Roy Chubby Brown. Steo must have watched *Sister Act 2* and *The Lion King* over a hundred times. It just did our heads in. I couldn't stand those movies so would spend my time up at the front of the bus watching the different cars. They did a whole lot more for me than watching Whoopie Goldberg.

The second leg of this particular tour featured five support acts: Rebekah Ryan, Peter Andre, Sean Maguire, Reel to Real and Kavana. We'd certainly come a long way from Toghers Café in Naas where we'd shared a toilet for a dressing room. Even so, we still tried to keep it real.

We never got into the outrageous backstage riders scenario we'd heard about. Some of the stories were legendary in the world of showbiz. Apparently, Oasis always asked for Monster Munch, Wotsits and Doritos, washed down with lots of Guinness, beer, red wine and a bottle of whisky. And if you think you that was excessive, P. Diddy demanded 204 towels, 20 bars of soap, two bottles of Hennessy cognac, two bottles of Santa Margherita Pinot Grigio, two bottles of Veuve Clicquot and a bottle of Dom Perignon, as well as white flowers, cheddar cheese and sour-cream crisps. In the face of that we were pretty low key, quite happy with a bowl of raspberries, a basket of crisps and mini-chocolate bars, lots of bananas, water and some honey and lemon.

Being on the road so constantly could be tough, but the actual shows were an incredible buzz. When we finally got to play Wembley, it was out of this world. We'd performed to over 250,000 fans that spring and summer the length and breadth of the UK, and our four nights at Wembley Arena were just the icing on a multiple-layered cake. We were there on the weekend of 13 and 14 July, then back at the end of the month for the grand finale to our UK tour – and there wasn't a seat left in the house. Deep down we'd always dreamed about having the opportunity to play Wembley maybe once, but four sell-out gigs? That was something else. We flew our families in from Ireland on the last night. There was no way they weren't going to experience this with us.

As we sang our hearts out, 15,000 adoring, screaming fans waved, swayed and sobbed, a heaving mass of energy and emotion stretching back through the auditorium as far as the eye could see. You needed that. It hyped you up. It lifted your performance even beyond your own expectations.

The preparations and build-up backstage before the show opened were all an integral part of each concert, but we were always desperate to get out there. As the lights dimmed to a semi-darkness punctured erratically by pulsating spots of light, the familiar music would begin to throb and the metal gates at the back of the stage complex swung open.

An intense wave of barely controlled excitement and anticipation seemed to roll towards us out of the audience at that moment. This was it. Kick-off time.

We stamped through the gateway, our heavy, black boots hitting the floor to the beat of the music – and the crowd erupted. In our metallic silver, oil-skin-type jackets, baggy red leather trousers and dark glasses, we must have looked more like cosmic firemen than a boy band. But the choreography and costume worked. There was real energy in that entrance.

We opened with *Together*, lively, pacey, one of those hard-to-keep-still-to songs. It was a relief to lose those silver jackets after that first number. We'd be sweating buckets before we were even half way through it. Then came the more melodic *Here To Eternity*, the heartfelt *Believe In Me*, and the punching, driving beat of *What Can You Do For Me?* The stage was on two levels and our meticulously rehearsed moves made the most of the impressive space. We danced in formation, sprinted from one side of the massive platform to the other, and bounced up the two light-lined stairways to sing from the upper level.

Fifteen or so minutes into the show, we took a break from singing to introduce the excellent musicians who shared the stage with us, clustering around each one and presenting them enthusiastically as they showed off what they could do.

There were quieter moments too. A glittering light display, with spots sweeping over the heads of the awe-struck crowd, gave us the quickest of chances to change costumes into white shirts hanging loosely over white trousers. Then, each sitting on a tall stool, backs to the audience, we turned individually to face them as we sang our own particular lines of *When All Is Said And Done*, before swinging away again. Each time a different one of us lads looked out front, we'd be rewarded by cheers and screams from captivated onlookers.

A narrow walkway led from the main stage to an illuminated platform jutting out into the crowd. Steo stood there on his own for his rendition of *If You Were Mine*. He put his heart and soul into that song – and the girls went wild. They were reaching up their hands, waving their arms, and by the time he'd finished, the floor around his feet was scattered with flowers.

The time out on stage always seemed to fly by. I suppose we had to be so focused, had to concentrate so hard on every little detail of the performance. Working together meant precisely that. Together. As one. We all depended on each other. No one could afford to look ragged or under-rehearsed. Add to that the amount of nervous energy there was buzzing around, radiating from us and from the audience, and I guess we would have been doing something seriously wrong if any part of the show had dragged!

When *Love Me For Reason* came round, we teased the audience that this was the end, the last number. Only, of course, it wasn't. After another manic quick change, we burst back on stage with a four-song finale ending with the stirring and evocative, *A Different Beat*. With the lights flashing, punching out the exciting percussion rhythms, it was a memorable and uplifting finish.

As soon as the performance was over, we were away back through the metal gates leaving a swelling volume of screams, cheers, applause and stamping feet. There must have been a lot of sore throats going home from Wembley on those four nights. But what nights they were.

In fact the entire tour had been amazing. With a spectacular set, live musicians, excellent dancers, fabulous costumes, expensive and sophisticated lighting and a crew of over 40 people, it was a show of which to be well and truly proud – at a cost of £2,000,000. After all the expenses, we earned about £20,000 each which, over the course of the 50 or so dates we'd played, worked out at around £400 a gig. Poor old Duffy ended up taking home a lot less than we did, though, because of his massive bar bill. Not that he spent that much on booze for himself, even though he did enjoy a good gargle. He just didn't keep track of what he was spending on other people. Mark Plunkett always took care of all the hotel tabs as we never paid for any of the necessities but, at the end of the tour, he announced that the total bar bill had come to £16,000. Considering all the after-show parties, we didn't think that was too bad. Then came the bad news for Keith as Mark pointed out that his share of the total was around £7,000 because he was always buying everyone else's drinks!

Back in the studios, we began work on recording our second album, along with *Words*, the next single. *Words* was a famous Bee Gees song and it turned out they liked our version so much they invited us to perform it on TV at *An Audience With The Bee Gees*. That was such a good time. Making the video, on the other hand, wasn't nearly as much fun and certainly not one of my favourite shoots.

Filmed at a studio in South East London, it was set in a sombre-looking café with a lot of dancers and other extras, and Boyzone's job was mostly to sit around looking moody and intense. It was all fine until the wet part. At a certain moment, rain was supposed to deluge down on us, presumably to add to the general sense of gloom, at which point water was poured down onto the set. They didn't even warm it up! We got totally soaked to the skin and that water was freezing. I'm not saying the end result wasn't really effective, but we'd been working on this thing all day and the last thing any of us fancied was getting drowned. In the end we had to go through it not once, but twice, because of an editing problem and a re-take.

On the plus side, we did manage to sneak a few props off the set. Mikey took a guitar and Ro tried to get away with a chessboard but he wasn't allowed to. It turned out to be an expensive antique. There was also a fish tank in the shoot and I took the goldfish home with me. They lived for years.

As it happened, getting caught in the rain turned out to be well and truly worth it. The fans loved *Words* and we finally had our first number one hit.

The release of our second album, *A Different Beat*, coincided with

Hallowe'en, so our record company held a themed launch party at a spooky old house in Hampstead, North London. Wearing red devil horns on our heads, we arrived in ultimate gothic style in a horse-drawn carriage. Our guests that night included Zoe Ball, Jamie Theakston and the lads from 911.

The mansion venue was huge and, as we walked through the archaic, wrought iron gates, the lawn was a mist of dry ice and smoke. The whole setting was straight out of a horror movie, and we could just about make out tombstones rising through the fog as if we were in a churchyard. It was all very eerie, with creepy crawlies and strange-looking vines hanging from the trees.

Inside the house, things were just as sinister. We made our way through the huge double entrance doors and across a dark red hallway. The lights were dim and the whole effect was definitely haunted. The house was decorated Hallowe'en-style throughout, there was a DJ playing music and it was a big party scene. The top execs were there in their designer suits, as well as the press, radio, television and other industry people. Different rooms were alive with partygoers, all standing around, laughing, chatting, and soaking up the bizarre atmosphere. Waiters would wander in and out serving canapés and drinks. It was all very relaxed, very informal.

But off one of the corridors upstairs was a small room that was different. I noticed the door was shut, and that intrigued me. Gingerly I pushed it open. There was no music in here. No chit chat. No crowd. Instead, just a handful of people were sitting round a table absorbed in something. It was a ouija board. Immediately I was interested.

I slipped inside the room and sat down. The light was only very dim and I couldn't see anyone's faces properly. I didn't know who these people were but I was fascinated as I sat there watching them working with this ouija board. The board itself was laid flat on the table and printed with letters, numbers and other symbols, and there was a movable indicator called a planchette which pointed, supposedly in answer to questions from people attending the séance. The fingers of the participants were placed on the planchette and it was moving about the board, indicating the different symbols to spell out messages. This was a spiritual gateway through which you could contact the dead.

It took me back to the caravan near Shannon when I was 14 and I'd messed about with a home-made board with Kaner and my sisters. All these years later and I was captivated again. It hooked me right in. I couldn't help becoming a part of this weird ceremony. Before I knew it, I was the one touching the planchette as it spun around the board.

Someone in the room was in charge and it was that person who was initiating contact. I didn't know what to ask, what to say. I just sat in there for four or five hours, mesmerized by this ouija board, this whole unearthly process. I wasn't scared, I was excited. I didn't think I was doing anything wrong. As far as I was concerned, we were just a few folk having a laugh, having a drink. Getting our thrills playing some kind of spooky board game.

But it wasn't a laugh. It wasn't funny at all. And though I didn't know it at the time, those few hours in that tiny, dark room were going to screw me up for years.

CHAPTER 9

Jet-Setting

"WE GAVE THE FANS ONE HELL OF A RIDE ON THAT
TOUR – AND THE SHEER VOLUME OF THEIR SHOUTING,
CHEERING AND STAMPING FEET SAID IT ALL: THEY
LOVED EVERY MINUTE OF IT."

On Monday 17 February 1997, Louis Walsh made an announcement on
Radio 1's *Newsbeat* that devastated Boyzone fans across the world. Even
our families and friends were left horribly frightened as he described how
we'd cheated death in an aeroplane crash: 'Boyzone were flying from
Melbourne to Broken Hill to make a new video. It was a seven-seater plane
and something happened. One of the engines blew out and they had to
make a crash landing and the guys were really, really scared. I phoned
the guys and spoke to Ronan and Stephen who were terrified. It was real
life drama and they wouldn't like to go through it again. But they are
absolutely OK and they are making the video as we speak. They want to
do it because they want to get home as they've been away for four weeks
all over south Asia. They are going to fly back.'

That was Louis's dramatic take on the incident. It certainly made a hot piece of news – and to be fair to him he wasn't far off the truth.

We'd been in Australia for a while and had to fly from Sydney to a place called Broken Hill to film our latest pop video. Broken Hill was way out in the Aussie outback and, when we arrived at the airport to make the journey, we were amazed at the stunning array of private jets on the ground. We stepped out onto the tarmac and started walking towards one of the planes. It was the kind of thing JR Ewing from *Dallas* might have used to wing his way to a meeting to clinch some deal or other. We thought that's where we were being directed. But, as we headed towards this sleek, glossy machine thinking, wow, we really have made it big, we suddenly heard, 'No, no, no, guys, that's not your plane. *This* is your plane!'

We turned. We gasped. We almost fell over. It had to be a mistake. In front of us was a totally beaten up, seven-seater propeller plane. It was a piece of junk, to put it mildly – and this was the transport that had been arranged to fly us to Broken Hill.

We were so horrified by the state of it that we held a brief, emergency band meeting. Our decision was unanimous. There was no way any of us was getting on that heap of rust. It didn't even deserve to be called an aeroplane. We got Mark Plunkett to phone the record company and ask how we could possibly be expected to get into this death trap they'd arranged when there was a beautiful-looking jet on the runway heading in the right direction *and* looking as though it might actually survive take-off.

The company explained that we could get on the better plane but it would probably cost us an extra £2000 each. That put kind of a different perspective on it and left us feeling that we didn't have a huge amount of choice. So, making the point that it would be on their own heads if anything went wrong, we gingerly climbed aboard. Keith sat up front next to the pilot and I took a seat behind.

Miraculously the take-off went smoothly. Even the early part of the flight wasn't as bad as we feared, the plane droning through the night, restoring our confidence a little and lulling us into some sense of security.

I remember sitting there munching my way through a red tube of ready salted Pringles and drinking a miniature can of Coke. Maybe we'd been worrying for nothing.

But then again, maybe not. All of a sudden, Keith turned and looked at us. He was as white as a ghost and there was panic written all over him. He was the one of us close enough to hear the pilot radioing ahead: 'Mayday, Mayday. We have to crash land.' I could see Keith's head twisting backwards and forwards. Whatever was going on, it was scaring the life out of him.

And that's when the announcement came over the intercom. That's when we all knew. One of the turbos had unexpectedly failed. This ramshackle old flying machine was going down.

By now, the other lads were wide awake and petrified. The sharp drop in altitude – we'd dropped 4,000 feet in a matter of seconds – was playing havoc with their ears and had jolted them harshly out of their sleep. They started shouting and screaming, thinking it was all over and we were going to die. I just sat there. I don't know what was in my head. At that precise moment, I knew we were still all right, so I was scared, but oddly emotionless. All I could think was, 'This isn't the end of us. We're not going to all die in a plane crash.'

We were flying over a remote desert and the pilot had requested a full emergency landing at the tiny airport nearest to us. As he made the approach, the plane was all over the place. It was pretty horrifying. All we could do was buckle up and pray that somehow we'd come out alive.

But that pilot did a good job, and in the end he managed to get us down. It wasn't exactly a crash landing, but we did come in with one hell of a bang. I still haven't worked out how he managed to miss the trees!

There were more than a few murmurings of 'Thanks be to God' as we clambered out of that rust-bucket of an aeroplane on a tide of super-charged emotion. We were safe. We might be marooned in a desert in the middle of nowhere, but we were safe.

Once the first shock waves had passed over, we began to relax and, after about half an hour, we were even able to have a laugh and a joke. We were getting hungry too so, not seriously believing it would ever actually arrive, we phoned a pizza delivery service and ordered a Plain Margherita. That was a regular feast for us. But, sure enough, about three hours later, this feller on an off-road bike turned up with our order. It was all very bizarre. There we were, having crash-landed in the middle of the desert, eating pizza at about 4.00am.

A couple of hours later, we were picked up by the very same smart jet we'd wanted to catch in the first place, and it flew us the rest of the way. That was some night.

The video shoot for *Isn't It A Wonder* was pretty tame compared to the excitement of getting to the location. After only about twenty minutes' sleep, we were there on set, having our hair cut, doing a bit of kangaroo spotting.

The filming started off in the mining town of Broken Hill on the edge of the New South Wales Outback. *Mad Max 2* and *The Adventures of Priscilla, Queen of the Desert* are just two of the movies that have been filmed in Broken Hill itself, as well as in nearby Silverton and the imposing stretches of surrounding desert. There were miles and miles of deep, red dust roads, and the scenery was breathtaking, although the heat and humidity did give it all the feel of a stifling sauna – with the added discomfort of swarms of huge, black flies.

Isn't It A Wonder was the most exotic video we had ever made, and certainly a far cry from that early days shoot in the gents' toilets at the POD nightclub in Dublin for *Love Me For A Reason*. The final result was sensational. Keith mostly sat astride a massive Harley Davidson motorbike, while the rest of us chilled (as far as you can in the heat of the desert) in a gorgeous, black, open-topped Chevrolet. Ronan and Mikey also rode on horseback for a while. The hot, dry, dusty colours of the land, the tin shacks that were a part of the backdrop, the elderly couple caught by the camera, the group of children in their tiny school running over to wave as we passed by – all of it combined to create an immense sense of peace yet extraordinary remoteness and isolation, enhanced by the lilting, evocative melody of the song.

* * * * *

Back in the UK in the summer of 1997, we found ourselves added to the long list of celebrities who'd officially opened the Harrods Sale with the owner, Mohamed Al-Fayed. I'd visited the Knightsbridge store a year or so earlier with Ronan to buy a cross for a gold chain that I had, but my reception then had been very different.

I'd been heading for Harrods but had stopped to look at particular crosses I saw on display in the window of a jewellery shop next door. This was a shop crammed with enormously valuable stock, and there were security men on the doors. As Ronan and I went to make our way inside, a man came through the inner door, opened the main door a little and said, 'Can I help you?'

I said, 'Yes, I want to look at one of the crosses you have in the window.'

The man looked at me and said, 'We don't sell crosses here.'

'No, no, no,' I went on, 'the one in the window.'

The man simply repeated himself. 'We don't sell crosses here.'

That's when we got the message. This man didn't want us in his store. We obviously didn't look right. But I thought, fine, fair enough. After all, I could just go into Harrods which was right next door and spend my money there.

I had about £2000 cash in my back pocket that day. Nobody made to stop us as we marched in through Harrods' doors and we walked straight over to the jewellery counter. In a cabinet underneath immaculately polished glass lay the most beautiful cross made by a celebrity jewellery designer called Theo Fennell. At the time, I'd never heard of Theo Fennell, but I just loved the look of this cross. There was a man wearing top hat and tails standing nearby so I asked him if I could have a proper look at it. He almost visibly flinched, took one step back from the cabinet, let his eyes travel superciliously from my head to my toes and said quietly, 'Do you know how much this is?'

As this came right on top of our treatment by the doorman in the next door shop, I wasn't in the mood to see the funny side. I was actually highly offended. I didn't give myself a chance to look at any of the other crosses. There may well have been something I'd have liked even better, but the man's look and comment angered me so much that I bought the Fennell cross anyway. I took out the £2000, rolled up in an elastic band, threw it on the counter and snapped, 'Just put it in a box for me.' The only thing that spoiled the moment as the words tumbled out of my mouth was the niggling doubt that maybe even £2000 wouldn't be enough. That would have been very embarrassing.

But I was saved a red face. I think the piece turned out to be around £900, so I was able to walk out of Harrods not only with a very smart cross, but, thankfully, with my head held high.

That was how it had been on my first trip to Harrods. This time, about a year later, I was walking in as a celebrity to open the summer sale. There was a real irony about that and I couldn't help thinking, wow, one minute they barely let you in and the next they're running after you with an invitation. I found it quite hard to get my head around. I know they had no idea who I was that first time, but it shouldn't have made any difference to the way I was treated. Someone looked at me and made a judgement. And, as far as I was concerned, that was wrong.

We arrived at the store in a horse and carriage, the streets lined with people – a lot of them Boyzone fans, I'm sure, but a fair few just eager to snap up a bargain – and declared the sale open. Mr Al-Fayed himself was very warm and welcoming, a proper gent. He gave us our own private tour of his incredible empire. It's more of a palace than a shop.

A little bald guy called B.P. Fallon was with us. He was a photographer and journalist and spent the year following us around, recording where we went, what we did. We had great fun with him that day, seeing what bits and pieces we could slide into his bag without him realising. When we stopped for a cup of tea with Mr Al-Fayed, we managed to slip the silver cream jug and sugar bowl, antique salt and pepper pots and even some knives and forks into B.P.'s little rucksack. We had a real laugh over that. There we were in the middle of Harrods, still big kids, still messing around.

To round the visit off, we were paid very handsomely through gifts to each of us of gold cards with a good chunk of money on them for use in the store. That's where I ended up buying my Bang and Olufsen television and stereo system.

The pace that year was fast and furious. Life was a constant round of private jets, helicopters, champagne, limousines and parties. Battered old Ford Transits with decorative pink elephants seemed worlds away. These days, the odd ramshackle, tin-pot aeroplane aside, it seemed to be glitz and glamour all the way.

We spent a fair bit of time in America, which was a very different experience for us. We were still relatively unknown over there, so it was a rare treat to be able to spend time shopping without being recognised and interrupted. That's not meant to sound ungrateful. The success we had was so much down to the loyalty of our fans and we were very thankful for what they'd done for us. There were just times when it was good to be able to turn the spotlight off for a moment and remember what it was like to lead a relatively normal existence.

We jetted all over the USA, appearing on countless chat and music shows to promote the American release of *A Different Beat*. Ronan and Mikey had family living over there, so the trip was especially valuable for them as a time when they could visit relatives they might not otherwise get to see.

From America, we headed to the Far East, by way of Cologne where we attended the German Premiere of the comedy movie, *Bean*, starring Rowan Atkinson. *Bean* is a feature film based on his hilarious television series, *Mr Bean*. It's set largely in California, and was directed by another comedy giant, Mel Smith. He and Rowan had worked together in the early

1980s on the BBC topical comedy sketch show, *Not the Nine O'clock News*. We were invited to attend the premiere because the Boyzone song written by Ronan, *Picture of You*, was used as backing music for the end credits. Rowan Atkinson even appeared with us in the video for the single, and that shoot was probably the most fun we'd ever had filming. He is such a funny man and it was a real privilege to work with him. We spent half the time dressed like Boyzone and the other half in drab, brown suits, just like Mr Bean, doing moves with Rowan, copying his peculiarly Bean-like antics. Six Mr Beans prancing about. It must have been a joy to watch – especially for the residents of the street we used. They had front row seats and made a day of it, setting up picnics on their lawns and watching the entertainment under blue skies in the warmth of a sunny July day. Poor Ro suffered by the end of it, though. Being so fair-skinned, he landed himself with a dose of sunstroke.

Louis was very serious about his bid to take over the world with Boyzone's music. 1997 was the year we danced, sang and interviewed our way through the Middle East, Asia and India in style, the crowds seeming to go crazy for us wherever we went. In just over three weeks in August alone, we visited the Philippines, Taiwan, Korea, Malaysia, Singapore, Indonesia, Hong Kong, Bahrain, United Arab Emirates and India. A typical tour day consisted of a lunchtime press conference, a photo session, a few TV interviews back to back, a meet and greet time with competition winners, half a dozen radio interviews and a signing session at a record store. And all that was before charging on to a venue for a sound check followed by a stadium show. We were worked very, very hard and it was exhausting. To this day I've never come across a band that's grafted quite the way Boyzone did.

But international tours weren't always comfortable for us. Once, when we arrived in Thailand, we found the army there ready to pick us up. A military general, no less, was waiting with his troops to escort us safely through the thousand strong crowd. What was really striking wasn't the numbers of people, but their size. They were all so small compared to us!

We shuffled forward with the army completely surrounding us and moving kids out of the way. It wasn't a good experience not being able to stop and talk to those people who'd turned out to meet us. Without your fans, you're nothing. You need them, and if you want to sell your music, you look after them. You appreciate them for what they've brought to your career. Arriving at that airport, we knew the right thing to do was to stop and sign autographs, say a few words and have photos taken, but we just weren't able to do it. It wasn't safe. We did wave, but we had to keep moving – which was so unfair when they'd been waiting for us for hours, so *un*like the way we liked to do things.

It wasn't easy in Bahrain either. A signing session outside the Diesel shop had to be abandoned. There were too many people jammed in. The heat was stifling, and the crush of fans surging forward trying to get close to us was putting them and us in danger. Our tour manager, Mark, sensed that things were getting out of control. We were speedily ushered away into waiting cars and led back to the hotel by a police motorcycle escort, with lights flashing and sirens blaring.

The worst time had to be in Italy. We'd made a TV appearance and then headed straight on to a record signing. As we came out of the store, we were escorted to our bus. But the bus was already surrounded by fans – and they were frighteningly hyped up. They weren't just waving and calling. They were banging on the bus with their hands, hammering with their fists, and the bus was starting to rock back and forth as if it was being hit by a hurricane. It was hysteria gone totally berserk. We sat there, cowering in our seats waiting for the windows to be smashed in. It was the riot police who eventually marched in and cleared the street.

We were kicked out of that town and told never to come back. They needn't have worried. As we made our escape, going back there was the last thing on our minds. It was a terrifying experience. It's scary enough arriving backstage at a venue to find fans have sneaked in behind the building and are banging on the windows. But that time in Italy was something else altogether.

Our trip to Brazil, on the other hand, was magical. On a rare day off, legendary racing commentator, Murray Walker, arranged for us to make a visit to the pits at the Interlagos Circuit during the Brazilian Grand Prix. For raving petrol heads like Mikey and me, it was a dream of a day out. We were able to check out the Ferraris and I even got to touch Damon Hill's car! That was one of the remarkable things about being a part of Boyzone. It opened so many doors like that, threw such a lot of wonderful opportunities our way. We found ourselves fortunate enough to be invited to do things other people can only dream about.

The camaraderie between us, both on and off stage, was something I wouldn't have missed for the world either. A simple glance between us during a show could say more than 100 words. When you made a mistake, the audience probably didn't notice a thing (at least, that was our frantic hope!), but it was blindingly obvious to the five of us, and all you could do was catch the others' eyes in an effort to say, 'I'm sorry!' It was never a problem, though – just something else to have a laugh about.

We used to mess around with each other on stage, too. The microphone stands we had weren't the kind that you raise and lower by twisting the mast. They had a trigger to adjust the height. Sometimes one of us might walk past a microphone stand, flick the trigger and send it down to the floor. We usually picked on Steo for that because he was tiny. The only problem was that someone always took revenge on the microphone saboteur. If it was me, I might finish my moves, get back to my own stand to find one of the other lads had got to it first and the mike was pretty well on the floor. That was a moment to get creative. If your microphone was down low, you had to be down low – so you'd just get on your knees and sing like that. The audience loved it. For them it was all a part of what they'd turned up to see.

We were also gradually becoming seasoned professionals in terms of the way we handled situations that had genuinely gone wrong. With experience, we found we were able to think quickly and find a way to get around unexpected problems somehow or other, and hopefully in a comic way that the fans would really enjoy.

Although we worked hard, we did play hard too. We felt we deserved that much. We didn't take things for granted exactly. They just became standard for us. We were on tour and a certain amount of luxury went hand in hand with the schedule. We needed a good hotel to relax in between appearances and help clear the head. It might be expensive but, as we were so constantly on the move, it was worthwhile if it offered us the space and comfort to keep our spirits up. The places where we stayed must have had the biggest beds in the world, the most accommodating room service, the best massages and the bluest, warmest swimming pools. In one hotel in Kuala Lumpar, my bath was made of glass with one face actually fitted into the outside wall of the building as a window. If that window got broken as you lay there having a soak, straight out and down 27 floors you'd go!

The Manila Hotel in the Philippines was another extraordinarily lavish stopover. It was like stepping into another world. Crystal chandeliers hung extravagantly down, their glass droplets tinkling tunefully, while in the main lobby, a string quartet gently serenaded passing guests. We each had our own exquisitely decorated suite, and our rooms allowed spectacular views of the old, walled city, the lushly planted gardens and the magnificent sunsets over Manila Bay.

Only four years before, when the band was first starting out, we were lucky if we made £50 a week – and even that was more in the form of a living allowance than an income. When we received our first advance of £20,000, we were raving about it. It seemed like an absolute fortune and we were quick to go out and spend every penny. But by 1997, even that was just a drop in the ocean. My dad always taught me to set my sights high and, that year, as much as £100,000 felt like just pocket change to me.

True to form, I spent most of my money on my cars. I started off with my 911 Porsche but, as I began driving myself around the UK, I found it was a little small and very heavy on petrol to say the least. That's when I sorted myself out with what must have been the biggest road legal truck in Europe. For the sake of fuel economy, I bought a twin cab Toyota Hilux. I had a few modifications made – body lifts put in to make it higher, and bigger wheels. But then I spotted a truck with an even bigger lift than mine, and the owner introduced me to a man called Nigel Morris, who builds monster trucks for, and owns the rights to, Bigfoot UK. I showed him the Hilux, told him what I wanted and must have ended up spending £50,000 on this £17,000 machine. So much for economy! By the time Nigel had finished, I had an incredible-looking vehicle with 44 inch tyres the height of your chest. At £500 each, they weren't the sort of thing you'd easily pick up down at Kwik Fit! I never changed the engine, though, so that little 2.7 motor was pretty well choked to death struggling to power those massive wheels. As for saving on fuel, forget it. It probably pumped more diesel now than my Porsche could ever have used in petrol! But I loved it. No matter what Porsche, Ferrari or Lamborghini I might own, they never turned heads the way that truck did. It was the ultimate business.

Most of the other lads were busy spending their money too. Keith was quite like me only a little wiser. He was another car-lover and paid out for a Porsche 911. I'm not sure if he was married at the time, but he had his girlfriend and their baby, and would have bought his first house for them all. I didn't think about buying a house at that time because I'd moved in with my then girlfriend, Easther.

Out of all of us, Ronan was perhaps the biggest fashion head. Clothes, watches, hats, jewellery – he lived and died for them, always searching out the latest trend, spending his money on looking good.

With Mikey, his hard-earned cash would go on music gear. He was a techy and always had the best and newest equipment money could buy.

I think Steo generally saved. He wasn't into cars and, when the money really started to roll in, he probably put a lot of it away. He was certainly the most sensible one of us as far as finances were concerned.

* * * * *

In May of 1997, it was Ireland's turn to play host to *The Eurovision Song Contest*. Needless to say, Louis had seized the moment and been frantically working behind the scenes to get us signed up to perform in the interval. After a lot of discussion, the producer, Noel Curran, not only agreed that Boyzone's presence would be a welcome and appropriate addition to the night, but also invited Ronan to co-present the show with local TV personality, Carrie Crowley.

A competition held every year among member countries of the European Broadcasting Union, *The Eurovision Song Contest* is a spectacularly staged event broadcast live on television and radio. Each participating country enters a song to be performed on the night, and then has the opportunity to vote for the songs submitted by other countries in order to select a winner. Since it first began back in the 1950s, the Contest has been broadcast every year, making it one of the longest-running television shows in the world. An incredible 300,000,000 viewers watch it internationally. Boyzone weren't going to be there to compete. We'd be there to provide the interval entertainment. And with viewing figures that high, we knew this was a massive opportunity for us. What we needed now was a very special song, so Ronan and Ray Hedges disappeared off into the studio together and, a few days and much blood, sweat and tears later, came up with the song we would be performing: *Let The Message Run Free*.

It was a desperately hectic week, with commitments still to honour in Germany and hours of rehearsal time needed for the Contest. We were flying backwards and forwards like idiots. Our choreographer, Melinda McKenna, was brilliant. She managed to pull in 15 dancers from Greece, Switzerland, Italy, Yugoslavia, Scotland and Ireland, making it a truly international performance.

Whatever anyone may feel about the legitimacy of *The Eurovision Song Contest* as a genuine popular music competition, actually being there on the night, being a central part of that extravaganza, did turn out to be a very moving experience. We were all immensely proud to have been involved. It was great for our families too. Our parents were all out there in the audience, cheering us on, as well as the President of Ireland, Mary Robinson. The UK won that year. Katrina and the Waves deservedly took the night with *Love Shine A Light*. And the champagne flowed into the early hours.

We toured twice in 1997 – in the summer, and then again in October when we took to the stage once more for our tenth UK tour. It had been a hard slog to get to this point, but we were rewarded by becoming one of the biggest boy bands of the decade, with a staggering nine top five singles and two number one albums.

Our *Different Beat* tour was the show we'd been wanting to give our fans for about the last three years, and now we were finally in a position to afford it. Five massive trucks hauled the vast amounts of staging and equipment from venue to venue at a cost of over £500,000.

The performances began with an intriguing video clip announcing the shocking news that all five of us had been lost in space. Then, giving the audience barely time to draw breath, we burst onto the stage dressed as spacemen and singing the opening notes of *Together*. The spectacle that followed was like a journey through time, with lavish scenery and costume changes depicting, among other things, a 1920s' nightclub, a 1970s' disco (complete with white trousers and big medallions), through to presenting Boyzone as we then were in the 1990s. We gave the fans one hell of a ride on that tour – and the sheer volume of their shouting, cheering and stamping feet said it all: they loved every minute of it.

CHAPTER 10

Cracks

"...THAT'S WHEN A PART OF YOU JUST WANTS TO TURN YOUR BACK AND WISHES THE WORLD WOULD DO THE SAME SO YOU COULD CREEP QUIETLY AWAY."

After the manic pace of 1997, it was unbelievably good to be able to take a break over Christmas. We'd travelled the world on promotional tours to the Far East, Latin America, North America, Europe, Australia and South East Asia, as well as undertaking two massive arena tours across the UK and Ireland. We didn't think we could possibly top that in terms of air miles and sheer frenetic activity but, as we sat and gazed at our itineraries for 1998, we looked to be even busier. The success we'd achieved in such a relatively few years was pretty astonishing but, in the fickle world of pop, we knew nothing could be taken for granted. If we wanted to stay at the top, we'd have to keep making the effort. Even our month off in January was eaten into as we were still in and out of the studio, tweaking and improving album number three, *Where We Belong*. There was never any real sense of let up, never a moment when we could truly feel, right, *now* we can relax.

The first gig of the year was a huge charity fundraiser back at our old stomping ground, The Point Depot in Dublin. We topped the bill at the sold-out Childline Benefit Concert and were joined by the excellent All Saints and Robbie Williams. It was a memorable night, both for the show itself and the outrageous shenanigans at the party afterwards. Most importantly, £100,000 was raised for Childline.

Then it came to filming the video for our first single of 1998, *All That I Need*. Gone was the previous year's glamorous international location. There were no scorching temperatures, no stunning Aussie scenery bathed in sharp, clear light. We were back to a regular Boyzone, nitty-gritty shoot, this time stuck on the rooftop of a derelict brewery in East London very early in the morning. To add insult to injury, it was miserably wet and blowing a gale.

As usual, the process was painfully slow and we had to do a lot of tedious hanging around, all dressed up in our leather designer gear. To pass the time, the other lads played on computer games while I fiddled around with a roll of gaffer tape, fixing up a director's chair that Steo had accidentally broken. Day two was marginally better. At least we got to shelter from the weather as we filmed the shots inside the building. Still, the discomfort of the conditions aside, *All That I Need* was a good song with a real swing beat and we liked it.

We liked it even better when it went straight to number one on 26 April. That number one was our third. We'd now had 11 top five singles which meant we'd broken Kylie Minogue's record for the biggest number of continuous top five hits in the UK. Some things are worth hanging around on wet rooftops for!

In March, Sir Andrew Lloyd Webber turned 50, and we were invited to be involved in a very special birthday party for him. Filmed live at the Royal Albert Hall, the event was a star-studded tribute to one of the world's most popular composers of musical theatre. The guests included Tina Arena, Michael Ball, Antonio Banderas, Sarah Brightman, Glenn Close, Julian Lloyd Webber, Donny Osmond, Elaine Paige, Kiri Te

Kanawa and Bonnie Tyler.

We felt slightly anxious as the day grew closer, wondering how we'd be received. After all, the majority of the performers were established musical stars singing highlights from some of the most popular shows ever written, including *The Phantom Of The Opera*, *Cats*, *Evita* and *Sunset Boulevard*. We'd be giving our first live performance of *No Matter What* from Sir Andrew's then newest musical, *Whistle Down The Wind*. When it came to our turn to sing, all we could do was get up on that stage and brazen it out.

And did he like us? He did. Thankfully we went down a storm.

The following May, our third album, *Where We Belong*, finally hit the shops. We felt a real pressure with this one. It needed to be nothing less than sensational if it was going to top the 2.2 million-selling second album, *A Different Beat*, and we put in a lot of hours refining it, getting the best sound we possibly could. It didn't disappoint apparently. The fans went out and bought it in their droves.

The album launch was celebrated with a big party inside a warehouse in London that had been ingeniously transformed into a fairground. We had dodgems, sideshows, hot dogs, even candy floss. A few fans managed to get hold of the hugely sought-after tickets, and spent the night rubbing shoulders with the 500 or so invited celebrity revellers, among them Sam Fox, Mandy Smith, UB40, The Corrs, Steps, Brian May, *Father Ted's* Mrs. Doyle, as well as my sisters, Keavy and Edele from B*Witched and Tara from FAB, all three of them now pop stars in their own right.

* * * * *

The summer saw us back out on the international circuit doing more exhausting promotional work. We crammed visits to Singapore, Malaysia, Taiwan, Thailand, The Philippines and Hong Kong into the space of just two weeks. We must have blitzed most of their morning TV and radio shows, getting up at 7.00am to make it in on time, only to find that we were then having to sit around waiting for the cameras and the crew to get the technical side sorted before we could go on and do our three minute slot.

So much of our time was spent like that, flying from country to country or being on the road in the bus, or simply hanging about waiting for something to happen. We still must have done between three and five shows in a day, with some at night – and then there were all the inevitable party invitations. We'd turn up to a do at whatever time of the night and be there until at least the early hours of the morning. Then it was back to the hotel for an hour or so of sleep before dragging ourselves up at 7.00am to begin all over again. I guess that's the problem with the life of a pop star. You do burn the candle savagely at both ends. You only really sleep when you're travelling – on the bus to the radio station, on the plane to the next country. I suppose we mostly used our exotic hotels for having a shower and getting changed. We didn't see that much of the beds, to be honest. Thinking about it, what with the work schedule and the ridiculous hours we kept, I'm surprised we didn't end up looking like five little old men. Or perhaps we did but no one was unkind enough to point it out!

Being asked the same question ten thousand times over was one of the worst things about being interviewed time and again. I didn't deal with it well. I was still very immature, I suppose, and found it hard to see what we were in as a business. I was a part of Boyzone but, more than that, to me I was still Shane Lynch. If anyone asked me a question, never mind what was good PR, I was going to answer it pretty much the way I wanted to. It was like that for all of us to an extent. You might get one or two good answers out of us in the morning but it could all go down hill after that. It got to the point where we weren't that bothered about being 'accurate'. We'd be making stories up, telling things wrong or stretching the truth, just for our own entertainment. It was one way we had of trying to keep sane because at times the monotony could be so unbearable.

On the other hand, for me, one of the enormous plusses to our success was being entertained by record company bosses across the world who always seemed honoured to have us as their guests. They would invite us to the craziest of restaurants, places where you might have to take your shoes off and sit on the floor, and we would be given the opportunity to sample startlingly unusual food. I remember trying duck tongue. Obviously the duck beaks themselves were small enough, but when the tongues inside came out, they were almost like peanuts in the bowl.

The other lads tended to go a bit green around the gills at just the thought of eating that kind of food, but I found myself thoroughly embracing it and enjoying all the new tastes and experiences. As well as duck tongue, I've also eaten goat's tongue (although I didn't enjoy that as much – it was a bit too jelly-like and furry), crocodile, snake and kangaroo. Wherever we were in the world, whatever was on the menu, I'd give it a try. Keith was the least adventurous of all of us when it came to food. He's very straightforward in his tastes. He likes his chicken and his chips and his hamburgers. You'd have a real job getting much that's unusual or exotic past his lips.

Those years being entertained in the far-flung corners of the globe actually turned me into quite a 'foodie'. One of my favourite restaurants is in Paris. It's called L'Acropole, which means 'The Dome', because inside the building the roof is formed into a large, rounded dome – a little like a very scaled down version of the one on St Paul's Cathedral. That restaurant serves the most incredible shellfish, and every time Boyzone were in Paris, some of the guys would go off to the Hard Rock Café, and I'd go to L'Acropole and order a plateau – for four. A two-tier silver dish stand would arrive, the bottom tier overflowing with winkles, cockles, whelks, oysters, other smaller shellfish and some little baby prawns. In the second tier would lie a full crab, full lobster, razor fish, huge prawns, enormous langoustines and I don't know what else besides. I'd sit there for two and a half hours until I'd munched my way through every last morsel. And I loved it. That has to be my favourite restaurant in the whole world – which is saying something because I've been lucky enough to visit quite a few.

Existing as Boyzone did under the relentless glare of the spotlight, we were bound to come into constant contact with people whose lives were similarly lit up. On 5 July 1998, we even came face to face with Prince Charles for the first time. Over 100,000 people gathered in London's Hyde Park that day to enjoy performances by some of the music industry's biggest names at the largest one-off pop event of the decade: Party in the Park, in aid of the Prince's Trust. We featured on a bill that was packed to the eyeballs with major stars like Shania Twain, Gary Barlow, Julian Lennon, Natalie Imbruglia, Louise, Des'ree, Del Amitri, The Corrs, Eternal, The Mavericks, All Saints, Tom Jones, Ultra Naté and Lionel Richie. It was an extraordinary range of talent and a brilliantly staged event.

After the show, we all lined up backstage to meet His Royal Highness. I'd already got changed out of the clothes I'd performed in, but the rest of the lads were still wearing their stage gear. As they stood waiting with everyone else, they all looked the part, very smart and showbiz, whereas I was fidgeting about in jeans, a tatty old jumper and a flat cap.

Prince Charles was regally making his way down the celebrity line, shaking hands, having a little chat with each performer. We'd had to learn to handle a lot of different situations since Boyzone took off, but this was perhaps one of the most formal. We'd certainly never had to talk to royalty before. Nobody had briefed us on what to do or what not to do. I suppose everyone assumed it would just be blindingly obvious to us – be polite, don't say too much, that kind of thing. And that's how the other lads responded as Prince Charles reached us.

It wasn't that I didn't respect the man; I just honestly didn't quite know how I was meant to be. Added to that, I'd had a few drinks. So, when he stood in front of me to shake my hand, give me a quick glance up and down and comment, 'Oh, I do like your hat,' I didn't just smile and nod, thankful that at least my scruffy sweater hadn't offended him, oh no.

I gave him one of my biggest, silliest grins and said, 'Thanks very much, Charlie. Any time you're going shooting, no problem, you can borrow it if you want.'

You could almost sense the horror of those celebrity onlookers creeping along the line and freezing their smiles to their faces. Fortunately for me, Prince Charles completely cracked up.

'I see we have a joker in the pack,' he was gracious enough to say as he moved swiftly on.

That meeting obviously made a significant impression on His Royal Highness because, a year later, I was at the same event – not in the backstage line-up this time (I can't imagine why) – when I literally bumped into him. Our paths crossed as he was leaving the venue.

He gave me one look, made no reference whatsoever to anything I was wearing (probably a wise move) and simply remarked, 'Oh no! Not you again!'

'Well, it's good to see you again, Charlie,' I replied. But that was the extent of our second brief encounter.

When our *No Matter What* single release shot to the number one spot in August, we were once again breaking records. We were now the first Irish group to have had four number ones in the UK charts, leaping ahead of legendary rockers, U2, who had so far had three. The composer of the song and our newest showbiz pal, Sir Andrew Lloyd Webber, was so delighted with the news, he even cut his summer holiday short so that he could appear with us on *Top Of The Pops*.

We were flying as high as we'd ever been, but, as the summer drew to its end, we knew we needed to knuckle down and concentrate on our big autumn arena tour. Other bands might take months to prepare for a major showcase like that, but we almost always seemed to end up with the worst, most stunted rehearsal time. We were so busy with everything else, doing promotional work, forever on the move, and just generally trying to survive a pretty impossible schedule.

The 1998 *Where We Belong* tour saw us working with a new choreographer. Shaun Fernandez was a very straight, good-looking guy, whose family was originally from Goa. He was amazingly talented and inventive – but the dancers absolutely hated him. He was a perfectionist. He wanted the ultimate best and that's not necessarily a recipe for good feeling among your artists. You didn't walk into Shaun's rehearsal room and simply mark your routine. He expected you to put everything into it and dance it how you'd dance it on the night. Maybe people don't always want to be pushed that hard. When there's no crowd out there watching, perhaps they just don't see the need.

We probably all moaned a lot, even though actually we loved it, but sometimes even Shaun did have to admit defeat. He might show us a particularly tricky move and we'd say, 'But, Shaun, that's rubbish.' In fact it wasn't rubbish at all. We just couldn't do it so that was our get-out clause. He'd always try and ignore us for a while, keep pushing us as far as he could, but in the end if we were finding it that bit too tough, he'd have to revert back to what we could do.

As well as being the choreographer, Shaun was also the show's producer, working with Steve Levitt, the production manager, who looked after everything from lighting rigs to front of house sound. Backdrops, staging and props were by now a hugely important part of any Boyzone tour, but we had to be cautious and approach all that accompanying paraphernalia from two points of view. Obviously, the more tickets we sold the better, so, from that angle, it was important that, tour to tour, the spectacle itself got bigger each time. On the other hand, we had to be mindful of not allowing the show to get bigger than our performance. It wouldn't have looked clever if we were out-classed by our special effects. Shaun's ideas were always fantastic, but there just sometimes needed to be that little bit of compromise. Mark Plunkett had a real eye for the right balance – and he was good at saying no. He knew when it was time to hold back on the extravagance and do the work ourselves. The effects were important to invigorate and dramatise the general feel of the performance, but the really crucial part was that we carried the show with our own energy, skill and individuality.

The *Where We Belong* tour was something of a celebration. We'd been together for five years and that deserved marking with delivery of a particularly special and unforgettable show.

Our guests included support acts Hinda Hicks and Christian Fry, and we also featured a band that was so new it didn't even have a name at the time the tour souvenir programme went to press. It was made up of Kian, Mark, Shane, Bryan and Nicky, five talented lads from our home country of Ireland. With a little help from Louis and Simon Cowell, it wasn't long before their career really took off – and everyone came to know them by the name, Westlife.

The Manchester tour stop was nothing less than brilliant. It was one of the largest venues we'd played on our 1998 excursion, and the last night of an amazing run. From very early in the morning, fans were beginning to mass excitedly in the streets outside the Manchester Evening News Arena, chanting the Boyzone name and waving their painstakingly made banners.

They weren't the only ones up and about early. Some 12 hours before the show was due to start, preparations were well under way. The huge lorries rolled up and all the staging and equipment was unloaded and carried inside so that the massive set up operation could begin.

Our performance space was arranged on two levels. The upper segment was reached via two stairways leading from opposite sides of the stage up and across a bridge that arched over a tunnel. Framed with lights, the tunnel made an intriguing focal point on the main lower level. It was through here that the dancers would eventually make their entrance as they opened the show. But before that, there was all the usual technical business to get right – the sound checks and lighting cues, the running through various routines with the dance troop and vocalists. The build-up to every performance was immense. It was hard to sit still and I guess we each needed to find our own ways of dealing with the pressure. That night, it was Steo who had to keep running to the toilet!

Finally the time came. The arena was packed to the gills with a vast sea of people as lights began to flash in the stage's central tunnel. Inside, the darkened shapes of the dancers started heaving and writhing before they burst onto the main stage, their movements pulsating with the percussion rhythms of the music. Then they reached down and each picked up a large torch, full on, with the light streaming out. They swirled the beams around as they danced before turning them dramatically upwards to a point over the auditorium. And there, caught in these hand-held spotlights and standing motionless on a platform suspended way over the heads of the crowd, were the five of us, all in black. As we were lowered slowly down towards the main stage, the fans were set to scream the place to the ground. The noise was truly deafening. It was one hell of a way to open a show. Forget all the gripes – Shaun Fernandez had done us proud.

As usual, we began with some up-tempo numbers, *Must Have Been High, What Can You Do For Me?* and *One Kiss At A Time*, to get the crowd in the party mood (as if they weren't already), waving their hands in the air and dancing along with us. Then Keith thanked all the fans for their support and we slipped into *All I Need*, which allowed us to slow down for a precious moment and catch our breath.

I guess that, over the few years we'd been together, we'd all grown in confidence and showmanship, and there were quite a few highlights in that show, memorable moments that would hopefully stay with the fans for a long time. Steo's solo spot, punching out his routine dressed in a metallic grey jacket and supported by backing dancers, before launching into *Games Of Love*, was a sensation. He's so gifted. So natural. His performances seemed to come from somewhere deep inside himself. I don't know what it was, but you could see it in his eyes. When he moved on to *Where Did You Go*, he somehow owned the whole stage. He just embraced that massive audience and had them eating out of his hand.

Then there was the *Grease* medley. That was such a blast for all of us. It always felt as if we might have been lifted right out of the stage show. There we were in our leather T-Birds jackets, acting out the little scenarios that went with each song, the dancers pounding out the moves. The set even included the front half of a 1950s car for *Greased Lightning*, and Viveen Wray, one of our excellent backing vocalists, guested for the duets,

Summer Nights and *You're The One That I Want.*

When you throw in Keith letting his hair down and playing some air guitar like a real rocker for *Where Have You Been?*, dancers carrying flaming torches down from the upper stage level to open *A Different Beat*, and Ro's most ostentatious costume of the entire show, an arctic tiger print suit and Stetson, you have a recipe for a stunning night out.

We finally closed with *Picture Of You.* Then, as columns of smoke burst up in front of us from the floor providing a momentary screen, trap doors in the stage opened up, and we were able to leap down through them and make our usual hasty getaway. Sweaty costumes off and dressing gowns on, we could finally breathe a huge sigh of relief as we were whisked smartly away on the bus and think, wow, we did it. There was always the odd thing that hadn't gone quite right, something perhaps forgotten somewhere, but it was moments like that that brought us together and made us laugh. Another night over, another show done. Until the next time.

Riding high on our success in so many other parts of the world, a few days later we headed back to the USA for a month. We were desperate to crack it over there. We even set out on a tour playing all the Hard Rock Cafés scattered across the country, pushing as far down as Puerto Rico in the Caribbean. But, despite all our efforts, we were still relatively unknown by the masses, and it was only the British and Irish tourists who would stop us for photos and autographs when they recognised us at theme parks or wherever else we might be appearing. They also came along to support us at the Hard Rock gigs after spotting us on posters, and that created a great vibe.

Any fleeting moments of freedom that happened to crop up between all the travelling, press conferences and shows were snatched at hungrily, and we'd try to use them to relax in whatever way we could. We must have spent several hours in various swimming pools along the way.

It didn't always work out, though. One afternoon, Steo spent his time off in a Miami hospital. Our stylist, Alex Delves, had managed to cut his hand quite badly on a wire fence. Because the rest of us were off being interviewed or taking a minute to do our own thing, it was Steo who was left to play Florence Nightingale and sit with him while the doctors bandaged him up.

North America is always going to be a tough place for any British group to get known because of its sheer size. It really is vast and, unless you have a pretty big record company promoting the hell out of you over there, you don't stand a lot of chance. I can't see how we could have done it without setting aside a few years for intense publicity and, to be honest, by then we were all getting to the stage where the last thing we wanted was to be away from home for more than two weeks, let alone two months, at a time, trying to break through. Realistically it was never going to happen.

That didn't stop Louis forever trying to boost our profile by coming up with a good story. When I happened to mention in an interview how much I fancied Madonna, his ears pricked up like two little radars. We were on a television music show in France and Madonna was there. She walked out in a long dress with a couple of minders round her and said hello. She was lovely – but so small! I really wasn't expecting such a petite little woman. People often say the same thing about me, how much smaller I am in real life to how I look on TV. The screen can be very deceptive.

That brief meeting with Madonna was all there was. We certainly never hung out together. But Louis, in his never-ending quest to keep us in the public eye, turned it into the suggestion of something that would make for hot gossip back home. One major tabloid proceeded to run a story about Madonna being the one who fancied *me*! Needless to say, the PR king was quietly delighted.

He might not have been quite so happy if he'd known about the fallouts Boyzone inevitably had. With all the time we spent in each other's company, as much as we were close as a band, we also knew how to wind each other up, how to get on each other's nerves and run them ragged. We were just five very young lads trying to exist in a highly pressurised environment. It wasn't surprising that tempers sometimes blew.

Steo once stopped speaking to me for about three weeks. It was after a certain comment I'd made when a press release went out announcing that he'd been asked to appear in the American TV series, *Baywatch*. We were at a radio station and the interviewer remarked, 'Stephen, I hear you've been offered a part in *Baywatch*.'

Steo nodded and said, 'Yes,' and I couldn't help adding, 'That's right, he's going to play a lilo.'

The rest of the lads just fell about laughing, but Steo freaked out and gave me the silent treatment for days afterwards.

Another time I remember him losing it was when we were in Germany. We'd been performing in the basement area of a theatre and, as we all sat there, it was either Keith or Mikey who started throwing little jelly bears at him from across the room. Steo kept saying, 'Stop,' but it would happen again. And every time he said, 'Stop with the jelly bears,' those jelly bears just kept on coming. Until one too many of the things came flying across at him. That was the point when he'd had enough. He lost it in spectacular fashion, picked up a steel bin and lobbed it across the room.

That's what the pressure did. We could push each other but only so far. But then, we were just kids. We didn't really know how to deal with any of what had happened to us. We were too busy getting on with it, keeping up with it, trying to survive it. They were good times. Incredible times. But when there's no let up and the scant resources you have for coping are starting to wear desperately thin, that's when a part of you just wants to turn your back and wishes the world would do the same so you could creep quietly away.

CHAPTER 11

Bleeding Life

"THE FACT THAT WE NEVER GOT BACK ON TRACK AFTER THAT INITIAL YEAR WAS A SAD THING. WE DIDN'T EVEN GO OUT WITH A BANG. IF ANYTHING, THE BOYZONE PHENOMENON JUST QUIETLY PETERED OUT."

As 1999 launched, Boyzone were massive. We were one of the biggest selling acts of the previous year and our single, *No Matter What*, came out as the nation's favourite in a national Record Of The Year 1998 poll. The world was on a countdown to a brand new millennium and we were at the very top of our game. Did we think it would last forever? Maybe we did. Maybe it was impossible to picture life in any other way than we'd been living it for the last few years. Professionally things couldn't be going any better.

But change was coming. We'd been riding dangerously close to the edge and there was only so far left to go before the balance was well and truly tipped. Whether you sit back and accept it or not, when your time's up, it's up.

Early in the year, we were once again involved with the Childline charity concert held in Dublin, and this was swiftly followed by more fundraising for *Comic Relief*. At a studio in North London, we recorded a version of Billy Ocean's hit, *When The Going Gets Tough, The Tough Get Going*, ready for release on 22 February. All the profits from the single were to go to the comedian-led charity which raises funds for projects in both Africa and the UK. And that song made a pretty tidy sum. It shot straight to number one and stayed there for a few weeks, making it the most successful *Comic Relief* single ever.

The video was the craziest we'd ever been involved with – as if that was possible after our stint with Mr Bean! In amongst singing the song, we were in there doing all kinds of daft things. Keith was drumming with a little help from Irish boxing champion, Steve Collins, Steo was a DJ, Ro was playing golf with a red nose golf ball, Mikey was doing a pretty realistic James Bond impression, and I enjoyed co-starring with a very flash car. We were joined in the shoot by a huge bunch of celebrities including Mel Smith, Harry Hill and a couple of badgers, Graham Norton, Mystic Meg, John McCrirrick, Jo Brand, Paddy, Mandy, Butch and Marlon from Emmerdale, Phil Jupitus, Davina McCall, Roland Rivron and Ulrika Jonsson. Snap it all together through some fast and furious editing and you had a very funny and totally wacky piece of video.

The fund-raising carried on in Modena, Italy, where we had an opportunity to sing with the legendary Italian tenor, Luciano Pavarotti, at his annual War Child Benefit concert. The night before we were due to fly out, we were performing at the massive RDS stadium in the heart of Dublin. It was an incredible experience, with an audience of around 40,000 people, making it one of our biggest ever shows. We didn't hold back at the party afterwards either, despite needing to be up and relatively alert the next morning to catch the flight to Italy. I was drinking red wine. I don't mean the odd glass. I swaggered around with a bottle in each fist. That way I didn't have to shake hands with anyone. I wasn't in the mood for small talk. I just wanted to enjoy the party with the friends I was there with. More and more often it was like that. I'd be rude and abrupt if that's what I wanted to be. I didn't care if it hurt people. Something was happening to me. Something bad. To the world I was a superstar. Personally, my life had got in a real mess.

Early the next morning, five badly hung over lads turned up to Dublin airport to catch our private jet down to Northern Italy. When we finally arrived at the hanger, it was a little like déjà vu. The plane sent to fly us over looked like something out of a scrap yard. It was a sixteen-seater disaster zone set to rival the rust bucket we'd got stuck with in Australia a couple of years before.

We got on board and had a look around, taking in the cockpit first and then the seating area. This thing didn't look any better on the inside, so Ro, Steo, Mikey and I decided on the spot there was no way we were flying anywhere on it. As far as we were concerned, it had 'death trap' written all over it.

Keith Duffy was steaming. He didn't care how tatty or old that piece of junk was. He was still unbelievably drunk from the night before, feeling sick as a dog, and all he wanted was to get on a plane, any plane. I think he'd have crawled into a bin bag that morning if he thought it would get him to where he needed to be.

GQ magazine were coming with us to cover Boyzone and the Pavarotti concert and, in the end, we were left at the airport waving off Keith, the press guys, our stylist, Alex Delves, and our minder, Barrie Knight, as they decided to take their chances with the private jet. We then hung around to catch a Swiss Air scheduled flight that went via Zurich.

That meant that Duffy arrived in Italy a fair few hours before we did. He told us afterwards how Luciano Pavarotti's PA kept coming over and introducing people to him, because he was the first one of us there: 'This is Luciano's wife, this is Luciano's daughter,' and so it went on. Duffy was more than a bit confused. He kept thinking, who *is* this coming over and introducing Luciano's this, that and the other? I thought we were here to meet Pavarotti. Who the hell is Luciano? He was wondering about it all day. He had no idea that Luciano and

Pavarotti were one and the same!

Once the rest of us had safely touched down and grabbed a few moments at the hotel to freshen up, Barrie Knight guided us onto the tour bus through the hundreds of fans who'd been waiting since dawn to catch a glimpse of the Boyzone boys.

The backstage area of the venue was shaped like a hexagon with a door in each side – and behind each door was a world-class artist getting ready to go on stage. There were posters everywhere and we were astonished to see ourselves billed above stars like Mariah Carey, Joe Cocker, Gloria Estefan, Michael Jackson and a host of other international performers. No one had the heart to bring us down off our cloud and point out that the listings were actually in alphabetical order.

In the middle of the backstage VIP area was a huge screen where you could see everything going on on stage. I sat in front of it with the lads, leaning back in my chair like I always did, watching the different celebrities walk out and do their rehearsals. There seemed to be supermodels and artists almost everywhere you looked. We waited where we did because we knew Mariah Carey would be coming out shortly and we wanted to make sure we saw her. Suddenly, a door opened and I turned. Out she walked – and it's amazing my jaw didn't just hit the floor at the sight of her. Then, as I gazed at her, she looked right back at me, and she carried on looking at me as she walked. It was a glance of maybe only five seconds but, as our eyes met, we held that moment. The rest of the lads were utterly gutted that it wasn't *their* eyes caught up with hers. It was one of those once in a lifetime, heart-stopping instants that meant everything to me and, I've no doubt, nothing to her. It stayed in my head, though. That was my claim to 'me and Mariah'.

The show that night was phenomenal, with the vast audience going wild for its slick parade of glittering performers. Thankfully our spot went without a hitch, despite the fun and games actually getting to the country. Right at the end, we were back on stage for the finale with all the other artists to sing *We Are The World*, backed by the momentous sound of a 50-piece orchestra.

And that was another after-show party to remember (or not as the case may be!), laughing, joking and sharing a drink with Lionel Richie, Joe Cocker and some of the rest of the biggest music stars in the world. Not bad for a bunch of back street lads from Ireland.

It was only a fortnight later that Stephen Gately finally came out. As a band, we'd always known that Steo was gay. It was fine and none of us had a problem with it, but I knew for years that he was always afraid somebody would out him before he was ready to make it public and had had an opportunity to explain it to his family. With the way the press so constantly liked to dredge up the details of our private lives, he was scared out of his mind almost all the time. His sexuality becoming public knowledge was a day he truly feared – until one morning in 1999 when he had to face it head on.

We were back from Italy and busy promoting and selling our *Greatest Hits* album when Steo got the news that a story on him was about to break. Someone who'd been on tour with us had gone to the papers trying to sell a feature about him being gay and having a boyfriend. The poor guy was in pieces, so upset, so emotional. But everyone was very much on his side and finally managed to convince him that he should tell his own story before it got out via anyone else. Louis was able to hold the press off for two weeks and spent time talking it through with him. But Steo knew it was only a matter of time before some version or other of the truth was splashed all over the papers so he decided that, at the very least, what came out should be the way he wanted the public to hear it. The headline, 'I'm Gay And I'm In Love', was organised with Steo's approval, and made a big spread in *The Sun* on 16 June 1999.

From that point on, the change in the guy was amazing. He'd been so depressed and sad, so plagued by worry and frightened of everything. Suddenly, the worst had happened. The truth was out there and, for him, that brought such a sense of immense joy and relief. He didn't have to hide anymore.

If the rest of us had any fears at all that the news might harm Boyzone and have a negative effect on our popularity, they were very quickly quashed. Steo's announcement was followed by the most successful album and the biggest tour we ever had. If anything, the fans loved us all the more. There's a Gay Pride flag in a multitude of colours, and those rainbow banners were flying all over the place at our gigs that year. Steo was delighted. He got nothing but support not only from our dedicated followers, but also from fellow celebrities like Elton John.

* * * * *

The MTV Europe Music Awards were held at the Point in Dublin in November. Ro hosted and Britney Spears was the night's big winner, being presented with four awards and performing a medley of her hits. The other multiple winners were Boyzone. We received two awards, for best UK and Ireland act and best album for *By Request*. It should have been such an exciting moment. Not that long before, it would have been. Far from starting to slide, the band just kept getting bigger and bigger.

But my head was gradually being so screwed up with the pressure we'd existed under for the last few years, the relentless media attention, the things I'd got involved with that I should have left well alone that, on that dark winter's night, I couldn't have cared less. And I didn't keep it to myself either. I let the whole world know it meant nothing to me. The other lads were all dressed the part, and there was I in my shabby jeans and sweater, as scruffy as you like. When we went up to collect the awards, I was steaming drunk and effing and blinding all the way. A worldwide audience of millions was at home watching on TV, let alone the huge crowd gathered in the venue itself – and I didn't give a damn.

I didn't even keep myself to myself at the after-show party. I picked a fight with Puff Daddy. My then wife, Easther, had performed with Eternal at the event, and I remember being outside the VIP room when one of her entourage came out to me saying Easther was being hassled by some bouncers. I hadn't a clue what was going on so I went into the VIP room and stood at the balcony that looked over the rest of the dance floor. I could see Easther having words with a burly security man so I thought I'd better go down and find out what the problem was.

I started to walk down the steps. To my left was Puff Daddy standing on a table. I glanced at him as I went by and found myself eyeball to eyeball with him. He was looking directly at me, but not in a friendly way. The man was cursing at me.

I didn't stop to wonder why. Being the kind of guy I was at the time, I didn't think to ask what was wrong, to see if I'd misunderstood. I just launched myself through the air right into him. Crash landing on the floor, the breath was pretty well knocked clean out of me, and all I remember is lifting my head up and seeing a wall of security men coming towards me – Puff Daddy's security men. They were huge, black guys, just the sort of heavies you imagine when you think of American bodyguards. They might not be the fittest men in the world but they had enough weight behind them to inflict a hell of a lot of damage. But, that night I wasn't bothered. I was so fired up. Something was going on with my wife and for some reason Puff Daddy was having a go. If I had to take these guys on, I'd take them on.

I never got the chance, though, which, from the point of view of coming away from the night with both my kneecaps intact, was probably just as well. As the heavy mob approached, the club's security intervened. I got lifted up from behind, taken out and downstairs.

Apparently Puff Daddy then seemed to decide that the VIP room was now his and proceeded to start kicking people out. Even Easther got caught in the thick of it, putting up a bit of a fight against the club's security men. But actually, they were all right. They were the good guys. They were the ones who said, 'Go on, Shane, don't worry about it, just get yourself home.' And that's what I did. I left.

To this day I don't know why Puff Daddy targeted me the way he did. I don't know what was going on with him. He came to play in Dublin some time afterwards and sent an apology and some flowers to Louis Walsh's management company. He even delivered an invitation saying he hoped I'd come to his show and that I didn't hold a grudge against him. It didn't happen, though. We didn't get together and shake hands and I haven't seen him since. The chances are he probably doesn't even remember the incident, all these years later. But then again, I didn't think Prince Charles would remember his brush with me either, but apparently he did.

The year and the millennium were drawing to a close. As for Boyzone, we'd begun to talk about taking a break. We'd changed so much as individuals since the early days. There were other things we wanted to do, other projects to get involved in. Ronan was already planning a solo album. The problem was that our band schedules left no space for anything else. It was getting to the point of being suffocating. Just the thought that we might actually be able to take some proper time off and have a bit of freedom was sheer bliss. I'd been driving myself mad for a while anyway. The whole Boyzone joyride had got pretty stale. Every day was just more of the same and none of us could honestly say we were enjoying it anymore. We were bored. Everything around us was shooting off at 100mph – the tours, the promotions, the album sales – but, dead-centre of that endless circle, it was empty.

The idea of the break was to recharge the batteries, to revitalize us as individuals so that we could pick up with Boyzone again in a short while with all our original energy and enthusiasm. At the time, it was such a relief. I didn't have a lot of things lined up that I was desperate to do, I just loved the idea of a holiday – a holiday in the sense of being able to go home and stay there. I'd bought a house early in 1998 and, getting on for two years later, all the work still wasn't finished because

I was always away. I was pouring so much money into doing this place up but, so far, I'd never been able to enjoy the beauty of it. Some decent time off would mean I'd be able to sleep in my own bedroom, wake up when I wanted to rather than when I was told to, feed the fish that I had, do all the other stuff that's normal about being alive.

When we decided to go for a temporary stop, Boyzone were still way up at the top of the tree. It wasn't that our popularity was waning. Record sales weren't dropping off. It was just that, as individuals, it wasn't working for us anymore. For myself, I didn't want to keep travelling the world going on tours. The thrill that used to be there was gone. There'd been a buzz about doing TV, a buzz about the concerts. Now there was nothing. I felt I'd been drilled into the floor. I was finished physically and mentally, so much so that by now I was drinking from pretty well first thing in the morning just to get me through, to get something out of the day. There was a lot going on in me that I wasn't able to deal with back then and, to some extent or other, each one of us was struggling. We had our own problems and were developing our own agendas. I don't think that, musically, there was a 'beginning of the end' for Boyzone. It was just that, whatever there had been between the five of us was slowly splitting apart.

We were definitely falling out more and winding each other up a lot of the time. I was a big player in that side of our breakdown. There wasn't a lot that was good going on in my personal life and my mind had grown very black. I'd go out of my way to upset people whether they were supposed to be my friends or not. I took a real pleasure in it. Add to that the utter exhaustion we were all feeling and the weight of the pressure, and I guess the only way we were heading was slam into disaster. Looking back, we had nowhere else to go. It was actually the perfect time to take a break, the best decision we could have made, given that we were getting into such a mess it was hard to make a right decision about anything. If we'd tried to push on any further, I can't begin to imagine what would have happened between us all.

That final, decisive moment came in a beachfront hotel. The five of us were in one of the bedrooms and I was sitting in the big bay window looking out onto a pebble beach. The window was beautiful, the kind you might see in a manor house, made up of rows of small panes of glass. I was gazing through it, not even looking at the other lads, but the conversation was going on and I was listening: 'We're going to take a year off. We're very, very tired. Most of us have wives and children and we want to be with them. We need a little bit of time for ourselves.'

And that was pretty much it. It wasn't, 'We're splitting up. End of Boyzone.' It was, 'Let's just take a breather.'

Louis was very good about the whole idea. He fully understood our reasons for doing what we were doing. Everyone was cool. So, we finished the tour we were on and went off to do our own thing. We didn't hold a press conference, didn't see the need to make a big, public announcement. After all, it was just a few short months off. We'd be coming right back. Nothing was really said about any of it until the final gig of the tour at The Point in Dublin.

Ronan was the one to come out with it. He'd always been the main front man so it seemed right it should come from him: 'We've come to the last song of the show, and myself and the lads have something to say. I'm sure we'll see you all later this year for another Boyzone show. They're not going to get rid of us yet! Thank you so much for the last six years. It's been unbelievable, thank you so much. But we're not going anywhere. We've all got some stuff to do on our own for a while but, believe me, Boyzone is stronger than it's ever been before.'

It was as simple as that. But even though we'd talked about it and were all agreed that it was the best thing (for our sanity if nothing else), actually hearing it, letting the fans know like that, was unexpectedly emotional. We knew what we were going to do; it was just that finally putting it into words kind of set the seal on it. It was real. Our year out was about to begin.

The time apart actually came as a hell of a shock. As Boyzone, we'd been living in some kind of a bubble. Almost every minute of every day was laid out for us, ruthlessly planned. We'd been scheduled to death. From our mid to late teens, we'd slipped into our twenties outside of reality. Normal life and the last years of our growing up had passed us by and suddenly, with all that stripped away, I was totally lost. I felt completely separated from the outside world because I'd been living on this other planet for so long. I had nothing to relate to. I didn't know what I liked or didn't like. I was so out of touch. Nothing about the way I'd been leading my life was ordinary. I didn't even know what TV shows I wanted to watch. I could remember the life I'd grown up with at 13 Grangemoor Drive, where my sisters were forever getting into trouble and I was forever digging my way surreptitiously out of it. There was my ma's routine and the programmes she liked to watch. She always knew when it was time for *Home And Away* and *Coronation Street*. Those were her moments to take a rest from the chores and sit back and relax. Things like that punctuated her day. Then there was my dad. He'd go to work and he'd come home. He'd plan the next holiday. My parents' existence had a rhythm to it, a structure. Mine had nothing like that anymore. My whole life felt like a void – as though there was no substance to it and it was just lying emptily in the dust, bleeding out the last few drops.

To begin with, I found I craved such simple things. I looked forward to pouring out a bowl of cereal or having a fry-up. I didn't want to be treated like royalty anymore. It sounds so thankless, I know, but I'd had enough of it. I actually didn't eat in a restaurant for about four years after Boyzone because that's what I'd done night after night. It was always the best restaurants and the best hotels for us. All I wanted now was normality – the freedom to do whatever I wanted whenever I wanted to do it, without that constant pressure of someone telling me what to do and where to go.

But there was an irony to that. I got my freedom. It was handed to me on a plate when the lads and I went our separate ways. Only, once

I had it, I didn't know what to do with it. I'd wake up in the night panicking, freaking out thinking, where do I have to go? What do I have to do? Of course, I didn't have to do anything because there was nothing going on. That went on for months. It was a very bad time. What I lacked in creative activity, I made up for by sitting indoors drinking. I drank on and off all day, stopping at about 8.oopm and hazily living on that drunken buzz till I went to bed at around midnight. The structure missing from my life I put into my alcohol consumption. I knew that if I didn't drink after 8.oopm, the effects would wear off just enough so that I didn't get the spinners. I made sure I was still drunk when I went to bed but, by stopping drinking mid-evening, I could wake up the next day without a hangover. A few months passed like that, indoors, locked up playing Resident Evil on the Play Station.

I didn't see any of the other lads for a long time. I was living in the UK in Surrey in a huge, £1,000,000 country house, but it might as well have been a filthy hole in the ground. I was miserable, depressed and angry. My marriage to Easther had turned into a complete disaster and I'd become a serious recluse.

Whether at the time of that initial break Louis really thought Boyzone would reunite after a year, I've no idea. It certainly never occurred to me that we'd reached the end. At some point between 2000 and 2001, I was expecting a letter or a phone call setting everything in motion again, saying, 'Come on, boys, let's get together.' But nobody made the call. I kept waiting but all I got was silence.

It wasn't until 2001 was under way that it became obvious that Boyzone was probably dead. The tour didn't happen. We weren't lined up to go back to the recording studio. In any case, Ronan had just released his solo album and was about to go out on the road on his own. He wouldn't be around to do anything because he was travelling the world promoting his own stuff. That was when it finally hit home. What was meant to be just a year out was turning into the end of the band.

At the time, I was very bitter about that and, being the angry, self-destructive person I'd become, I took it intensely personally. I was furious with Ronan to start with. He was just doing what was right for him but all I could see was what the end of Boyzone meant to me. What was *I* going to do? How dare Ronan go off like that and spoil it for the rest of us! I'm ashamed to say that was how I saw it. It was totally wrong and I said a lot of things that I regret. The press, on the other hand, were delighted. They were only too happy to document the malice that poured off my loose and viciously sharp tongue.

But it wasn't just Ronan who I was angry with. It was anyone and anything that got in the way of us going back out on tour. We'd been together for a lot of years – a lot of our growing-up years – and I missed it all very, very much. Yes, I'd got sick to the back teeth of the life we lived. We all had. We'd pushed ourselves to the limits of our endurance and had paid the price for that. But, as a band, we'd never parted on the basis that it was all over. It wasn't like a marriage breakdown because it never finished. That was the confusing part about it all. If we'd been told it was over, no going back, there would have been all that sadness and disappointment but, at the same time, an inevitable moment of acceptance. Without that, it was very hard, certainly for me, to move on. We were at the top of our profession. We'd ridden the most astonishing breaker to success. We were massive but we'd chosen to walk away. And now there was to be no going back.

Maybe it was obvious to most people that Ronan was bound to want to pursue a solo career. On our final tour, he'd already released the single, *When You Say Nothing At All*, which he'd written and recorded for the film, *Notting Hill*. He even sang it during his solo spot in our concerts. That was really the beginning of a whole different journey for him. The first year apart from Boyzone launched him in a brand new direction.

Things weren't so straightforward for all of us. Mikey got into a similar situation as I did. Without the band, he seemed lost. He took the whole thing very badly, getting on the drink and becoming reclusive and depressed for a number of months. Things changed for him when he finally built his own recording studio. It was music that managed to lift him out of his black hole. He did try for a solo career but, unfortunately, that didn't quite work how he wanted.

Steo, at least, had some kind of focus. With his natural ability for singing and dancing, he was desperate to get into the West End and spent a lot of time going along to auditions. Keith was also pretty strong – in terms of business, probably the strongest of all of us. He quickly found a way into television and eventually landed a starring role in *Coronation Street.*

I didn't have any plans. For me, the big attraction of time out was being in a position to do nothing. Only, in the end, doing nothing did my head in too. There wasn't really anything I wanted to do with music to begin with. If I looked for any opportunities, they were in motor sport. In that respect, I was the same as ever. I just wanted to get in cars and drive.

A meeting about the future of Boyzone was eventually held, but not until getting on for a couple of years after the initial break. We sat down together in a place in Kings Road, London, looked at what each other was doing, talked about what was going on. And, as we walked out again some time later, I guess we all knew that nothing was going on at all. Nothing could happen in the next year because Ronan had just made his second album and was going off on tour. He was a busy man now. Busy with something other than Boyzone. It was plain to see there'd be no picking up where we left off. The band's days were definitely over.

It was hard to believe how far we'd come since 1993 – or since that first embarrassingly inane appearance on *The Late Late Show,* followed by countless, highly insignificant gigs at some decidedly dodgy venues the length and breadth of Ireland, playing to little more than a handful of people. Those were the days when a broken smoke machine was our pride and joy. But from those less than promising beginnings, through sheer hard graft and the dogged determination of our management company, we'd somehow hauled ourselves up to the ranks of A-list celebrity. We'd had three number one albums and an uninterrupted succession of smash hit singles, establishing ourselves as one of the longest lasting, most successful boy bands ever, not to mention being the first band in history to have 16 singles get into the top three. We'd also developed both in showmanship and musically, to the point where true song-writing ability had emerged and was rewarded with an Ivor Novello award for *Picture Of You*. Our five times platinum third album, *Where We Belong*, even seemed to appeal to all ages, older fans swelling the ranks of the younger ones, and adding to the thousands of devotees who turned up to support us in their droves wherever we went.

It had been a rocket ride to superstardom. We didn't always understand it. We couldn't possibly have foreseen it. And in the end we didn't break away from it because we were failing but because we were worn out. We couldn't take the pace anymore. The fact that we never got back on track after that initial year was a sad thing. We didn't even go out with a bang. If anything, the Boyzone phenomenon just quietly petered out.

CHAPTER 12

Meltdown

"EVENTUALLY THE DIVORCE WAS FINALISED. I GOT MY
PAPERS – AND, SAD TO SAY, IT WAS A PROPER RELIEF."

The charity fashion show we did for Bono's wife in Dublin back in 1996 wasn't only memorable for being the time I got on the catwalk and famously dropped my trousers! It was also the night I met Easther Bennett. She was one gorgeous part of Eternal, a London-based R&B girl group. The band had become well-known in 1993, and went on to enjoy incredible success not only in the UK but way beyond. The original line-up with Easther included her sister, Vernie, and friends Kéllé Bryan and Louise Nurding, who'd both trained at the Italia Conti Academy stage school.

Louise was already a good mate of Boyzone and, around the time Ronan and I were looking for a flat we could share in London, she'd suggested we all move in together. We found a stunning place in William Morris Way in Chelsea, a three-bedroomed apartment on the river. Ant and Dec had a place in the same building. We did try to persuade the record company to pay the £550 a month each, rather than forking out for hotels, but they wouldn't go for it. In the end, we decided it was too beautiful to lose so we decided to stump up the money ourselves. To us it was pure magic. There was a concierge and underground garages, and inside it was plush cream carpet wall-to-wall and the most lavish of furnishings. The bedrooms each had their own luxurious en-suite, and the sitting room was straight out of a lifestyle magazine – everything in its perfect place with huge, sliding glass doors opening out onto a balcony overlooking the river.

Still, in spite of the location and who we were, this wasn't what you'd call a showbiz party house, although Louise did have her particular friends who'd come around. They were lovely girls, too, with their own off-beat take on life – and definitely interesting, to say the least. They had their tongues pierced, their nipples pierced, and God knows where else pierced! But they were always such a laugh and fun to be around.

Louise mostly just did her own thing. She was already seeing Jamie Redknapp, the football star she later married and, despite the fact that we were flatmates, our paths didn't seem to cross that often. If she and Jamie came in late I was usually in bed and, the next morning, I'd tend to be up and out before they even stirred. And I didn't really socialise much with other showbiz mates. At that time, the way of life was all still pretty new. Ro and me would hang out together and visit local bars, but we didn't know where to look for the serious party scene. I remember once we decided to go out and make a night of it, and we spent the time wandering around Chelsea and finding it so dead. I thought London was rubbish! That was before we got to know about Browns Night Club and all those party places Louise introduced us to.

When I met the Eternal girls at the fashion show in Dublin that February 1996, I was attracted to Easther almost immediately. Our eyes met and there was just this spark. Instant chemistry. As that first day we were there was all about setting up and rehearsing for the gig tomorrow, we had plenty of time just to sit around and chat, and we got on really well – so well that I thought I'd ask her out for dinner that evening. She turned me down. She said she had to go and do something with the band. It wasn't until later I found out she'd said no because she thought I was joking, just winding her up.

But the following day, with the show getting under way in the main auditorium, there the two of us were, hanging around again backstage in the corridors, laughing and joking. In the end we exchanged phone numbers. We both lived in London and said we'd meet up some time after we got home and go out and do something. Which is exactly what we did. Back in London we went bowling and started to find out about each other. Easther was quite a staunch churchgoer and very moralistic when it came to relationships. She wanted to take things slowly and I thought that was fair enough. I was perfectly happy to get to know each other as friends, and take things from there.

It wasn't until a couple of months after that that we finally got together. We were both performing in Birmingham and, after our shows, we met up and sat up all night playing cards. It was such an intimate time that I eventually asked her out. Properly. And that's when we became a couple.

Easther used to come round to the flat in Chelsea, but unfortunately it was a little awkward. Louise had actually quit Eternal in 1995 and things were still just a bit sticky between the girls. There had been some controversy over the fact that she was the only white member, and she was the one leaving. The press had suggested she'd been dumped to give the band a better chance of making it in America. This was something Eternal's management hotly denied, and Louise always maintained that she simply wanted to pursue a career as a solo artist, apparently signing with EMI six months before she actually left. Whatever the truth was, it didn't make things all that easy on the domestic front. The girls were pleasant with each other and there weren't any catfights in the corridors, but I found I did start to spend more time at Easther's instead of her coming over to my place. Then, in early 1997, I moved out of the flat altogether and in with Easther.

We'd been together for a year by then, which was quite an achievement in showbiz circles, especially as both our bands were incredibly busy. It wasn't unusual for us to be apart from each other for two or three weeks at a stretch. We weren't quite ships in the night, but not far off. Still, even though we had to spend so much time away, in our own minds we must have felt as if we had something pretty solid going for us, because 1997 was the year we got engaged.

We used to talk about getting married – having kids, living in the perfect house with a gorgeous garden surrounded by that storybook white picket fence. We could picture the whole fairytale. Then, on Sunday 8 March 1998, we did it. We got married at the magnificent Leez Priory, a stunning sixteenth century Tudor mansion near Chelmsford in Essex.

Beyond the dream, I don't know what we both thought our life together would be. I suppose most people stand at the altar with the idea that everyone else's marriage may fall apart around their ears, but theirs is the one that will work. Theirs is the one that will stand the test of time, staying rock solid no matter what.

Whatever was in our heads, the reality of being together was very different. Instead of our commitment bringing us into a real intimacy, we seemed to drift apart. We wanted different things and I felt very rejected. I couldn't help it. I had a wife but we just weren't close somehow. It grew into a big mess in my head. I battled with it every day, starting to question everything about myself. My main experience of marriage was what my parents had had. They always seemed so strong. So together. That's how I imagined my life with my wife would be. Not like this. It was actually a very confusing time and I found myself slipping into some sort of depression. This wasn't made any easier by my growing fascination with the occult which, although I wasn't aware of it early on, was causing disturbing changes to my personality.

Those were not happy days. I was very insecure in the relationship and, the fact that Easther was still very friendly with some of her ex-partners didn't help. It made me constantly suspicious – even jealous. One day I gave her an ultimatum. I didn't stop to think whether I was being fair or not. All I could see was that when I was away with the band, she'd be off with old boyfriends, going for dinner, that kind of thing. In my head, that was all wrong. If I'd been able to think rationally, I'd have known there was nothing for me to worry about. But that wasn't the way I felt at the time because there seemed to be so many barriers between us. So one night I told her. We'd had yet another argument over it and I spelt it out: 'Look, knock around with them and do what you do, or do you want to be with me? You have to choose. If you carry on this way, it can't work.'

Although I wasn't banning her from seeing them, I was telling her to make a choice. Whatever she really felt about that, I don't know, but she chose me and all ties with old boyfriends were cut.

By late 1999, things were still far from right. That's when it all got messy and I ended up cheating on her. My wife. The woman who I was supposed to love and respect. The woman I'd chosen to spend my life with.

I'd gone to my brother-in-law's stag do. He was marrying my sister, Tara. A gang of us lads went to Liverpool where we got drunk out of our minds and ended up hitting strip clubs. It was just meant to be a good time. I certainly wasn't planning on what happened. But I finished the night by going back with one of the lap dancers.

A couple of days later, I get a phone call from my lawyer in Ireland saying, 'Look, Shane, there's a story going in the papers on Sunday. What do you want to do?' Unknown to me, the lap dancer had sold every sordid detail of it to the press. That was a desperate moment of, 'Oh, my God.' Although my relationship with Easther had never really got off the ground, when she found out what I'd done, that drunken night was obviously pretty much going to be the kiss of death to whatever we had left. Still, I had to call her and warn her that the story was about to break.

I was away at the time, in Anglesey in Wales, and I remember sitting in the car for hours trying to work out how I was going to sort this situation, how I could explain it. When Easther picked up the phone I began to talk: 'It's a no-brainer. It is what it is. Plain and simple. There's a story going in the papers about me and this lap dance girl and there's no point in me denying it.' What else could I possibly say?

Of course I had to go home and see her face to face. To begin with, she seemed to take it quite well. What happened had happened. I was in a marital relationship. I'd taken vows and I'd ended up committing adultery. I couldn't change it. But, from that point on, things went even further down hill very quickly. We were in the middle of a hopelessly bad time, and it was plain enough for anyone to see that our marriage was in big trouble.

I moved into a different bedroom after that and life became very weird for me. Easther and I still watched the same TV shows together, ate dinner together, did all the same stuff we'd always done together, but now we weren't even sharing a bed. How were we ever going to mend this and at least try and find some kind of middle ground? There wasn't just a coldness between us now. There were solid walls. It was as if we were looking at each other across this huge chasm that I couldn't work out how to get across. I spent a lot of days outside in the garden, trying to make sense of life and the world I was living in. It was a very depressing time. I wanted to understand but I couldn't. I knew I'd done wrong and it was my duty to make it right but nothing I did seemed to change things for the better. All I was doing was clinging on, just hoping that one day everything would come good again.

I must have been losing heart, though, because it got to the stage where one night we sat down together and I laid my cards flat out on the table.

'Look,' I said, 'I'm not being funny but I'm going to get to the point where this is over for me. I can't try any harder to make it all better. What I did was wrong, but all I want to do now is move forward.'

Easther just sat there looking at me, saying nothing. Maybe she didn't know how to respond. I went on, 'If you want to move forward together we can do that. If you don't, then it's time for me to leave. I haven't reached the point where I want to leave yet, but when I do, there'll be no going back. I'm hoping I don't get there. I'm hoping you'll come round to me first.'

We had the same conversation every week for about six months, but nothing changed except that I was sinking deeper into depression. I began drinking heavily – the blue cans, super strength 9% alcohol – just to get away from life, to shut out what was happening in my world. I spent most of my days drunk, locked into Play Station games, trying to run away from this situation that I couldn't work out any more and didn't seem able to put right. I went out and spent money pointlessly on cars to try and find a way to feel happy again. I might buy a new Porsche, a Ferrari, a Jeep, anything just to get a buzz and feel good about myself. Maybe it worked for a moment, but then the next morning, it was always the same thing. The cloud of depression would roll back over me and I'd feel empty and worthless.

When I think of everything Easther and I had, being so low and despondent must have looked crazy from the outside. We had the ultimate lifestyle. We lived in a beautiful five-bedroomed mansion that I'd designed and built, set in 20 leafy acres in Surrey. It was originally an old stable house and was an incredible place, custom-built of reclaimed stone brought down from a castle in Scotland. It had beautiful sandstone floors, with the kitchen crafted in solid oak and the size of the entire ground floor of most people's houses. There were hefty island units and massive American style fridges dispensing drinks and ice cubes. Upstairs, the main bedroom was enormous, with a lounge and a bathroom the size of two double bedrooms, a walk-in wardrobe and hidden closets. Then there were the guestrooms with en-suites. We even had a 15 foot aquarium.

I loved my gardening and tending to my fish. We hadn't been able to get planning permission for a pool, so I had a lake instead where I used to swim. But my favourite place had to be my garage, where I kept all my cars, bikes and tools. Deep down, I was still the same small-town Irish lad I'd always been, enjoying nothing better than being up to my elbows in grease, tinkering away on an engine. I had a Porsche out there, a BMW, five Toyotas and three Corollas, two of which I used to rally in.

I was earning a huge amount of money and, on top of all those cars, I'd got myself a JCB, which I still have. The way I saw it, what was the point in spending hours digging a hole with a shovel when you could do one scoop with a JCB!

Looking at my life objectively like that and all the things I'd been able to buy to fill it up with, how could I ever have been unhappy? I had everything I could possibly want. The life I lived in that house was every boy's dream. The lads used to come round and we'd get out and get dirty on the motor-cross track I had in one of our fields. In another, there was a rally course and we'd get beered up, light big bonfires and race cars. It was one way I had to keep everything going, to try to deal with the emptiness I felt and the anger that was building up inside of me. The problem was, it was only ever a temporary escape, and not a solution at all.

I was never suicidal, but it did come into my head now and again just to leave everything behind and go and live on the streets. I nearly did it, too. I almost took off one night to give it all up and be homeless. A wanderer. After all, none of what I had had made me happy, and I got to a point of such desperation and misery that I just wanted to forget about it.

Then it happened. One day in 2002. Completely out of the blue, Easther suggested going to a marriage counsellor. My heart almost skipped a beat. I couldn't get my head around it. I was thinking, at long last we're going to sort this mess out. We're going to find the fairytale.

But I was getting ahead of myself. No matter how much we both might have wanted to turn a corner at that moment, to find some common ground, by then it was too late. We were too far apart. All of a sudden, I couldn't see a way through anymore. Inside myself I made the decision that there was no point to it all and I simply said, 'Right, that's the end.'

Easther seemed genuinely surprised. 'What do you mean?' she asked.

'It's over,' I answered. 'I've said to you for a year that when I say it's over, it *will* be over, and hopefully we'll manage to sort it all out before that happens. But we haven't. And now it's over.'

It didn't take me long to buy another place to live, and I moved out of our Surrey home, even though that wasn't what Easther wanted. All of a sudden, she seemed desperate to try and hold us together. She even said she wanted to have children with me. But I couldn't go back. Not now. Our marriage had been a very bad time. Every day I'd wake up and feel like nothing. Worse than nothing. It wasn't any good for either of us. The best thing we could do was just let it go.

We were separated for quite some time before I told her I wanted a divorce.

She said, 'OK. But will you do me a favour and let me finish some exams first?'

She was in college and wanted to concentrate on her work there, which did mean having to put things on hold for about eight months, but I didn't argue. As far as I was concerned we were separate people. Finished. In my head we were divorced already.

The eight months passed, the summer came and Easther did her exams.

The following September, I gave her a call and said we needed to sort everything out. I couldn't believe her response this time. She told me she just didn't want a divorce.

When I spoke to my lawyer, he said she had to be served with official papers, but I didn't have her address anymore. In the end, I had the divorce papers sent to her mother's house. They were swiftly returned to my lawyer with a note stating that she didn't live at that address. I sent other letters and they were sent back too.

In the end, I resorted to hiring a private investigator to find out where she lived and, at last, I got hold of the information I needed. I passed it on to my lawyer and he must have instructed the investigator to make sure the divorce papers ended up in her hands. Slickly doing his job, he'd apparently walked up to her front door with a bunch of flowers, pretending to be someone from a florist. When he'd asked, 'Are you Easther Bennett?' she'd said, yes, she was – which is when he'd dropped the flowers, handed her the divorce papers and said, 'You've been served by Her Majesty's Court.' I didn't know until after it had happened. It wasn't a nice thing for her and I didn't feel good about it. But I had to get those papers served.

The divorce didn't come through quickly. There was a lot of negotiation, a lot of battling it out between our two lawyers. Then, two weeks before everything was sorted out, Easther sent me a text. She wanted to know if we could stop everything, the whole messy process, and have another try at working on our relationship. I couldn't do it though. I think, by then, we'd put each other through too much.

Eventually the divorce was finalised. I got my papers – and, sad to say, it was a proper relief.

CHAPTER 13

Dark Is The Moon

"I WAS IN A FILTHY PIT AND I COULDN'T CRAWL OUT.
NOT ON MY OWN. NOT WITHOUT HELP."

The fame, the fortune, the constant attention from adoring fans who just couldn't get enough of Boyzone, it was all astonishing – extraordinary when you think of where I'd come from, a kid with no proper direction, struggling even to read, and kicked out of school for being a waste of time. It should have been so perfect, and one in the eye for that head teacher back at the Grange Community College who'd given me up as a bad job. A truly charmed life.

But, for me, it wasn't like that. I had it all but it felt as though I had nothing. Deep down, I was a very troubled man.

My first brush with the occult was meant to be just a bit of innocent fun, kids messing around and getting their thrills. I was 14 years old and on a family holiday in a place called Terryglass in the Shannon region of Ireland. We used to pack up and go there water skiing. It seemed so inconsequential when it started, just a stupid game with my sisters and Kaner to pass the time.

But meddling with the occult is nothing like playing games. Without realising it, we opened the door to something very sinister.

We found a couple of pieces of paper, scribbled out the alphabet and created this homemade ouija board. We put a coin down on it and, as my sisters spoke to what they assumed was some sort of spirit, asking it questions, it actually moved across the board, spelling out words supposedly in answer. To be honest, I can't remember exactly what they were asking, but I do remember one thing. It was a couple of words that the movement of the coin spelt on the board: *Kill Shane*. I freaked out. I didn't know if it was real or not, if maybe the others were just pushing this coin around to wind me up. I never asked them. But it was my first encounter with the occult, my first insight into power and darkness. And it really put the frighteners on me.

It was six years later at the launch party for our second album, *A Different Beat*, that I found myself dragged into what I can best describe as 'the dark side' again. You'd think the experience when I was 14 would have scared me off ever having any more to do with it. But somehow it hadn't. When I came across a group of guests at the party, getting their Hallowe'en kicks huddled round a ouija board, I couldn't stop myself joining them. I wanted to be involved. It was as if something was sucking me in. Not that I was really taking it all that seriously, but a few drinks, a laugh, a bit of spiritual communication, where was the harm?

It *was* harmful, though. Deeply harmful and very dangerous. It changed me and messed me up for a long, long time.

Soon after that second occult encounter, I started to have disturbed dreams. I would wake up completely paralysed. I could just about manage to force my eyelids open so that I could see, but I couldn't move the rest of my body no matter how hard I tried. My arms, my legs, even my tongue were totally frozen. It was terrifying. Although the whole experience would go on for maybe only five to ten seconds, when I was lying there petrified, panic-stricken, not knowing what was going to happen to me or if I'd ever move again, it felt like so much longer. This on and off state of paralysis went on for perhaps two years, and I guess, in a way, I got used to it.

I never really tried to work it out, to see if there was some sort of pattern to when or how it happened. I would just wake up time and again, able to see but unable to move. Then, one night, the whole experience became even more horrific.

I was staying in a hotel in Germany. We'd just finished a great gig and had headed back to our rooms with a chicken and chips take-away. It was midnight and, after enjoying my food, I went right to bed. I was feeling exhausted and hoping I'd get the chance to catch up on some much needed sleep. The room was as comfortable and spacious as we'd come to expect while we were away touring and, as usual, I'd left the en-suite light on. I spent so many nights in different hotel rooms that I always left the light on, and pulled the door closed. That way, if I woke in the middle of the night and needed the bathroom, I'd know which direction to go in because of the shaft of light shining through the gap at the bottom. It could be very disorientating otherwise.

I was in a really deep sleep when I was woken suddenly by the sound of a door opening. My eyes were open but, as usual, my body was frozen. I couldn't move a muscle. I was lying with my back towards the bathroom door, but I knew that was the one I'd heard open because the wall in front of me was flooded with the light I'd left on. Then the door closed again and in the darkness I could hear footsteps padding across the bedroom. They came right up close behind me and I sensed someone or something leaning over me. I could hear breathing. I couldn't feel the breath but I could hear it whispering in and out.

I suppose five or six seconds must have passed like that, I don't really know how long it was. I was so scared I just closed my eyes. I couldn't move or shout or scream. I couldn't have turned to face whatever it was even if I'd wanted to. I just remember the sound of breathing stopping, the footsteps retreating and the door opening and closing again. I didn't open my eyes. I probably could have moved by now but I didn't. I stayed exactly as I was and willed myself back to sleep.

How I managed to drift off again, I have no idea. I'd never been so frightened in my whole life. But when I eventually woke up the next morning, all I could think was, did that actually happen? Was that real? It had seemed real enough in the middle of the night and I was very confused. The chain was on my door. Nobody could possibly have come in. In any case, I knew whatever it was had come and gone through the bathroom. So did I dream it? Was it just some sick nightmare? I didn't know. And, to be honest, I was just glad it was over with and I'd come through it.

Apart from my usual spate of paralysed night waking, nothing more happened for a couple of months after that, until one night at the apartment I shared with Ronan and Louise in Chelsea. I was in my bed which was pushed up against one wall, and there were some double wardrobes at the end and a door to the en-suite. I'd woken up in one of my usual frozen states, lying on my back. In the blackness of the night, my eyes slowly focused on three transparent-seeming shapes. They were very small, each no bigger than a pint glass, and they circled over the door that led out of the bedroom to the corridor. Nothing happened. They just stayed where they were, hovering on the air. I stared at them. It's all I could do. Then, I don't know if they just disappeared because I must have closed my eyes and pretty much drifted back to sleep.

When I woke up the next day everything seemed fine. Normal. Or as normal as possible given that something unearthly was happening to me and I had no control over it.

But that wasn't the end of it. Another night when I woke, I found myself gazing at a chilling red aura that floated backwards and forwards across the room. There was no sound. No contact. It just drifted silently above me.

Then I had a third night-time encounter. I opened my eyes to find the face of a very old man looking down at me. It didn't look evil, just ancient, and for the first time, it was an apparition with a voice. It had something to say: 'Did you enjoy that one?'

The only thing I could think was that it was talking about my dreams. They'd been so real that night, so vivid. I couldn't answer because I still couldn't move. There wasn't a muscle in my body I could get to respond. The apparition didn't ask again, it simply said, 'All right, see what you think of this one.'

But there was nothing more. There didn't seem to be another dream. And after that strange and mysterious contact, nothing more happened for a very long time.

Since the Hallowe'en launch party, I'd been dabbling more and more, not necessarily in the occult as such, but in witchcraft. It fascinated and absorbed me. I began watching horror movies, becoming obsessed with all kinds of devilment. After a couple of years, my life was dangerously steeped in so much that was demonic that things progressed to a terrifying level.

It was night again and I was in a hotel room in Los Angeles. I could see the bed I was lying on, the walls, the ceiling, but then suddenly they were gone. Whichever way I looked, that particular surface was transformed and I'd be faced with a scene inside someone's house, or outside in a park, or there would be a television screen. One image was of a corridor, and there was an old woman standing there in Victorian headdress. She walked across the hotel room two or three times before the scene seemed to dissolve away and I was able to move again. That was the first time that I didn't go back to sleep. That time I woke right up and actually snapped out of it.

During another episode, I had actual physical contact. A little boy was pulling on my arm. I could feel him tugging at me. It wasn't spooky or ghostly like you see in films. It was very real. But it was the reality that made it terrifying. It all felt so troubled, so disturbed. I could see what I assumed must be the boy's mother and father – a man and a woman – calling him, saying, 'Come back, come back!' The boy suddenly let go of me and just turned and ran. Then the scene disappeared.

When I travelled on to Hong Kong with the band, I had my first daytime encounter. I was up in my hotel room, chatting away on the phone, when, all of a sudden, the bed I was sitting on rose up from the floor. It lifted about a foot in the air then settled back down on the carpet, landing from left to right, just as a feather might come to rest on the ground. I was wide awake, the sun was streaming down outside, and there I was, having a conversation with an old mate on a floating bed.

I said, 'Something weird's happening. Let me call you back,' and put the receiver down.

I couldn't speak about it. I hadn't spoken to anyone. No one knew what was happening to me. I just sat there for a while, trying to work it out. The bed was now sitting squarely on the floor. Not for the first time I had to ask myself, did that really happen?

That same night, I had yet another physical contact. It was so bizarre because the woman who appeared in my bedroom was someone I'd known for years and years and she was still very much alive and well.

It all started in the same way. I'd been dreaming and when I woke up unable to move, there was this familiar lady standing at the end of my bed, watching me. She was friendly, and I didn't feel scared as she moved closer and leaned over me. But then she touched me, put her hand on my side and, as she made contact with my body, she turned into the most horrific demon I have ever seen in my life. It was so shocking, so disgusting. This woman I knew, who wasn't even a dead person, was violently transformed into some kind of creature that looked like cross between an alien and a predator, with coarse hair and a hideous long snout and jaw jutting out.

Although the other encounters had been very unnerving, very frightening, this was the first time I was well and truly freaked out. I was face to face with the most repulsive being I'd ever seen. I couldn't scream or curse or shout. I couldn't yell at the thing to go away because my tongue wouldn't work. My brain was willing me to cry out at the top of my voice, but my lips were forced to stay silent.

Like all the others, this apparition disappeared as suddenly as it had come. But this time I knew I couldn't let things go on. I was going to have to find some help. Before long, I could see myself getting to a stage where I'd be scared to go to sleep.

The next day, I decided to confide in my tour manager, Mark Plunkett. He went off and spoke to somebody he knew from a record company, and when I'd explained everything to them, they said that they knew an American medium who might be able to help me. We got in touch with her and she came over to my hotel room. She listened to what I had to say, and then claimed that she knew exactly what was happening to me and how to put a stop to it.

'No problem,' she said confidently. 'I know what's wrong with you. You are possessed by a spirit.'

Fair enough, I thought, so I'm possessed by a spirit. What do we do about it?

This medium seemed to have all the answers. She said, 'I'm going to carry out a ritual over you. Then the spirit of the demon will leave you and everything will be fine.'

She sounded as if she knew precisely what she was dealing with, so I lay on the bed in my hotel room and let her place some small crystals down round my belly, my chest, around my neck and on my forehead, and she put two more in one of my hands. Then she took something out of her bag which looked like a miniature chalice which she held in her hands, and told me to close my eyes whilst she performed her ritual.

As I lay there with my eyes shut, she started speaking to me in a low, calm voice, instructing me to visualise my body being wrapped carefully in a protective white cloth. She went through the process from my ankles, to my knees, to my hips, to my chest, even my fingers and all the way up to my head. I could hear her walking around the room as she spoke, murmuring all the time about the wrapping in the cleansing cloth.

The session lasted about an hour and a half, and when the medium had finished, she proceeded to take the stones off my body. She'd barely begun to gather them up when she had to drop them because they were so hot. She couldn't hold onto them. I picked them up for her and to me they felt cool. But to her, they were burning and she started to look worried.

'I had a bit of a problem with you,' she said finally. 'Usually I feel the spirit leave and it's very clear to me. But with you nothing like that happened. I've never seen this before. What I'm going to do is take your picture and use it to continue with the ritual after I leave.'

Then she told me that this psychic photo would cost $100. At that point, I told her not to worry about the picture. Obviously it wasn't a question of not having the money. It was just that, as far as I was concerned, if whatever she'd done hadn't worked, then it hadn't worked. I thanked her for her time, but said not to bother any more, and she left.

I told Mark what had happened. By this stage all the lads knew that something weird was going on with me, and that a strange American lady had been in my room performing some mysterious ritual. They didn't kid me about it or treat me as if I was seriously losing the plot. They were actually very supportive, taking it all quite seriously with a kind of 'we always knew there was a reason for your madness' attitude. Maybe it would have helped me to talk to them before, but I just didn't want them to know.

The one person I did want to talk to was my wife, Easther. I was married for quite a lot of the time I was experiencing the paralysis and the encounters and, as we shared the same bed, she'd be there in the room when something happened. She knew when I woke to a demonic visit, and I could hear her voice telling me calm down, saying that everything would be all right. On the mornings that followed the disturbed nights, I always wanted to talk about what I'd felt or seen, but she never wanted to go into it, so it wasn't something we ended up discussing. I found that very hard. It was odd in a way because she came from such a strong church background, but she never suggested that perhaps the Church could help me. Maybe that was just part of the way she was. She had her beliefs, but she never tried to force religion onto me, which was fine. That's not what I had a problem with. What got to me was that she didn't want to talk to me about what was happening. I was going through something and needed her help, but she didn't seem to want to know.

After a while, I turned to a friend. She was one of the dancers on tour, a beautiful black girl. We got on really well with each other. I found it easy to confide in her. She had a grandmother in Africa who used to be involved in voodoo and, when she knew that the medium's ritual seemed not have done its job, she said she'd find somebody else who might be able to help me. This turned out to be a big African witch doctor in Brixton and, as soon as we returned from Hong Kong, we went over to see him. I paid over £100 for the session, then did my best to answer the questions he put to me as he sat down on an old seat that looked like an antique wooden chopping board. The questions and my attempted answers did gradually begin to shed a little light on what was happening, but they didn't seem to be offering any solutions.

The man asked me if there was a pattern to the visitations. Did each cycle of encounters begin as something fairly harmless then become more and more disturbing? I told him that was exactly the way of it. Everything would build and build and, in the end, there would be physical contact that was so bizarre I found myself wondering if it had actually happened at all. Then he asked if the apparitions appeared at any particular time in a month. I didn't know the answer. I wasn't keeping a record, so he told me to mark on my calendar the next time something occurred.

He went on, 'Usually something like this will happen in and around the full moon, so that can mean anything up to a week before or a week after the time when the moon is full.'

He said it was to do with the moon being high and the tide being low. That was when spirits were able to roam free. I didn't really understand what he was trying to explain, but his words did seem to make sense in my situation. When my friend and I left his house, we perhaps understood a little more, but we still didn't know what to do with the information.

A short while afterwards, the African man was proved to be absolutely right in what he had said. Around the time of the full moon, my next visitation happened. I marked it on the calendar and then, working forward, had some idea of when it might be going to happen next.

Because the witch doctor had understood what I was saying and could explain how it was happening, it somehow made the situation even more real for me. I wasn't imagining things. The apparitions I'd seen weren't to do with sleep deprivation or having bad dreams. This wasn't some kind of junkie's trip or temporary madness. I drank alcohol but I didn't do drugs. No, this was real. I knew I had a very big problem in my life.

As time went on, I was also very aware that, inside me, I was changing. There were moments when I thought I was going absolutely out of my mind. At other times, I think I found a certain amount of comfort in my involvement with the occult. It was a weird phenomenon in the same way that I was weird, and that's why it constantly drew me in. The occult was mysterious, dark and edgy, and I felt like that about myself. I was this dark and edgy guy, with an emptiness looming up inside me.

I definitely played on that image. I used it in the band. I projected myself that way in the media. That was my persona and how I wanted to be perceived. People knew Shane Lynch as a bit dark, a bit restless. They saw me as very unpredictable and were never quite certain what I was going to do next. I don't know if people were actually afraid of me, in that they felt intimidated, or whether they were just never sure of what might kick off when I was around. For example, there was the night when we'd been invited to the MTV Awards. Everybody else arrived dressed in their smart gear, and I turned up in a scruffy pair of jeans and a sweatshirt. Then I got up there on the stage and started effing and blinding, not giving a thought to the other lads and what that might be doing to them. It wasn't that I didn't want to be there, it was just that I didn't care. I was doing what I wanted to do. It was totally selfish and obviously the others didn't deserve that, but I was completely bound up in Shane's world and doing what Shane wanted to do.

At least, that's what I thought. But the truth of it was that I wasn't in control at all. I was in a downward spiral of self-destruction and there seemed to be no way out of it. Some of the moods I'd slip into were unbelievably vile. I could be very sharp-tongued, feeling so cold and evil at times that I couldn't wait to tear somebody down, slag them off, crush them with some home truths. If I thought a girl looked ugly, I'd tell her she was ugly. If I saw a fellow performer who, to me, didn't seem to have a lot of talent, I'd tell them so to their face. I didn't bite my lip and stay quiet for the sake of being polite. I said exactly what was on my mind with the deliberate intention of upsetting people and bringing them down. At that time, my whole purpose seemed to be to hurt those around me. I wanted everyone else to feel the pain I was feeling because I'd fallen into such a dark and hopeless place. I'd become a horrible, horrible man.

On top of that, it took next to nothing to get me into a big argument or a fight. I wasn't glassing anyone or taking a baseball bat to them, it was nothing like that. There were just so many times when I should have simply turned and walked away – and I didn't. I'd get into fisty-cuffs when people would have a go and say something derogatory like, 'Boyzone, you're rubbish' or, 'Shane, you're a dick head'. That gave me the perfect opportunity to start a ruckus. I was the young, immature hothead who couldn't wait to fight back. It was almost as if I felt I had something to prove. I might prance about in this boy band but I wanted to show that I wasn't weak or effeminate or feeble. I was one of the lads and, to get my message well and truly across, I made a point of going out drinking and fighting and causing grief.

My tattoos reflect some of the things I felt going on inside me back then, some of the emotions I was grappling with. I didn't get tattooed to be hard, that's for sure. Those tattoos were my journey. I've got ropes and chains, and there's a broken crucifix on my chest. The crucifix symbolised a particularly dark and evil time. There was a period when I was anti-God, anti-Bible and anti-Jesus. I wanted the cross broken because to me it was meaningless rubbish and had nothing to do with real life.

Anger churned around inside me almost all of the time and I was weighed down under the influence of the dark things I'd been messing with. A lot of my moods became so weird, so intense, that it would get to the point where I wouldn't speak for days. I could be in a car travelling with the lads, or whoever was around at the time, and I just couldn't say a word. Someone might ask me a question and I wasn't able to respond. I wanted to, but it was almost like another form of paralysis, except that this time it was just my mouth that was frozen. I simply could not speak. Whether that was some kind of depression, or I'd ended up withdrawing so far inside myself that I couldn't be bothered to make the effort to respond, I don't know. But it was all so bizarre and so unlike the person I used to be.

By that time, it was as if whichever way I turned, there was nothing but blackness. I knew I was in deep trouble, that there was something fundamentally wrong with me, but that's not where it finished. My marriage was a disaster, Boyzone had pretty much come to the end of its run, and the drink was sinking me even further into the mire. Everything was destruction and more destruction, and all I was doing was sliding deeper and deeper into this state of angry, empty nothingness.

The African witch doctor I'd been to visit in Brixton had pointed out to me the changes that could take place in people when there was a full moon. Hollywood and the movies have made light of what can happen at that time and the demonic realm that's curiously interlinked with it.

They've turned it into some kind of adrenalin rush to get the heart pumping and the spine tingling as they project terrifying images of men undergoing hideous transformations into werewolves. In reality, it's all pretty impossible. But on another level, a far more insidious and dangerous level, I was being transformed. I'd once been an ordinary, rational human being but, bit by bit, I was changing into a thoroughly nasty piece of work, a hopeless, evil man. I was almost like a werewolf, tearing people apart, only I was using my tongue. I was attacking them at every opportunity. I was in a filthy pit and I couldn't crawl out. Not on my own. Not without help.

That's pretty much how I found God.

CHAPTER 14

Release

"I HONESTLY BELIEVE THAT HE WAS PUT IN MY PATH TO SHOW ME THE TRUTH. HE POINTED ME THE WAY TO GO AND THEN STAYED CLOSE, OFFERING ADVICE AND SUPPORT."

On 13 November 2003, I got baptised. I remember walking into church and scratching around in my head for any excuse I could come up with to get out of it. There was a fierce battle raging inside me that day. I kept asking myself what on earth I thought I was doing. This was absolute madness. But I guess that was the dark and the light meeting each other head on. I'd made my decision to step into the world of Jesus, to connect with Christ and to be under His authority, and the darkness that had tormented me as I'd got deeper and deeper into the occult and its evil, was fighting back. It didn't want to let me go. Not ever. So the struggle going on in my head was really very powerful, very intense.

For the last few years, in the eyes of the world it must have looked as though I had it all. Let's face it, materially speaking I had, thanks to Boyzone. I was an enormously rich man and I'd used my money to try just about everything in my search for a wonderful life, a life that had some meaning, some sense of purpose. But still I'd wake up every morning wondering what it was all about. The fortune I spent on trying to find happiness was leading more to destruction than to anything else. All the booze that I drank to help me escape was devastating for my body. A great night out might be just that, but a lifetime of partying is a total wipe-out. You'd think it would be a fantastic thing, but the reality was I was killing myself. I'd fallen head first into the evil of the occult and everything I tried to get me away from it just dragged me in deeper. I suppose that's really where my whole journey stems from – the heart of darkness, and a good friend of mine called Ben who one day threw me a lifeline.

Ben Ofoedu sang lead vocals on *Turn Around*, a big hit in 1999 for Phats and Small, the band of two Brighton-based music producers and DJs, Jason 'Phats' Hayward and Russell Small. I first met him several years earlier on the 1994 *Smash Hits* tour, when he was in a band called Benz with Tony Thompson (aka Darkboy) and BJ (Benjamin Balogun, aka T.I.M. Shade). They were signed to RCA records and had several hits over the next three years.

I'll always remember those guys as seeming so much larger than life to me. They were such big, commanding characters. Although I was in a band, a band called Boyzone that was really going places, I still looked at those three as being more powerful then I could ever be. There was just something different about them and the group of people they hung around with. I noticed it every time we met. Being in their company was a very positive experience for me. Somehow or other, they made me feel that I had support. I never understood what it was until, one day, Ben and I got into a conversation about God.

In 2001, Ben and I formed a pop/rock band called Redhill together, with two other friends, Rodney Williams and Mark Brightman. Because we were going out on the road to do some small gigs around the UK, I decided I ought to tell the other lads about the turmoil going on inside of me, the anger I couldn't control, my violence and the black moods. These guys were going to be living in close proximity with me and I suppose I wanted them to know so that they'd understand. I needed to warn them about possible changes in my character. I tried to explain how it all seemed to be linked to the full moon but, as I talked, I was very aware of how *Harry Potter* it sounded. I thought, they'll never understand. You can't possibly relate to the reality of it unless you've been into those things and lived that kind of life.

They listened to every word I said, listened and took it in. As I tried to explain my experiences of the occult, the visitations, the torment, the intense grip the whole dark side now had on me, it was Ben who told me there was a way to break free.

He said, 'You have to try telling these evil spirits to go away in the name of Jesus.'

I didn't know how to react. For years I'd been existing in some kind of black hole under the influence of demons. And I'm not speaking figuratively, those demons were real. A lot of the time I felt as if I'd fallen into hell. Nothing had ever worked to get me out of it. No well-meaning suggestions. No crystal therapies. And all of a sudden, there was Ben telling me to use the name of Jesus – a name that I was deeply against. It wasn't that I was a raving atheist who wanted to stand against God and the Bible, but I just didn't have any time for it. My limited experience of church was those obligatory Sunday morning visits when I was growing up, which had been so dismal, so nothing. Jesus hadn't done anything for my life at that time. I just couldn't see that He had any relevance to me and to what I was going through. In Hong Kong in 1998, I'd even had that broken cross tattooed on my chest. It sat over my heart, defiantly symbolising to me the fact that I didn't need religion. I didn't need God. I didn't need any of that whole thing that went with what I understood to mean 'being a Christian'. I thought all I needed in my life was true friendship and unity.

But one night after that conversation with Ben, I found myself experiencing a terrifying visitation. I was effing and blinding like I did, just willing it to end, and in sheer desperation I thought, I've got to try this. I've got to try telling it to leave in the name of Jesus. So I did. And it blew my mind. The moment those words were out of my mouth, the visitation stopped. It was gone. To be honest, that in itself was a shock. It kind of frightened me. I'd never had any control over the apparitions before, no matter what I'd tried. What kind of authority was there in this Jesus that the thing just turned tail and ran?

I couldn't ignore what had happened. That was the point when the turn around began in my head. I started to investigate the power of Jesus and the truths the Bible was supposed to hold. I read all the stories I'd been so familiar with as a kid. With our Catholic upbringing, all my sisters and I had learned about Mary and Joseph, about Noah's Ark and the Prodigal Son. But suddenly, they weren't just stories anymore. They became an authoritative history to me. They were real. They leapt off the page and came alive, and I began to be conscious that I had a hunger for God. I'd never felt anything like it. Nothing I'd ever done in my life had led me to feel hungry for knowledge in that way. For the first time in my life I was starving for something, starving for the Lord. So I decided I had to put myself in a place where I could learn.

Initially I started going to a Catholic church in London. It's what I thought I'd be familiar with from my childhood and, to be honest, I wasn't really expecting more than something a bit boring, a bit dull, with a few old ladies dotted around in the pews like you often see on TV. Only it wasn't like that at all. It was a full house. There were so many people, so many families. When I walked in, I couldn't get over it. All I could think was, wow, this wasn't what I was expecting. It certainly wasn't how I remembered the services my dad had taken us to back in Ireland.

I went to that church for about three or four months and, although I was learning, it got to a point where it just wasn't feeding me enough.

I wasn't getting what I was going there for anymore. To begin with, it had been such a sanctuary for me. It had offered me comfort and some kind of happiness. That hadn't changed; it was just that the teaching time, the 10 to 15 minutes when the priest gave his word for the day, was too short. I needed more.

At around this time, I had a girlfriend called Sheena. When I first met her, she was only 21. I spotted her in the choir backing Westlife at Party In The Park one year in London. The moment I laid eyes on her, I couldn't help being so drawn to this stunning girl, so attracted by her. But when I got into conversation with her afterwards, I wasn't so sure anything should happen. Something just didn't feel right. Maybe it was the way she spoke. Maybe it was simply the wrong time for me. Whatever the reason, I came away thinking, no, she's just too young.

It was quite a while before we bumped into each other again and, when we did, although the powerful physical attraction was the same, I still couldn't see us going anywhere.

Another few months slipped by. Then, one night, I was sitting in a pub having a drink by myself and, I started thinking about her. I sent her a text and, to my surprise, she texted right back and we agreed to meet a few days later.

I don't know what I was expecting but in the time since I'd last seen her, Sheena had grown up. She seemed so different to me now, so strong and self-assured. She spoke with real intelligence and authority. While I'd been looking the other way, that beautiful young girl I'd met some time before had turned into a woman. And she rocked my world. I just couldn't get enough of her.

Because of Sheena's singing and acting work, she wasn't tied to the usual 9.00 to 5.00 routine, and I wasn't working then so I'd spend a lot of time at her house. She came from a very active church family – her father was a bishop and her brother a church pastor – but we never really talked about what they did or what she believed. It wasn't until I found myself needing to move on from the church where I'd been going that I started asking her about the Bible class she went to. It was run by her pastor brother which, to be honest, was one of the reasons I'd been nervous to go. I was a bit scared of him. In most people's eyes I was a very public face, a pop star, and I imagined they assumed Sheena was just the next in a long line of women that I preyed on – another notch on the belt. I wasn't that kind of guy but that's how I felt I was perceived. It made me afraid to go to her church because her brother was the leader. I imagined him thinking, now this man's with my sister he's going to start coming here so it looks as if he's fitting in.`

But when I heard Sheena's brother was going away on holiday for three weeks, I thought this could be an opportunity for me at least to go along to the Bible class. I could sit there without worrying about what he might be thinking – even though he probably wouldn't have been thinking any of the things I imagined.

The speaker at that class was dynamic. He gave the most amazing explanations of how the truth of what was written in the Bible connected to today's world. I must have just sat there with my mouth open. Every Wednesday it was Bible class and every Wednesday I'd be there, even after Sheena's brother got back, never missing a night for several months. My hunger to know more was insatiable. I couldn't get enough. I bought Christian teaching tapes and listened to them over and over driving from my house to Sheena's and back again. All I wanted was to soak up this knowledge.

Then, one day, I realised I wanted more than just the Bible class, and that's when I decided to go to Sheena's church with her in Lewisham.

This was a big moment for her because her church was very lively, the complete opposite to the quietness and calm of the Catholic Church I used to go to. She was uncertain how I'd react. As it was, I was stunned. The first three or four Sundays I was there, I think I spent the entire time gaping, just gazing around at everybody else. I didn't hear one word of preaching, one note of singing. I just stared.

The building itself was in Gothic-style, with room for 400 to 500 people. It was always so packed you had to get there early to get a seat. There was a choir on the stage and a live band with everything from drummer to bass, and every week it was the most sensational event. It was nothing like going to mass, or even like going to church in the conventional sense, the way I always pictured it in my head. It was phenomenal. No one turned their noses up at me. No one seemed suspicious of my motives for being there. Everybody welcomed me with open arms. They didn't know who I was. To them, I was just someone else walking into church. I was so surprised. People came up to me and shook my hand – men, women, kids. They were all so warm, so friendly.

Despite the very public life I'd lived as a member of Boyzone, underneath I was still the kind of guy who preferred to take a back seat. I always headed straight for the back of the church (even today I don't like being up the front) and from there I could watch without feeling that *I* was being watched. It was all so charismatic, so full of fun and life. There were young people and old people all together, anything from hooded teenagers hugging to pensioners dancing. What surprised me as much as anything was that the well-dressed, smart people were just mixing in with the denim-clad youth as if it was the most natural thing in the world.

And those kids and young people were so into God. When I was growing up, I didn't care. I wasn't interested. I didn't want to be in church. But in this place, the kids were packing the place out even if the parents weren't there. This was their choice and they obviously loved every moment of it. The longer I spent there, seeing people getting excited, lifting their hands to God in praise and adoration, the more I realised how powerful and absolutely beautiful it all was.

At the end of each service, the pastor and his team would invite people to the front of the church to be prayed for. I saw so many people walk down there, watched prayers spoken over them and gazed as they broke down and were touched in a very real and remarkable way by the power and love of God.

As the weeks passed, I began to settle in to the church and to stop looking at what was going on all around. I gradually focused on what was being said, what was being sung, and I started to get a very real connection with God. I realised that, as much as I was learning and filling my head with knowledge, I was also becoming much more aware of my feelings, my emotions, and how I was being touched in a profoundly personal way.

The first time I lifted my hands to God, it was incredible – something like warmth and energy and power flooding through me. I went through this battle with myself before I could actually do it. There was a whole tug of war going on, with one voice inside me going, 'Okay, now's the time,' and then another piping up and saying, 'No, no, no!' The pastor would be teaching from the Bible, and I could see hands stretching up towards God as people listened, nodding their heads and saying, 'Hallelujah!' in response. I wanted to do it with them. I wanted to join in. But I'd hesitate and then it was always that second too late and the moment was gone. I'll do it next time, I'd think to myself.

It sounds like a crazy comparison, but it was like everything I ever felt when I did a bungee jump. It was the same experience of throwing myself off something solid and safe with just the bungee attached to me, that exhilarating sense of fear and indecision – one, two, three … no, not this time!

Then suddenly I just did it. I don't even remember what the pastor said. Inside my head the voice whispered, 'This is the time,' and I lifted my hands with all the other people. My heart was racing and I was so scared, but I was saying, 'Hallelujah!'

Once I'd done it that first time, I found I could join in more freely. I was beginning to be part of what was going on, to belong to this church, to these people. I was understanding and feeling what they were feeling, realising that reaching out to God physically and calling to Him was all about making a connection, getting close to the Lord.

The more I got involved in the church, the more I wanted to go up for prayer at the end of the service. I kept seeing the pastor and his team talking with the people who'd gather at the front, laying their hands on them, praying with them. I couldn't hear the words but I'd watch intrigued as men and women just broke down in tears. I kept thinking I'm going to do it. I'm going to walk down the front. But again, I had to fight with myself and, just as I'd decide now was the time, the altar call would be over and I somehow hadn't been able to move.

In the end, my longing to get down there must have been stronger than my fear because, one Sunday, I remember just letting go. I walked down to the front and suddenly one of the leaders was there. He laid a hand on my head and started praying for me. For the first time, all those words I'd seen being spoken over people but had never been close enough to hear were being said for me. The leader was asking God to help me get hold of myself, get hold of all the things I'd been struggling with and find strength. I don't know what happened but my heart seemed to sink to the bottom of my heels and the tears started to flow from my eyes in rivers. I was an emotional wreck, sobbing and sobbing, overwhelmed by a sweep of emotions that had never touched me before. It was so beautiful, so unreal and yet the most real thing that had ever happened to me.

When the leader had finished praying, I sat down near the front. There was a lady next to me. As I huddled there, tears still pouring down my face, she put her arm around me while the pastor closed the service. I couldn't really understand it all, but I knew that day I'd been touched by the Lord, touched by God.

That wasn't the only time I went forward for prayer. Every so often at the end of the service, I'd go up. I was learning so much, not only about God, but about the kind of person He wanted me to be, and I wanted to take whatever steps I needed to get the control and discipline into my life that were so lacking.

What I realised early on was that, when you start going to church and making a connection with God, that doesn't mean things are going to change overnight. It's a long, long process. I'd spent years and years of my life going my own way, allowing a kind of madness to take hold of me. It wasn't just that I'd ignored God or not given Him any particular thought one way or another. I'd gone off in completely the opposite direction. I'd got involved with the occult. I'd messed around in what was evil and opened myself up to God's enemies. The walls I'd built up around myself weren't going to melt away in the space of a few weeks. They had to be taken down brick by brick. Everything I was dealing with inside me, the visitations, the anger, the confusion, the excess, all those struggles and bad habits and the things in my life that needed fixing – it wasn't all going to mend with one click of a finger. This new life with God was about commitment and maturity. It was about understanding that I couldn't actually live my life by myself, because I'd tried that and so far all I'd made was a total mess. I needed something to give me a sense of purpose, to teach me control and respect. It might take a while, but I knew God could do that for me. He'd touched me hard with emotions and with insight and now it was up to me to respond and follow Him.

As time went on, I was able to build up a strong and close relationship with God. I could trust Him because I'd been told He'd never let me down, and He never did. He was always there. Every step I took, every decision I made, I would ask Him to be a part of my world and to make me a part of His. He opened my eyes and my ears, showed me what I should be doing and helped me to do it. I'd been such a wreck of a person, torn apart by the wrong choices I'd made, and my heart was very black. But God had forgiven me and gradually I was being set free. This was the way I wanted to move forward with my life. And that was why, four or five months after I'd been going to the church with Sheena, I decided I wanted to get baptised.

When someone asks God for forgiveness for the wrong things they've done, and for Jesus to come into their life, all their sins are washed away and they can start again with a clean sheet. Baptism represents this cleansing from sin, and being baptised was something that Jesus commanded his followers to do. It's an outward expression of an inner commitment to follow Him and it was something I so much wanted for myself. But I was still a kind of back seat person, so I asked if mine could be held in private rather than on a Sunday as part of the service.

I knew how I'd been touched by God and all the things He'd shown me but, as I drove to the church that day in November 2003, once again the voices were battling it out inside of me: 'What do you think you're doing? Don't be so stupid, this isn't the way forward for you. It's just church, just something you're going through at the moment.' But then I could hear my heart saying, 'Open your eyes. Look what this has saved you from.' It was such a clash of good and evil; such a powerful moment of choice and decision.

But, as I stood inside the church, no matter what inner struggle was going on, I knew one thing: I might not yet be the man I was meant to be, but I certainly wasn't the man I used to be – and that was such an important transition for me that I couldn't wait any longer. Sheena and her mother and brother were supposed to be there as my witnesses, but the whole thing suddenly felt so urgent that I couldn't hang around. I threw on the clothes I'd brought to wear in the water and I remember one of the leaders, Elder Williams, asking, 'Do you want to wait for anybody?'

'No,' I said. I didn't even hesitate. 'No, just get me in that water. All I want to do is get baptised.'

We stepped into a tank. The water was warm. Comfortable. Elder Williams gently lowered me backwards until, for that brief moment, I was submerged. When I stood up again, I remember looking around and seeing Sheena. She and the others had arrived during the ceremony, but I hadn't noticed them come in. I hadn't looked to the right or the left. I'd just kept my eyes fixed on Elder Williams as he talked to me, prepared me for what was going to happen.

When I came up out of that water, I can't honestly say I felt any different. I think that was one of the things that was so strange for me first of all. I'd gone in as Shane Lynch and, as far as I could tell, I'd come back out as Shane Lynch. I found myself asking, is this right? Am I meant to feel different? I spent hours asking questions, and the leaders gave me plenty of perfect answers and fitted all the pieces together for me in my head. I grew to understand that this process is different for everybody. My baptism was just another step in my journey. No one could tell me what I should or shouldn't be feeling because this was my personal experience, no one else's. This was about me and God.

In the days and weeks leading up to my baptism, the demonic visitations that still plagued me started to get much stronger. The intensity was horrifying. Instead of one demon, there would be 20 in my room trying to torment me. There was a spiritual war raging for my soul, and the demons didn't want to let me go. The difference was that now I was covered by God. I'd said yes to Him and let Him in. As far as I could see, the next step was to be filled with His Holy Spirit.

In 2004, I was meant to be going out to the jungle. I was offered a chance to take part in the hit Australian reality TV show, *I'm A Celebrity, Get Me Out Of Here*. I had a medical and blood tests, signed all the papers and even arranged a fee but, somehow, I wasn't happy about it. The timing was all wrong for me. I knew I still had a lot of things in my life I needed to get sorted. So, in the end I chose not to go. I'd heard Sheena talk about a 'tarrying' meeting for the Holy Spirit and, instead of flying out to the jungle, I organised one for myself.

The idea of 'tarrying' for the Holy Spirit came out of the Pentecostal Revival which started around the turn of the twentieth century. It began in a church on Azusa Street, in Los Angeles, California, where God began to pour out His Holy Spirit. The people there not only received His Spirit, but also began to use the gifts that came with it – gifts of healing and prophesy, and being able to speak in tongues, a heavenly language used to worship God. It was exactly the way the early church was written about in the Bible. From that church in Los Angeles, the Pentecostal revival spread around the world like wildfire, and there were countless signs and wonders and healings.

A 'tarrying' meeting for the Holy Spirit was a time to get together with other Spirit-filled Christians and ask God to fill you with His Spirit too. That's what I wanted – for the Holy Spirit to fill me, to take control of me. And I so longed to receive the gift of speaking in tongues. As far as I was concerned, it was very black and white. Once I had the Spirit inside me, I'd have my connection with God. I'd already prayed, 'This is what I want, Lord. I'm not interested in hanging around. Just get me in there, fill me with Your Holy Spirit, and get me out.' I never thought for a moment that God would say no. It never even occurred to me that I wouldn't receive what I'd asked for.

I went into the meeting not knowing at all what was going to happen, but I was so expectant, so ready. Some ladies began by telling me to visualise Jesus, what I thought He might look like, and His goodness. Then they asked me to call His name, and I did. I was on my knees as they were praying for me and I started joining in, saying, 'Hallelujah!' It was almost as if I couldn't stop myself, as if there was some kind of a momentum to this process and, as I let go, I was just being carried along with it.

Before I knew what was happening, there were other words coming out of my mouth but, this time, I didn't know what they were, even less what they meant. This was a language I'd never heard before and yet it was coming from inside me. I knelt there on the ground and the strange words continued to tumble out of my mouth and then, as my lips gradually fell silent, I started to become aware of myself in the meeting room again, conscious of the people gathered round me. It was the strangest feeling – as though I was returning from some indescribable journey, some place where I'd been lovingly transported.

When I arrived back, I found I was crying like a baby. Through my sobbing, I remember one of the ladies asking me if I'd understood anything I'd said. For a moment I wanted to say yes. I thought perhaps

I was meant to understand. But I had to say no because that was the truth of it. When I looked up at her, she was smiling.

'Fantastic! Brilliant!' she said.

The meeting continued with worship. It was all very joyful but, to be honest, I didn't quite know if I'd been filled with the Holy Spirit or not. As far as I was concerned I'd prayed to God and He'd taken me on some kind of a journey where I'd spoken a language that was completely new to me. It wasn't until I arrived back at Sheena's house that the reality of it hit me and I was able to say, 'Yeah, I got filled.'

Sheena threw her arms around me and said, 'Congratulations.'

As it turned out, she already knew. Someone from the church had phoned her to let her know.

At every stage of the journey to receive His Holy Spirit, God was right there with me. He never let me down. I asked and He gave. And He goes on giving to me. For years I was an anti-God man. I couldn't see the point in this belief that some people seemed to have or in the teachings of Jesus. But now I work for Him. I go into churches and to different events and I speak about Him. I let people know what He's done for me, about the evil He saved me from, about the person I was and the man He's teaching me how to be. It's only my story I'm telling and I'm not preaching to people, but I'm working for the Lord and it is the most incredible thing ever. I think in life it's so easy to understand and to focus on what you don't like and what you're against. That's where I was for a very long time. But now, I feel so privileged to know who I am and what I stand for. And what I stand for is God.

My family were absolutely delighted with the changes they could see in me. I don't mean necessarily that they were over the moon because I was now a 'born again' Christian. I guess I'm not really sure exactly how they feel about that part. I don't think they quite understand yet about the power of Jesus and that love of God that I'm so connected with. What I do know is that I'm no longer that evil, angry, foul-mouthed, bad-actioned guy. I'm not out to hurt people anymore. I'm such a very different man now and, whether they understand it or not, my family are just happy and grateful for that.

I phoned Ben Ofoedu to tell him I'd been baptised. Benny could hardly believe it. He had already seen a transformation in me from that selfish, out of control idiot – a proper unruly head case – to something more or less human. And now I was telling him I was baptised. Having seen so much of what I used to be, it must have been a lot for him to take in.

Since he'd first told me to speak out in the name of Jesus, Ben had helped me so much. His knowledge of God and of the Bible is enormous. I honestly believe that he was put in my path to show me the truth. He pointed me the way to go and then stayed close, offering advice and support. I found God and I found life, and in all of that phenomenal journey, Benny was certainly the biggest player.

CHAPTER 15

Revving It

"IT WAS OVER AND DONE WITH. WE'D GOT SO CLOSE
AND THE TITLE WAS ALMOST OURS. BUT THAT WAS THE
DAY THE BRITISH GT CHAMPIONSHIP SLIPPED RIGHT
THROUGH OUR FINGERS."

Back in late 1998, I received a letter from a guy called Rob Phillips asking
if he could come and see me. I was performing with Boyzone in
Liverpool when we first met. Rob was an accomplished rally driver and
he simply wanted to know if I'd like to be his co-driver in a rally he was
doing in his Ford Cosworth. At the time, as far as I was concerned, I was
a driver, not a co-driver. The idea of being in the passenger seat didn't
hold a lot of appeal for me. I rang him up and explained that I'd rather
drive the rally car more than anything else and, over the next few
months, we stayed in touch but nothing more came of it.

Then one day I got a call to ask if I'd like to take part in a celebrity
race at the National Exhibition Centre in Birmingham. The car I'd be
driving would be a Caterham 7, which is like a kit car build, based on the
1960s Lotus Seven sports car, still with rear-wheel drive, but a different,

modern engine. The rear-wheel drive was right up my street because that's what I'd been used to with the GT twin Corollas I'd driven. It all sounded pretty good to me so, in 1999, off I went to the NEC show where I met up with my fellow competitors for this celebrity race.

That's where it was all a bit of a shock. The line-up was certainly impressive: British touring car driver, John Cleland, Le Mans 24 Hours driver, Allan McNish, Alister McRae, a world rally driver and brother of the sadly now late, Colin McRae, who was the first British competitor to win the World Rally Driver's Championship in 1995 – plus two other drivers also none too shabby on their wheels. Great credentials, yes, but not quite the celebrities I'd been expecting. These guys were the real thing, big in the world of motor sport, and far from the selection of soap or pop stars I thought I'd be up against. I was actually very scared.

We were taken off to get helmets and gloves, and then the clerk of the course, who was head of the event, came over and spelt out the rules.

'This is a corporate day, boys, a corporate event. There are a lot of big cheeses here to see this race, so keep it clean and tidy, and just go out there and enjoy yourselves.'

Then he glanced over at me. 'Now, you, Shane,' he went on, instantly separating me from the 'proper' drivers, 'we're going to put you at the back so you don't get in the way of the other lads.'

Fair enough, I thought. They all knew far more about this than I did, so it seemed like the best idea.

As I sat in the car, waiting there on the start line, it took me right back to that first BMX championship of years ago, with Kaner and me on our beaten up bikes in amongst the flashy set, not having the first clue what was going on. The guys in the Caterham 7s in front of me were professional, paid, world-class drivers – and there I was, Shane Lynch from Boyzone, stuck at the back. The rampant nerves were the same as ever too and, as the green flag went down, I felt that familiar adrenalin rush coursing through my body. I'd had a word with one of the mechanics earlier in the day and he'd told me to start off in second gear to get better traction. So that's what I did, and I found myself flying away from the start.

On the first corner, I passed Alister McRae. I don't know how. I just put my foot down and went for it. As the second corner came up, there I was shooting past Allan McNish. Then, on the third, unbelievably I managed to overtake someone else to end up third across the finish line! No one was more astonished than I was. I was a rank amateur and I'd beaten a couple of world-class drivers. What was that all about? I hadn't worked my way up from the smaller stuff the way race drivers do. I'd never trained, never go-karted. I was just a street-racer, one of those kids every policeman hates.

What emerged that day can only have been some kind of natural ability fuelled by my life-long passion for cars. And that's how I got properly into motor sports. It must have been obvious after that race that I knew how to handle a car, so the men with the power to make it happen put their heads together and seemed to decide, 'Let's get this guy rallying.'

I signed with Ford first of all, and began to do some rallies for them up and down the country, trying to get my licence to be a professional driver. I even got to race in France at Le Touquet, competing on the roads of the Opal Coast in the Nord-Pas-de-Calais region. There was a lot of rain around that day. Having to drive fast in the wet was a real challenge for me because the surfaces were so slippery. There was obviously real power in the car but I had to be able to balance that with absolute control.

I remember one night rally I did in a Ford Ka. It was all a bit frenetic. The rally was being held up towards Lincoln, but I had to be in London that morning rehearsing with Boyzone for the Brit Awards the following day. We were doing a Motown medley with Peter André. I finished the rehearsals, got in the car and drove up to the rally meeting point, arriving there about 7.00pm, with the rally due to start two hours later at 9.00. I then drove in the rally until 7.00am – and finally got my professional licence.

On my journey back to London, I was stopped by the police on the M25 for not wearing a seat-belt! It cost me £30.00 and was the first fine I'd ever had. But in spite of the interrupted journey, I still managed to arrive back from the all-night rally in time to get on stage to perform for the Brit Awards. I even joined in the party afterwards. When my head finally hit the pillow, I must have gone almost 48 hours without sleep.

Into 2000, I was offered a lot of celebrity drives. I had the opportunity to race a car called a Legend, a small kit car type build with a fibreglass body and a 1300cc motorbike engine. The racing was fast and very close and tight. I also raced a Genetta G27 which is a two-door, two-seater sports car. It's essentially a coupe version of the roadster Lotus Elise. I entered my very first race in those championships at Pembury race track.

The Genetta was fitted with a brake bias control valve – a device for distributing more of the braking force to either the front or rear wheels. The car was all set up and ready to go for this particular race but before I went out to the starting grid, the man who was looking after it at the time started tinkering with the brake bias valve. I didn't know much about the engines of racing cars back then and I don't know exactly what he did, but I do remember that he seemed to twist this valve. I didn't question it. He was a mechanic and I assumed he knew what he was doing.

I drove around the track ready to line up with the other cars, concentrating on warming everything through, alternately accelerating then braking hard, only something didn't feel right. I couldn't understand what was going on but the back tyres kept locking up. At the start of the race, I hurtled down towards the first corner, into a hairpin, stood on the brakes enough to steer myself round – and all I did was keep going straight! Whatever it was the guy had done when he twisted the valve, I now seemed to have no front brakes, only at the rear. It was a bit like pulling on a handbrake at 100mph – you're really not going to stop. I smashed hard into one of the other cars, and didn't come out of it well. My Genetta was a total wreck. The drive shaft came right up through the middle of the car. It was well and truly destroyed. Back in the pits, the man who'd fiddled with the valve looked the car over and said grimly, 'No, that's it. It's over for the weekend.' I couldn't believe it. This was the first of two days of races and, already, it looked as if I was out of it. Fortunately, my motor sport manager at the time, Peter Griffiths, wasn't going to be put off that easily. He knew a couple of boys living in the Welsh hills from back in his early days in racing. They were proper hillbillies but had an absolute genius for fixing cars. He got in touch with them, told them we needed a hand with a Genetta and, luckily for us, they said, 'No problem.'

We got what was left of the car onto a trailer, took it to the garage, and those lads worked on it until 4.00 or 5.00am. They took pieces off, welded different pieces back on. I think they might even have used the hinges off their garage doors, anything and everything just to get this thing back together. And the following morning when I arrived, that car was ready to race again.

I'd explained what I thought had happened with the brake bias to Peter Griffiths. He couldn't believe it. And there wasn't a lot he could do about it because nobody could prove it.

When I finally found real success in racing, it was with a different team: Eclipse Motor Sport. They were an amazing bunch of guys who said they would run my car for me and do it virtually for nothing. They'd looked at the Genetta that Peter Griffiths had had put back together, had set it up for the race, and they were the ones who were able to tell me that it had no front brakes. They said I couldn't possibly race it like that, and then they went ahead and sorted it all out. I stayed with them for the rest of the championship – and ended up doing very well.

After that, they invited me to drive a GT car. I was over the moon! So, the next year, we started the whole process of testing a Marcos Mantis with a big V8 5.5 litre engine. There was also a 3 litre model, which, I suppose is the junior version. I tested both cars but began actually racing in the smaller one to get some experience. I started at the back (as usual) and nothing very spectacular happened for a while, but I wasn't unhappy because I was learning all the time. Then in 2001, I moved up to the big Marcos Mantis GT. It raced incredibly well and I was teamed up with a great partner called Shane Bland.

I learnt a lot from Shane. He was a brilliant driver, always pushing, always out there on the edge. But then, during one of the last races of the British GT Championship we were driving in together at Donington Park, he had a terrible accident.

In GTs, you race for anything from one to up to 24 hours. You get in the car and go out, drive for your allocated number of laps, then come in and hand over to your partner. Shane and I had made our change over and I'd been sitting out for a short while. He'd done no more than two laps when something went horribly wrong. He was shooting along a straight, then round a corner called Redgate, when suddenly the car spun around backwards, flew across the gravel, smashed into the barriers and burst into flames. It was a devastating crash. The back wheel actually thrust itself inside the car and Shane's neck was virtually broken.

As it turned out, he was lucky. Unbelievably lucky. He was rescued carefully and painstakingly from the remains of the car and rushed to hospital to undergo a series of in-depth checks and x-rays. Over time, he was able to get his neck rebuilt with vertebrae cages. He can walk and talk, and thank God for that. But he'll never race again.

It took a while to get over that incident. You know motor racing is a dangerous sport, only I guess in some weird way the risk is all part of the appeal. But when a bad accident happens, particularly when it involves a team mate, it shocks you.

For its next car, Eclipse decided to buy a brand new TVR Tuscan R 400. That was what you might call a serious bit of kit as a racing car. Out it came, fresh from the factory, all sleek and gleaming, and I jumped eagerly into it for the brand new 2002 season of the British GTs.

Normally at the start of a race, as the engine noise built to a deafening roar and the cars kicked off the starting grid and began to burn their way around the track, I was used to being way down the line. There were always at least 10 to 15 cars in front of me. But this time, as I sped along in the TVR, all of a sudden I was driving with only three cars up ahead. How in the world I'd got there I have no idea, but I seemed to be in fourth position! At those speeds, you need to stay focused yet, at the same time, I was looking around me, wondering where everyone else was and thinking there must have been a big accident.

I drove around hard for a few laps. There was no sign of a crash and still there were barely any other drivers in sight. It wasn't until the TVR suddenly developed a major throttle problem and gave up on me that I realised I had actually been sitting in fourth position because the team had picked out a truly competitive car. There might have been a mechanical fault that knocked me out of that race but, for sheer power and speed, the TVR Tuscan had been up there with the front-runners.

I pulled over and there were the rest of the boys, catching up, shooting past me. Obviously I was disappointed to be out of the race but, at the same time, I was amazed that I was driving such a hot competitor.

The rest of 2002 turned out to be a pretty mixed bag in terms of driving success. Out of 13 races, the car let us down a good six or seven times. But whenever it ran to the finish, I came in fourth. It was a brilliant position, a fantastic result, and all the time we were working on the car, developing it to try to overcome the technical problems that were holding us back.

At the start of 2003, I was training hard. I was boxing. I was down at the gym, getting fit. This was serious business for me now. I knew I had to be in peak physical condition. I had a superb car and I wanted to give it and the team everything I possibly could. GT racing is so much more than just sitting in a fast car and driving. It's all about strategy – knowing when to step it up and when to calm it down, getting to grips with all the tricks to save your fuel, your brakes, your tyres, and your gearbox. Over the winter the team had developed the car incredibly. Now it was up to me to drive it right.

It was the start of a new season and we were up against a brand new challenge. Two Moslers were in the new line-up for 2003. One was a 5.7 litre and the other a 7 litre. Mosler Automotive is an American supercar manufacturer founded by Warren Mosler in 1985 and based in Florida in the USA, with a European branch in St Ives, Cambridgeshire in the UK. At Eclipse, we had a 400 bhp TVR Tuscan. It was no match really for the Moslers. They had far more power. But I wasn't going to let that get to me as we were revving up on the starting grid. After all, once I got out there, anything could happen.

Donington Park was the first race of the season. As the flag dropped and the cars hurtled forward, the pace was set – and it was furious. I had a new partner called Piers Johnson. He was quicker than I was by about half to three-quarters of a second, and it wasn't long before the TVR and the Moslers had a real battle going. For the whole race, we were pretty much swapping places from first to second to third. It was a brilliant feeling, tearing up the track at the front, giving those power packs a flat out run for their money. We were fit, focused and strong, and we were driving really well. The car was sensational, and we finished that first race in third position. That was the very first GT trophy we won as a team.

For the rest of that season, that's what we were doing – shuffling between first, second and third place, battling it out against those two Moslers. We scooped a couple of second places, a few thirds, and we even won two races. I was ecstatic. Any one of those three cars was in with a chance, our TVR Tuscan or one of those two Moslers. There was Shaun Balfe driving with Jamie Derbyshire, Martin Short teamed with Tom Herridge, and, of course, there was me and Piers Johnson.

I can't begin to describe the excitement, the sense of anticipation and expectancy just knowing we were in the frame for the title, British GT Champion. It was unbelievable. I was a guy from a boy band. Those years spent in the pop spotlight were like living on another planet compared to this. This was such a different world, something else that had come along and I'd thought, yeah, I'll give that a go, why not? I'd somehow made this leap and yet it all seemed so unreal. So unlikely. The people around me had been driving for a long time. They had a real history in motor sport. I think at that point they still looked on me as another Andrew Ridgeley, that other half of Wham!, the pop duo that shot George Michael to stardom back in the 1980s. Ridgeley had raced cars for a while but without any success to speak of, so, to the seasoned professionals I was now driving with, I was probably just another pop star who thought he could drive.

But, all of a sudden, as finishes in the top three mounted up, I was getting recognition. I was getting a bit of praise. People were coming up to me, congratulating me and shaking my hand. This was such a male-dominated arena. It wasn't teenage girls I was out to impress anymore, it was men. And men began saying, 'Great drive,' and, 'Fair play to you.' I got a real buzz out of finding acceptance there.

I don't know what it is about speed. Maybe it's the feeling of being in control of this machine that's burning up the tarmac. I love that thrill. When you're driving, you're so caught up in the moment. You have to be. On top of that there's the knowledge that 2000 nuts and bolts may be holding it all together while you're out there doing 180mph, but all it takes is for one thing to break and it's all over.

I never feared for my life, but you'd have to be pretty stupid if you climbed into a racing car thinking that you were invincible. You have to get in knowing there is always that possibility that you could die in there. It might sound like a grim approach but it's important to think that way. If you understand that, you'll treat the car, the race and the drivers around you with the level of respect and awareness that's so vital to avoid major accidents.

That 2003 season was a beautiful, fast and joyous experience for me. Until the last race of the championship.

I was in one of three cars going head to head for the title at the world-famous Brands Hatch motor circuit in Kent. What a stunning position to find myself in. But there was something about that day. As I got into the car, I somehow had the notion that, this time, it wasn't going to turn out well. Maybe it was just a gut feeling. Maybe I sensed God saying, 'This is going to hurt. You'll be all right, but it *is* going to hurt.'

I could feel myself on the edge. Every nerve in my body was tingling, strung tight. But it was a very different set of nerves to the ones that kicked in as I got on stage with Boyzone. Yes, there was that same release of energy, that powerful surge of adrenalin, but with this, it wasn't a case of standing in a line with four other fellers. This wasn't about just making sure I played my part. I had something I was hugely responsible for. I was in control of a car and, as much as that was about me and my driving performance, it was also about everybody else. I might be hungry for a win, desperate to clinch the title but, with 20 to 30 other drivers out there on the track, I couldn't afford to make a mistake because that could result in seriously hurting one or more of them.

As the race began and the cars thrust their way out onto the circuit, the Mosler/TVR Tuscan format found its usual place out at the front, with the three of us pretty much neck and neck as we powered round the track. The car was handling well. I was so focused, so alert. But then something happened. The Moslers disappeared. Suddenly they were nowhere to be seen. There had been an incident. Shaun Balfe had crashed out and the other Mosler was now running at fourth to fifth place. I was in first! I was racing for the championship title and I was in the lead, followed by a Corvette and another TVR. For 25 minutes, we hammered round like an express train.

I was racing as fast as I could make the car go. I couldn't move any quicker. Nobody could get past me. I knew I was doing what I was out there to do and I honestly couldn't have driven any better. I'd nearly completed my allocated number of laps and I was close to going into the pits to make the changeover to Piers, the quicker driver. My heart was pelting flat out along with the car. We were going to win this championship. We were flying. With the Moslers apparently out of it, how could it possibly go wrong now? Piers Johnson and me, we were going to be the 2003 GT Champions!

I entered the last lap and sped into a corner called Dingle Dell. All the time, I was watching one of the back-markers in front of me (one of the guys virtually a lap behind). He happened to be driving a Marcos Mantis. It was ironic, really. This same Mantis had blown up in practice and, because as a team we ran a Mantis too, we had a spare engine. The lads at Eclipse were fabulous. They were able to help out and went ahead and lent this guy an engine so that he could race.

I was coming up fast behind this Mantis driver and I wanted him to get out of the way. He was traffic. He needed to let me through. He knew that I was bearing down on him with the other two front-runners, the three of us nose to tail, and he made to move aside. But the manoeuvre went badly wrong. Somehow he swerved off to the left and put two wheels on the grass. Then he lost control. The car was veering left and right all over the place.

I'd been around Dingle Dell. The Corvette and TVR were hot on my heels and I was heading down a small straight into a left-hander. I must have been doing about 140mph and I could see the Mantis sliding slowly into my path in the middle of the track. To avoid a collision I needed to go to the right or to the left. It was my choice – and I had about a half a second to make it.

The Mantis in front of me was cutting across from my left to my right so I chose to go left, behind it. It was moving away from that side of the track and I shouldn't have had a problem slipping through the gap. But that's where it went desperately wrong. The moment I turned the steering wheel and fixed my path, the Mantis suddenly stopped in the middle of the track and rolled backwards. There was nothing I could do. Nowhere for me to go. It was a sickening moment of inevitability. And I slammed into it.

The Mantis just seemed to fracture into pieces. All I remember was a huge bang and my TVR getting spun viciously around and thrown headlong into the tyre wall, before bouncing back out onto the track. Miraculously it was still the right way up and even facing in the right direction!

Somewhere inside myself I must have been saying, 'Come on, it's not so bad.' In my desperation to win the race, I still thought I ought to be able to get the car back to the pits for Piers to take over. I was frantically trying to select a gear. I really believed I could get the TVR back in the running. But that car was going nowhere. It must have been obvious to everyone else that it was finished. I just didn't want to believe it. And when I managed to pull into the side by the tyre wall, I had to radio ahead to say, 'Lads, I'm so sorry. It's all over.'

It wasn't until I went to open the door that I began to see the extent of the damage. There *was* no door anymore. It had been ripped off. The car itself was lying on the grass – literally. Most of the back of that TVR was gone. There was a back wheel missing, no axles, and the roof had been torn clean off. There were bits and pieces just hanging off the trees. It was as if somebody had used a giant paintbrush to splash the nearby greenery with bright orange. That fibreglass car was destroyed and, until I was standing on the outside, I didn't have a clue.

That's when it hit me. The realisation. The shock. That's when reality started to sink in. I'd lost the championship and I was damn near killed. The losing felt so personal. I was the one driving. It must have been my fault. But it wasn't, of course. It was just one of those racing incidents. No one was to blame and there was nothing I could do about it.

Suddenly I'd torn off my helmet and was kicking at the car. I could see my foot punching through what was left of the fibreglass. I was so angry, so frustrated. Then I must have collapsed on the ground, in shock and totally devastated.

The medics came and picked me up, checked me over and took me back to the team. I don't really remember what anyone said. I was simply overcome with this dreadful, painful sense of disappointment, and all I could do was go into the trailer, sit down with my head in my hands and cry and cry.

The British Championship was finished for us. We'd lost. We were out of it whilst the other guys were still racing round that track, still battling on. My dad was there and I remember Sheena coming in. She'd watched it all. She must have been so shaken up. But there was nothing anyone could say to make me feel better. Nobody could make things right for me. It was over and done with. We'd got so close and the title was almost ours. But that was the day the British GT Championship slipped right through our fingers.

CHAPTER 16

Game On

"WHETHER I WAS HAPPY ABOUT IT OR NOT, IT WAS DEFINITELY TIME TO HANG UP MY PURPLE LEOTARD, PACK MY TRUNK, AND SAY A FOND GOODBYE TO THE CIRCUS."

By 2004, apart from the odd small-scale project, I'd been out of the music industry, away from TV and pretty much outside any form of major public arena for four years. I'd been getting on with my life, piecing it back together after the Boyzone era came to an end. It was a time of real searching for me, a time to rediscover myself and start to build some structure into the days, months and, hopefully, years that lay ahead. I'd been approached to do reality shows like *I'm a Celebrity, Get Me Out Of Here* and *Celebrity Big Brother* but, although they offered a good way of getting my face back out there, that kind of television wasn't really something I wanted to be involved with.

Then *The Games* came along. It was still reality TV, but somehow it was different. It seemed to have a point to it and, with the competitive nature that I had, I got it into my head that I might stand a good chance of winning.

The show was basically an all-round sports competition. I'd be one of 10 celebrities invited to compete against each other through training in a series of Olympic-style events including weightlifting, gymnastics and diving. Gold, silver and bronze medals were up for grabs at the end of the show's run for the contestants with the most points from each round. Jamie Theakston was the presenter, with Jayne Middlemiss and Kirsty Gallacher reporting from the track side, and the filming was largely done in Sheffield, at the Sheffield Arena, Don Valley Stadium and Ponds Forge.

A lot of people turn their noses up at the idea of reality TV, and I'd certainly had my reasons for not wanting to be involved before. But, with *The Games*, it seemed to me that it wasn't just about being on show. You were there to achieve something and, at that time in my life, perhaps that was what I needed to do. Mel C from the Spice Girls had taken part in the previous series. She's a high profile, intelligent girl who I guessed would have thought long and hard about taking part. The fact that she'd gone ahead with it made me think that perhaps it would be a good way forward for me too. So I signed on the dotted line and pitched myself into the ring with Jarrod Batchelor (Mr Gay UK), Charlie Dimmock (BBC TV *Ground Force* gardener), It girl Lady Isabella Hervey, Katy Hill (presenter), Charles Ingram (the controversial *Who Wants To Be A Millionaire?* contestant), Linda Lusardi (former model and actress), Jodie Marsh (model), MC Romeo (member of the So Solid Crew) and Pat Sharp (radio DJ).

We trained for three months, working at everything from speed skating to javelin. I'd get picked up at 8.00am ready to start on the first discipline at 9.30am. We'd keep going on that until lunchtime, and then we'd move on to practising a second discipline in the afternoon. That was the pattern, two a day. At around 5.00pm we'd finish – and get taken home in severe pain!

To begin with, I must have been the least fit guy on the team. Even

Major Charles Ingram, who was 56 at the time, could perform better than I could. I remember one of the coaches commenting on how unlikely I was to do well because of my poor level of fitness. I suppose I'd always been lucky physically in that I had quite a good general body shape without having to work at it. But, in spite of all those rigorous dance rehearsals with Boyzone, good, solid stamina was never really there for me.

As time went on and the training grew more intense, the coaches' view of me began to change. They discovered that I was actually able to pick things up very quickly. Behind that undisciplined body lay a natural ability for sports. Come the live competition week, I was pretty realistic about what I was and wasn't good at. I knew I wasn't going to do so well on stamina. The wrestling, for instance, was one and a half to two minutes of pure, stamina-based energy. In the end it went better than I thought, and I came second to Romeo who was fitter than I was.

I wasn't the best runner in the world either because I had shin splints, so the pain factor was an issue. But where I knew I could really perform was with the javelin, the diving, and the weight lifting. Those were different events. They required moments of more explosive power, and I had the upper body strength and control to deliver it. With the diving in particular I knew I had ability. I was able to focus very tightly on technique and that was what helped me get the moves just right.

The line up of contestants was terrific, both in terms of the people they were and how we all got on together.

To begin with, all I could see in Major Charles was a man who'd put himself in that place to win. But then I watched him with his family – and that stuck the biggest smile on my face. As soon as he was with them, he changed almost instantly from being that serious, focused, 'I'll do anything to win' kind of guy, to a gentle, loving father and husband. I had a lot of respect for him after that. He was a man who got on and did what he had to do, a survivor like myself, but as much as that was a part of him and drove him to act the way he did, he also had a genuine heart.

Pat Sharp, the radio DJ, was one of the funniest people you could ever hope to meet and we got on like a house on fire. He was very good in the competition itself, but lacked confidence in his ability, and that's what held him back. It was a shame because, when he really put his mind to it, he was excellent. Out of all of us, I think he was the one who came the furthest. Not only that but he gave me a real boost in my weaker moments. He helped me through a lot of the pain and agony of the training and, even when I was at my wits' end, he could always force a smile out of me.

MC Romeo from the garage act, So Solid Crew, was another great guy. Without a doubt he was one of the lads, straightforwardly down to earth, and very able in athletics. He did end up missing a lot of training sessions, I guess because he couldn't be bothered to turn up, but that worked in my favour. It put him that little bit further behind. If he'd been there every day, I reckon he would have been unbeatable.

We didn't spend those three months before the competition with the female competitors. They were off training somewhere else and we didn't actually see them until the live week. Katie Hill and Jodie Marsh were brilliant. Charlie Dimmock was fantastic too and came a long way in the events. I got the feeling that, like Pat, she didn't quite believe in herself but, even so, she managed to achieve a lot. Isabella Hervey was incredible, a real competitor and so focused. Then there was Linda Lusardi, and she and I had some wonderful conversations together in amongst all the filming.

On one particular evening during the live week itself, the competition event was gymnastics. I'd heard that my little sister was going to be in the audience, and there was also a chance Stephen Gately would be there to cheer me on. I was pleased in the sense that having it would be great to see them both again and maybe the chance of da craic. But that part of me that was distinctly uncomfortable about doing what I had to do in front of friends and family hadn't really changed from when I was a kid. I could sing and dance on a stage in front of thousands and I'd even been known to prance around wearing tights in a panto, but put anyone I'm close to in the audience and I have a real problem with it. Maybe it has to do with some kind of shyness. Perhaps it's about vulnerability. But I never want the people who really know me to see me looking silly or doing anything that's uncool. I didn't even like it when my family were out in the audience for major Boyzone events. I was glad for them but for myself I just wasn't comfortable. It was always like that. Any kind of sport that I ever did, whether I was running or swimming for the school, if I was BMX racing in a championship or driving racing cars – I never wanted anyone I knew to come and watch me.

So that evening, as my name was called and I walked out to do my presentation, I was determined not to look out to my left into the stands because I knew that was where Steo and my sister would be sitting. I figured if I couldn't actually see them, maybe I could carry on as if they weren't there. The trouble was, I wasn't going to be allowed to get away with it. The floor manager was getting on to me to look out front. I flatly refused. I wasn't going to do what I didn't want to do. I just wanted to focus on the job in hand – doing the best I could in this round of the competition.

But the floor manager was as stubborn as I was. He kept on at me to look left until in the end he was fairly leaping out of his skin. I wasn't left with a lot of choice. When at last I forced myself to glance over, I could hardly believe it. Steo wasn't the only Boyzone lad who'd turned up that night. Ronan, Keith and Mikey were all sitting there too, and in amongst them was Barrie Knight, our personal minder from the tour days.

I was utterly stunned. There I was on live TV, a whole crowd of people cheering and screaming, and everything around me seemed to disappear apart from those five faces. It was like diving under water. You're still aware of some kind of faint noise above you but below the surface, it's quite silent. When I'd managed to drag myself back to the reality of where I was, with the lads still shouting and waving their hands in the air, I went down to say hello. But the whole thing really choked me up. I started crying. There was something about the five of them making the effort to be there that evening and wanting to see me perform that deeply touched me.

That was the first time that all of us had been in the same room, sharing the same air space, in three years. It was so incredible to me that they were there, so much the last thing on earth that I was expecting – and it totally threw me for the whole of that evening's competition! How in the world was I going to get my focus back now? As delighted as I was, I was also terrified. All I could think was, I've got to do really good now. The lads are here. I've got to win.

As luck would have it, I did win – thanks to a good half-somersault off the vault.

Usually, the live show on Channel 4 was followed by the 10 competitors going on to appear on E4 in *The Games: Inside Track*. After that we were always taken straight back to the Village where contestants stayed all week in full view of the cameras for the benefit of the TV audience. But that night it was different. I was allowed to stay behind for a couple of hours to share a few cans of Guinness with the lads. Keith was drunk as a skunk, but it was a brilliant, brilliant evening of reminiscing, going over times past. It was worth being on the show just for that.

From a physical point of view, *The Games* was definitely one of the hardest things I've ever done. It was enormously challenging not only having to learn seven different disciplines in such a short space of time, but then having to go and compete in them for a week. It's a journey I wouldn't have missed for anything, though. It gave me a huge amount of respect for athletes that I never had before. To maintain their levels of fitness, to achieve what they do in their specific speciality must demand such complete commitment. I can't say that I'd want to live my own life that way. It's way too much dedication for me, and more than I could ever possibly give. But I have nothing but admiration for those who can.

When the live week came to an end and I found I'd won *The Games*, it was a real boost for me on so many levels. For a start, there was the obvious sense of achievement. I'd put in the hours and worked through the pain and managed to walk away with the gold medal. But more than that, so much more than that, I'd shown the watching public that I'd grown up. Until that moment, all they knew, if they knew of me at all, was the Shane Lynch I'd been at the tail end of the Boyzone days – loud, aggressive, outspoken and immature. Now I was someone completely different and it felt good to have the opportunity to reveal something of the person I'd grown into. A few years before, I'd been banned from live television because of my foul mouth and unpredictability. Now I'd been allowed back through the doors, and it proved to be a totally positive re-introduction – but, man, did I ache at the end of it!

In 2006, a special champion of champions' event was held following *The Games* that year, in which the top two male and female contestants from series two, three and four competed against each other in a 50m freestyle swim, a diving contest and a freestyle relay at Ponds Forge in Sheffield.

Javine Hylton, Julia Goldsworthy MP, Jade Jones and MC Plat'num represented the 2006 team; Kirsty Gallacher, Chesney Hawkes, Kevin Simm and HRH Princess Tamara were there for the 2005 team; and our team 2004 brought together Lady Isabella Hervey, Linda Lusardi, Romeo and myself.

At the start, I wasn't happy. All we were going to get to prepare for the diving was two practice sessions. The thought of diving on live TV after such a short training time, when I hadn't actually done any in over two years, to me was ridiculous. So, along with Romeo, Kevin and Chesney, I decided to pay for some extra tuition. We got together and hired an Olympic coach.

Obviously I wanted to put on a great show, but it wasn't all about looking good. We were going to have to jump off 10 metre high diving boards. That's a dangerous thing to do. If you made a mistake, you could break your back or your neck. You could end up doing untold damage to yourself and we wanted to be safe, so we forked out for extra training because the TV company wouldn't.

Before the actual competition, I'd still never been off that 10 metre board. As the contest got under way, Chesney Hawkes, the oldest competitor, was the first to make a dive from that height. Then Jade from Damage took it on. There was no getting out of it. I knew I'd just have to face it.

I started to climb up and I couldn't believe I was actually going to do it. That was when I thought, damn it! Why have I got involved in this? And I actually hated being anything to do with *The Games* at that moment. But if there's one thing I'm very good at, it's getting my head around things. If I'm going to do something, then I'm really going to do it. No half measures. So I reached the top, walked straight out onto the platform, looked at the judges, got the nod – and I dived. I didn't hesitate, didn't pause to think about it. What would be the point? I just had to get on and do it.

Remarkably, that dive was pretty much perfect which gave me the highest score – 84 points out of the available 90. That meant I could go last in the trick dive, the most difficult dive in *The Games*. It was a one-and-a-half somersault and I'd been used to doing that from 5 metres. This time I had to take my chances off the 7.5 metre board. Oh well, you only live once, I thought – but I was scared witless!

I looked at the judges and got the nod again, then somehow managed to pull off a really slick dive. It was quite funny watching the footage back. I could see myself starting to turn into the somersault, then coming out of it as I must have been thinking, no, that's way too early. Then, there I was hooking back into it again. It certainly wasn't perfect by Olympic standards, but apparently it was perfect enough for *The Games*. I scored an unbelievable 108 points and, supported by a strong show from my team-mate, Romeo, our 2004 crew took the overall victory. But I still hated every minute of it!

* * * * *

Once you're seen to be up for the odd bit of reality TV, maybe that's why the calls keep coming. After *The Games* I did a stint on *Love Island* and, some time after that, I got a phone call from my agent asking if I fancied a turn on *Cirque de Celebrité*. This was another very hands on, extremely physical show and I felt quite excited about it. I'd watched it the year before and found the challenges it threw down and the achievements of the celebrity participants pretty inspiring.

The programme was broadcast on Sky One and followed contestants as they learned and then had to perform a variety of different circus acts. Points were collected from the judges and from public phone votes, and the two celebrities with the lowest scores were the ones who faced expulsion.

I was invited to join the 2007 series. The live show on a Sunday night was to be hosted by Jenni Falconer from GMTV, and the three judges were Louie Spence, professional choreographer and director, circus director, Phillip Gandey and the television personality, Gaby Roslin. I knew it was all fairly formulaic reality TV. There'd be the usual banter from the host, footage from the training sessions and interviews to reveal the inside story. But the idea of it still gave me a buzz. These days, I like to push myself, and I could see that this was an opportunity not only to do just that, but also to learn a range of new and demanding skills.

The next step was to meet with the show's producers to set everything up. As it turned out, I was going to be away on honeymoon for the first two weeks of training, but the only person my early absence seemed to cause any problem for was me. It really didn't help my fitness levels. I ate and drank so much while Sheena and I were away together that, at the start of the competition, just as with *The Games*, I found myself to be woefully unfit, and the training was absolutely gruelling.

The show had raised the stakes on last year's run and the demands presented by the different disciplines were huge. My competition was made up of Kyal Marsh from *Neighbours*, Hannah Waterman, the *EastEnders* star and daughter of Dennis Waterman, Stacey Cadman from *Cavegirl*, Lady Isabella Hervey and Princess Tamara, both from *The Games*, Olympic athlete, Dwain Chambers, Antonia Okonma from *Bad Girls*, footballer, Dean Holdsworth, Ritchie Neville from 5ive, Luke Bailey from *Casualty*, and model, Emily Scott, who I'd got to know the summer before when we were doing *Love Island* together. We all knew we were going to be pushed to our absolute limits.

The atmosphere was nothing less than electrifying as Jenni Falconer opened the first show under the Big Top. There were 1,000 people squeezed into that tent, not to mention the hundreds of thousands watching on television at home. This was genuinely nerve-wracking stuff. I wasn't up there singing and dancing with the lads. For my first act, I was literally going to be playing with fire.

I'd had a week to get a routine together with something called a 'fire poi'. Poi is a Maori word for a ball on a cord. The people of New Zealand used to use that kind of mechanism to improve flexibility and strength in their hands and arms. Being able to manipulate it proficiently also has a lot to do with good co-ordination.

When you're learning a new skill, you have to listen to your trainers. They're the ones with all the technical ability. They have the experience and should know exactly what they are doing. But there's this big part of me that can't seem to help wanting to go my own way – even when I'm being told to do something different by the experts. With my fire poi routine, I very much wanted to be left alone to do my own thing. This was a 'circus' and what you had to give the audience was a performance. It was different from *The Games*. With pure sport, there's a lot of discipline, but a real internal focus. Performing a routine is something else altogether. Obviously the discipline still has to be there, but the whole presentation should be much more about character and entertainment. You should be opening up a dialogue with the audience.

My trainer, Rob, was very able and knowledgeable but, as far as performance was concerned, he didn't seem to understand the energy that I wanted to put into my act. Yes, he had moves that I could probably never learn to do in my life. He was sensational at what he did. I just couldn't help feeling that it lacked something from the point of view of being spectacular. On television, I didn't think that simply swinging a ball of fire around relatively slowly, up and down, side to side, was going to come across as anything particularly stunning. So, I continued to develop my own routine, putting a lot of myself into it, my own personality, along with plenty of speed and energy.

Once I was happy with what I'd worked up, Rob came and had a look.

Very quickly he said, 'No. You need to put some tricks in there, some different crossovers. You need to display the skill behind what you're doing. That's what will get you the points.'

I didn't agree and we had a bit of an argument over it, but he was the trainer after all, so finally I had to go along with him. I went away and worked out where to start slowing things down a little, putting in a few tricks.

When the show went live, I got out there and threw myself into my routine, storming through my own, pacey opening, then easing off so that I could concentrate more on the technicalities, just as Rob had told me. And that was such a big mistake.

One of the judges, Phillip Gandey, who'd run circuses all his life, began by saying, 'Amazing start. Explosive beginning.'

I was thrilled. Until he made his next comment: 'But you ran out of steam.'

At that point, I was distinctly less than happy. The only reason I'd 'run out of steam' was because I'd listened to my trainer who'd told me I should slow the whole thing down! If I'd just followed my own head, I'd have been way up with the best of the rest.

During the second week, I had to tackle the art of the floor cube. A Russian girl came over to teach us – and she really was as dry as the

Sahara Desert. You certainly had to go some to crack a smile out of her. I managed it a few times but only because I kept messing around. The night of the performance was a lot of fun. My stint on stage seemed to go pretty well and I managed to keep control of that large, steel cube, which did actually demand a fair bit of skill. All in all, I must have been doing something right because Gaby Roslin, with a glint in her eye, commented, 'Shane, I can't keep my eyes off you!'

Week three saw me hanging around on the bungee. It made me feel wickedly sick and, in the four to five days of practice, I simply couldn't get the routines together. Finally I had to say, 'Look, I'm just going to go out there and wing it and do my own thing.' There was a certain format I did try and stick to but, on the performance, I didn't manage to pull off some of the tricks, and a few of the ones I attempted went wrong. The end result was that the routine didn't look as though it had any structure to it – which was exactly the case. I just bounced around doing random flips and somersaults. It was the best I could do.

Cirque de Celebrité proved to be far more challenging than *The Games*. For *The Games* we had three months to learn and to train, before we had to compete. With *Cirque*, we had four to five days at most, and that made such a huge difference. We were all sustaining injuries of one sort or another but, because time was always so tight, there was no letup to allow anything to heal. If you got hurt, you simply had to work through it, or with it, or try to find a way round it.

Being up on the cloud swing was the first time I remember thinking, 'I'm getting old!' I climbed up there – and I was really scared. It wasn't an excited sort of scared where I'd be shaking like a leaf but still thinking, I want to do this. I honestly didn't like it, and I just wanted to get down.

The cloud swing is a soft rope suspended between two rigging points to form a u-shaped loop. This loop is the focal point for an energetic swinging aerial act. Technically, it requires enormous core, back and hand strength. I don't really know how, given the terror that filled me when I was up on this thing, but I learned to sit, stand and hang from the loop, performing dives, rolls and drops.

I was used to heights but this act was all about seriously defying gravity. It was so different to the bungee, where you were high up with your heart thumping, but somehow you couldn't wait to jump and get on with it. With the cloud swing, my heart was still thumping but all I wanted to do was get down. It was a little like facing the diving in *The Games*, only much, much worse. I felt so bad I just wanted to finish with the whole thing and stop all this messing around. That was quite hard for me to face up to. I was 31 years old and it was the first time I'd had feelings like that in my whole life.

For one particular move, I had to learn to drop from the standing position with the ropes wrapped round my ankles, and swing underneath. I imagined it would probably hurt – and it did. All I could think was, I'm not interested in being hurt, and I want to get down. I built up a real mental block about that cloud swing.

But something inside me always pushed me to keep going. In the end, I managed to get a routine together that I was actually fairly happy with. There was just one move that I got slightly wrong. I had to form myself into a star shape on the loop while it swung to the back of the tent but, in doing that, I must have braced myself badly, using the muscles in my chest and upper body to keep myself upright and stop myself from falling off. As a result, I took a bit of a strain in my chest muscle on the right hand side. I managed to finish the routine, but it was a viciously sharp surge of pain that shot through me.

When I turned up for training on the Tuesday morning, I had a word with the doctor because it still didn't feel right. He proceeded to press the muscles around and then pronounced that I had strained myself a little, but that I was fine to continue with the programme.

My next event was the swinging trapeze. I felt slightly more confident with this one. It was more stable than the cloud swing and I found I was feeling quite good about working with it, thinking I could maybe build up to quite a spectacular routine. I was taught how to get the trapeze swinging from a still position, and then how to use that momentum to execute my moves. There are dozens of tricks that are only possible on a swinging trapeze and most of them are far more difficult than anything you might do on a static trapeze. They are usually performed on the peaks of the swing, and the moves are complicated, requiring perfect timing and great flexibility and strength.

As I attempted to build up a routine, I realised my chest wasn't feeling at all good. The pain was growing very intense. I came down, described what was going on and said that I needed to rest for a day. I ended up resting for two days, but I found I really had to fight for the time off. The trainers and the people running the competition weren't really very happy. I was telling them I was injured and needed to try and get better, and the doctor was saying that the strain wasn't too bad. They didn't seem to know which one of us to listen to. All I knew was that my body was telling me it didn't want to be pushed any further.

I came back to training on the Thursday. That only left me two days to work up a proper routine because Saturday wasn't really classed as a training day. That was when you had an opportunity to practise your performance of the finished moves once or twice.

I got up to do one particular move called a tombe´ where I had to drop down beneath the trapeze from a standing position and grab onto the bar. As I went into it, I had a feeling it was going to hurt. I was so right. I grasped the bar and that was it. The pain was unbearable. Something tore inside my chest. If it hadn't hurt so much, it might actually have felt very weird. There was no sound like a bone breaking. But it felt exactly like a piece of steak being ripped apart down its length – in slow motion.

I screamed. That's how much it cut through me. I let go of the bar and fell to the ground. A gang of people raced over to me. I was in tears. I've got a pretty high threshold for pain, but tears actually came to my eyes. I lay on the floor thinking, this isn't good, and when I could speak,

I shook my head and said, 'I'll be very surprised if I can continue in this competition. I think it's over for me.'

I was taken to see the doctor and the physiotherapist. They had a look, prodded me around and said they'd send me for a scan. Sure enough, the scan revealed a tear, but the producers and trainers still wanted to keep me in the competition. In one respect, I could understand that. I was a big part of the show. But, on the other hand, I didn't think they were concerned enough for my personal safety. They wanted their competition to continue with me in it, and I had to fight hard not to carry on and end up injuring myself further.

The doctor told me that, with an injury like I had, there were three stages. Stage one was a bad strain. That's what I had to begin with and that's when I should have rested for two weeks, as soon as it happened. Stage two was a rupture, which was what I had now. Stage three was when the rupture was so severe that you had to go and have surgery. Luckily it didn't come to that for me.

In spite of the pressure not to quit, I didn't see that I had a lot of choice. I didn't want to end up needing an operation. It was a shame because I'd pushed myself pretty ruthlessly, both physically and mentally, to get as far as I had in the competition, and I never liked having to give up on anything. But this injury was something outside of my control. Whether I was happy about it or not, it was definitely time to hang up my purple leotard, pack my trunk, and say a fond goodbye to the circus.

CHAPTER 17

Where The Heart Is

"I'D BEEN WAITING FOR JUST THE RIGHT MOMENT AND WHEN IT CAME I GRABBED IT. IT DIDN'T HAPPEN QUITE LIKE I'D IMAGINED, BUT IT WAS EXACTLY THE WAY I WANTED IT TO BE. PERFECT."

Early in 2006, my girlfriend, Sheena, and I seemed to have run down a blind alley. We'd got to the point of 'are we going to get married or not?' and, uncertain about the future and how marriage might pan out for me this time, I'd made some wrong decisions. In the end we temporarily parted. After that, I guess I was going through that phase of just wanting to get away to try and sort myself out, clear my head. The offer to appear on ITV's reality show, *Love Island*, seemed to give me the perfect opportunity to do just that.

Love Island saw celebrities fly out to the tropical island paradise of Fiji for a couple of months, where the cameras would follow their antics 24 hours a day. I'd initially been approached to join the crew in 2003, when the show was first being talked about, but it never happened. Then, in 2006, I was invited again for the second series.

It wasn't an easy decision and, despite things not going well on the home front, I was still very much in two minds. I knew *Love Island* wasn't exactly what you'd call a constructive game show. It meant putting myself up for scrutiny in a very judgemental arena. I had to weigh up whether I thought I was strong enough mentally to go into that place and still keep a level head. I needed to be sure that I wouldn't let it get to me. Only when I felt I could honestly say, yes, I'm strong enough to do this, did I finally agree to go. So, on 3 July, that's how I found myself taking that long flight out via Australia to Fiji. It was my thirtieth birthday and stretching in front of me were up to seven weeks of palm trees, white sands, crystal clear waters – and I had no idea what else besides.

My fellow contestants were certainly a varied bunch and initially consisted of model, Bianca Gascoigne (the stepdaughter of Geordie footballer, Gazza), ex-Eternal star, Kéllé Bryan, dancer, Brendan Cole, Chris Brosnan (the adopted son of actor, Pierce), model, Sophie Anderton, Lee Otway, the former *Hollyoaks* star, *Playboy* model, Colleen Shannon, Leo Ihenacho who'd been a backing singer with The Streets, 'It Girl', Lady Victoria Hervey, and glamour model, Alicia Douvall. In the days and weeks that followed, we were joined by other contestants; models in the forms of Calum Best, Emily Scott and Emma and Eve Ryan, together with *Big Brother 3* winner, Kate Lawler and actor, Paul Danan. Then there were the celebrities who only came to the resort for a short time: singer, Abs Breen (formerly of 5ive), basketball star, Dennis Rodman, and Steve-O from the American TV series, *Jackass*, a dangerous stunt show. Throw me in there as well and, all in all, it was a pretty mixed bag.

When you put the whole thing together, I guess it did sound like the dream job. Up to virtually two months of blissful island living – sun, sea, and stunning girls wandering around in skimpy bikinis. But I arrived there as a Christian man, a God-loving Christian man, and that put kind of a different perspective on things for me. In any case, at that point, my personal life was very much up in the air. I certainly wasn't going to Fiji with the idea of meeting someone and getting involved. As far as I was concerned, I was there to be on a TV show, and I said as much to the interviewers intent on probing my motives before I went out: I'd been to a school with 500 girls and never ended up dating one of them. I might be flying off to an island with ten women, but, really, what were the chances? Probably very slim.

As it turned out, I did meet some lovely and interesting people, but I didn't feel attracted towards anyone. Whether the producers of the show really believed that any of their celebrities might actually fall in love with each other during their paradise experience, I have no idea. What I do know is that the whole thing was very sexually orientated. The other lads spent a lot of their time talking about sex and I think, for the TV viewers at home, *Love Island* was seen very much as Sex Island. It was quite a challenge to me in many ways. I was coming at this from a totally different standpoint from almost all the other contestants and, somehow, I wanted to make it clear what I stood for. To me, this was about getting to know people. All right, so it was in full view of an audience of several million, but I wanted to show that sex didn't have to be the ultimate aim. It was tough, though. After all, it was TV. The producers wanted the ratings, and more than a fair bit of manipulation went on to try to sensationalise the situation so that they got them.

I probably spent most of my time with Kéllé Bryan. She is a beautiful woman and, like me, a committed Christian. Spiritually, we were very good for each other, although it was an odd situation in a way because I'd been married to one of her best friends from Eternal and that hadn't turned out so well. There was a deep, Godly sense of strength about Kéllé and she definitely helped me to keep my head together. But I knew from the start we were only ever going to be good friends. Nothing more.

I also got on really well with Colleen Shannon, *Playboy* magazine's Fiftieth Anniversary Playmate, although these days she's also an actress, DJ and musician. We had some great conversations but there's no way I could ever see myself getting together with someone like her. Where she was aiming to go with her life just wasn't where I wanted to go with mine.

Each evening, viewers back in the UK would vote for celebrities to spend the night together. I ended up going out on a date with Emily Scott, officially Australia's sexiest woman, because the audience had cast their votes and put us in the love shack. (I'll always think of it as the 'Shane shack' because I seemed to wind up there almost every night!) Emily was a cool girl and we hit it off pretty well. Our 'date' was a trek through a tropical forest to a hot spring and a sumptuous picnic. It sounds idyllic, but there was more to it. On the way, we had to have an encounter with, as I see it, the evil troll. It was a bit like a fairytale quest – the hot spring and the food were the prize but, to reach them, you had to run the gauntlet of the forest demons. In this case, the demon in question was a woman spiritualist.

Of course it was all very set up. There were blankets and cushions, and it was made to seem romantic and cosy as we met with this so-called medium or spiritual something or other. I didn't know what her professional title was and I didn't really care. What I did know was that this wasn't just a bit of fun to me and I had a big issue with it. I used to be deeply embedded in that dark side of life. This might have been a perfectly nice woman who believed she was doing the right thing by using the stars to tell people about their connection together as a man and woman. But, as far as I could make out, what she clearly didn't understand was the power of what she was dealing with and the detrimental effect she could have on those she was 'counselling'. She didn't see that what she was messing around with was evil.

This lady had a book with her that she consulted as she talked to us, and she pointed out various stars here and there. The whole meeting didn't get shown on the TV, but I remember asking her some very simple questions. I could see her becoming quite agitated and abrupt with me, I guess because I wasn't prepared to accept what she had to say. I was challenging her about her sources and she didn't like it. She was telling Emily and me to be open and free, that we should be prepared to allow things into our lives, and I told her point blank I didn't believe that. Quite the opposite. I said you have to be very aware and cautious about what comes into your life because, if you let in the wrong thing, it can destroy you. You have to be much cleverer than that. Life shouldn't be about taking your soul into your own hands and stepping into uncharted territory. You have to be so much in control of the influences that come your way. You have to know how to make the right choices because, in the end, it's your choices that can make or break you.

After a while, the lady could see that she and I obviously weren't going to find any common ground in this discussion, and it got to the point where she asked me to leave. Emily wanted to stay and, of course, that was up to her. But as I walked away, I remember I said something about being protected in the name of Jesus. Then I went off and spent some time praying for Emily. She wasn't aware of the evil inherent in what the woman was saying, in the forces she was using. After all, to her it must have all seemed so harmless. It's just that I knew it wasn't. I'd been drawn in through something I once thought of as a bit of fun. Drawn in, then tormented by demons and dragged into a black hole. Emily was just innocent prey. The dark side of life lies in wait ready to pounce on people like that, just as a hawk shadows a field mouse before plunging in for the kill. I wanted to pray for her to give her that little bit of protection.

In a sense, although it was our choice to be there, I guess we were all prey on that show to one extent or another – not necessarily to evil, but to the whims of the producers who obviously had to grab onto whatever means they could to give the TV audience the scandalous viewing they were hoping for.

Sophie Anderton was perceived to develop some sort of crush on me, and the hosts, Patrick Kielty and Fearne Cotton, lost no time in latching grimly onto it and making it out to be a huge deal.

As far as most people were concerned, it was Sophie who made the show and, looked at from a certain point of view, her antics did produce great television. She could be very volatile, but her portrayal on *Love Island* was definitely distorted. She was shown as a deeply needy girl who went around upsetting everyone, as opposed to a deeply needy girl who was crying out for help. Sophie had been through a lot of trauma in her life. At 11 years old, she'd been so seriously injured in a car accident that she'd had to undergo 18 operations. It took her four years to recover and the pain was so intense that, for much of that time, she was on morphine. That meant that, from a very young age, she'd grown to depend on something. But it was an unhealthy dependence. It set up a pattern of dependency in her brain and the way she functioned as a person. It threw her into eventual drug abuse and became her everyday 'habit', spilling over into her relationships. That's what people didn't understand.

Sophie revealed on the show that she had bipolar disorder, a dysfunction that causes sufferers to flip from bouts of mania to periods of deep depression. I've upset a fair few people in my time with my anger and black moods, but maybe it was those past, deeply personal experiences that gave me a little more understanding of her character than some of the others on the island. Whatever it was, it seemed to me that she didn't deserve the portrayal she was given. She was at the receiving end of some wrong publicity and I really believe she's a better person than the manipulated version of herself the viewers saw.

As for her supposedly 'big interest' in me, I don't think that's what it was. What I feel she locked onto was the Christ in me. Without actually mentioning God when I talked with her, I always tried to speak in a Godly way. I tried to show her about hope and understanding and control and discipline, all those things I'd been learning in the last few years. In the end I'm sure what she had for me wasn't to do with sexual attraction. It was about finding someone who maybe understood her a little, about discovering a sense of peace in someone else and reaching out to try and grasp that peace for herself.

Little Lee Otway was another one who seemed to find some connection with me. He was known for his portrayal of David 'Bombhead' Burke in *Hollyoaks* and had also appeared on *Soapstar Superstar* and *Celebrity Stars In Their Eyes*, but he was still very young and didn't quite understand who he was other than this full-on, party guy. I had a lot of time for Lee and I didn't like the way some of the others treated him. I suppose in my own way I tried to look after him, but I wasn't there to control him. It was his choice how he behaved and he seemed to have to go and do what he had to go and do. There were moments of real madness with him. But when it came to his broken times when the tears wanted to take over, I just made sure I was there. I think he'll be a powerful guy when he finally gets hold of who he is.

A few weeks into the show, *Jackass* star, Steve-O, arrived to boost the ratings – and he certainly stirred things up. He was a lunatic! I realised that what you see of him on TV is very much how he is in real life – packed with energy, living right out there on the edge. He seemed to me to be a very unsettled man. He couldn't sit still for two minutes without creating a situation. It was impossible for him to chill. He was going flat out at 100mph the whole time, to the point where it got very out of hand. Right from the start there was an uneasy sense of, uh-oh, this is Steve-O from *Jackass* – what in the world's going to happen next? Almost the first thing he did was to pick up a huge kitchen knife and start balancing it on his nose. Then he was suddenly messing around in the kitchen/bar area, playing a game with Paul Danan where you had to climb up onto the high stools and knock each other off. If there was any peace to be had on that island, Steve-O's arrival saw it well and truly shattered.

But I've learned that people tend to be the way they are for a reason. When he and I got into a conversation, he explained that his father had been in the army and they'd had to up sticks and move every year and a half. So he'd never settled, never had a long-term friend. His whole life was about getting up and moving on, and that's what you see in his character. He can't sit still. His mind never rests.

The two of us did have one fairly major altercation. Steve-O had barely arrived in the place before he was verbally laying into one of the other guys, viciously pulling him to pieces. It was all very negative, very unnecessary and I didn't like it – especially as I'd become close friends with the victim of this attack. I began to get very angry, so angry in fact that I found myself leaping up to go over and give him a thump on the head. I'm a Christian man, and my fighting days are behind me, but there are times when we all get pushed to our limits. Somehow I managed to stop myself. I managed to think about what I was doing. It was hard because this man, Steve-O, had just about tipped my balance but, instead of punching him, I walked away.

The bathroom in the house was about the only private place there was for us. So that's where I headed. When I got there, I didn't scream in frustration or start kicking the walls. I prayed. Inside me, I was still raging, but I said to God, 'Please don't let my anger get the better of me. I don't want to fight this man. I don't want this bad feeling. All I want to do is have the opportunity to speak to him and get things sorted out.'

A short while later I was back sitting in the kitchen. Steve-O left the table almost immediately and walked over to me. It was a perfect moment to be able to talk to each other and maybe clear the air.

I didn't want to make a big deal out of it. All I said was, 'Look, Steve-O, I don't agree with what you've said. You're an intelligent guy and you're speaking a lot of sense. But a lot of what you say is also pure nonsense and I don't like it.'

At that moment, I watched that wild, reckless guy lose his devil-may-care, 'I don't give a damn what anybody thinks' front, and become a humble man. He couldn't seem to apologise enough. It was as though he was really knocked off balance by someone challenging him. He seemed to realise that I'd almost stuck my fist in his face but had managed to stop myself.

'Dude,' he said in his American drawl, 'you know what? I really respect you for that because you could have taken my head clean off.'

For those few moments, we made a real connection with each other. But it was by no means the end of Steve-O's havoc-causing on the show. A few days in and he lost it in a sensational way.

The producers had given us a challenge. We had to build a sandcastle bigger than seven feet in two or three hours. If we were able to do that, we'd get a reward: beer, wine and chocolate. To us it was a prize well worth getting dirty for so we picked up our shovels and spades and headed down to the beach to complete the challenge.

I didn't see what happened next because I'd been voted into my second home again, the love shack, and I was away from everything else that was going on for the next two days.

When I got out, Kéllé came right up to me and said, 'Thank God you're back. Steve-O has gone mad. He's flipped out, he's gone crazy.'

He had too. He'd been ranting and raving, and throwing glasses at the big mirrors hiding the cameras. He seemed to have gone totally berserk. He'd only been on the island for a few days and he was out of control. When I knew what the problem was, I could pretty much understand why. The producers had said we'd be rewarded if we completed the sandcastle challenge, which we'd gone ahead and done. The problem was that they weren't prepared to give us the promised booze and chocolate there and then, not even when Steve-O had gone and asked them for it. They made it clear that they would decide when we could have it and this was what had sent Steve-O into his fury. It wasn't so much that he was stamping his foot because he wasn't getting his own way. It was a matter of principle for him. As far as he could see, we'd all done our part but now the producers weren't keeping to their side of the bargain.

In amongst the shouting and crashing about as he was throwing things and smashing the place up, I got a call to go into the beach hut. That's where we each got an opportunity to talk to the people supposedly in charge about how we were feeling and the things that were going on. I told them I was pretty disappointed with the way they were dealing with, or rather *not* dealing with, this episode. Steve-O had got himself into such a state of madness that I felt they really should have come in and talked to him, taken him out even, to try and calm him down. But they'd done nothing. It was an interesting concept for a TV show that one of the contestants should be allowed to lose it in such spectacular fashion and we were somehow supposed to know how to deal with the situation.

But there was more to it than that for me. As I watched Steve-O throwing himself around, unable to control the fury that had got hold of him, it all felt horribly familiar. I couldn't help seeing myself in him. Everything he was right then was everything *I* had been only a few years before. His violence, his anger, his rudeness, his sharp tongue – I was so familiar with all of it because I knew what it was like to feel that dark. I felt as though I knew this man because I knew myself and the person I used to be. That's when I realised I had to make a stand with him. It was almost a sense of, 'Let's take on the world together.' So we joined forces. I wanted him to know that he had somebody there with him and didn't need to feel out on a limb. I thought it might calm him down and he'd feel better.

I took my microphone off. Steve-O did the same. That started the programme people battling with me, calling me into the beach hut and demanding, 'What's going on? What's happening? What are you doing? Put your microphone on.' But I wasn't going to be pushed around. I was pretty furious with them by that time about their lack of concern for what they'd sparked off in Steve-O. They kept saying, 'Put your microphone back on,' and I kept replying, 'Look, I ain't putting it on till he's either left the show or you guys have sorted the situation out. You want me to wear my microphone, then tell me you'll deal with this.'

I stayed with Steve-O and eventually he calmed down enough to curl up on the deck and go to sleep. He preferred sleeping outside to being in the bedroom.

Everything had got way out of hand but through it we'd found an interesting connection, me and this wired, restless guy. As it turned out, there was something good in there for me. I felt as though I'd been able to help Steve-O come through his rage in a peace-making kind of way because I understood where the anger was coming from – and that was because, after all these years, I could finally say that I understood myself.

Dennis Rodman, the six foot seven inch tall basketball star, stayed on the island for just four days. In the short time he was there, we never spoke once. Not a single word. I think he knew that my views as a Christian weren't for him in the sense that he was the complete opposite.

I'll always remember one particular moment with him, though. We'd been given a challenge to match personalities with the different contestants. We all stood in a line, the personality trait was read out, and Dennis had to say who fitted each particular statement. He'd point and say, 'That guy on the end,' or, 'The girl in the pink bikini.' He'd been there for three days but didn't seem to know anyone's name or, if he did, he wasn't prepared to use it. Until it got to me. A characteristic was read out that matched with me and he said straightaway, 'Yeah, that's Shane.' It was quite weird for me. Mine was the only name he actually spoke and yet Dennis and I had never even talked to each other.

The 2006 series of *Love Island* ran for seven weeks, with Calum Best and Bianca Gascoigne emerging as the eventual winners. But I wasn't there to see them clinch their victory. I'd walked out during week five. It wasn't through anger or personality clash or just getting fed up with the whole business. It was simply a spontaneous decision that I knew I had to make. Paul Danan had just been evicted and, as he was saying his goodbyes, I found myself thinking, yes, that's it. My time's over here and I've got to go home. There was nothing in that place for me. I'd stayed with the show for a fair few weeks, just getting on with the same old nonsense and taking it as it came day by day, but all it did was make me think about what I could have back home.

I did find love on *Love Island*, but not with any of the girls there. It was with Sheena. 100 per cent. And everything about me was suddenly screaming, 'Look, Shane, just go home!' – until all I wanted to do was get back and find a way to work it all out with her.

I went to the beach hut and said, 'I'm going to leave. It's my time to go home.'

The programme people didn't make it easy. They must have gone over it 30 times, asking the same question, 'Why do you want to go home?' But I knew my own mind and I just kept telling them, 'There's somebody at home I want to fight for.' They didn't want me to leave but, that same evening, I was gone.

I must admit that breaking the news to the others was a lot harder than I thought it would be. I've watched a lot of reality shows and seen people come to the point where they want to leave. There always seems to be this turmoil going on for them over their decision, and they become very emotional. I've sat there in front of the TV and thought, what a load of nonsense. But, all of a sudden, there I was in the same position. I'd spent five weeks with these guys and, despite all the ups and downs, I'd formed a real bond with some of them. It had been an incredibly intense experience. The emotion took me by surprise and I couldn't control it. I imagined people watching back home and thinking, look at that idiot, shedding the tears. But, when you're actually there living through that situation, what you feel is very, very real.

I asked the others one by one to come and sit at the table with me. I remember saying something like, 'I'm leaving the show. I've got some stuff to deal with at home, so I'm saying good-bye.' I'm sure there were some of them who didn't really care in amongst the ones who were sad to see me go. But it felt very much like the end of something for me, and it was hard. I wanted to get home. I needed to get out of there, only I didn't want to hurt anyone. Suddenly I was faced with little Lee, who I'd been trying to look after, saying, 'Please, Shane, don't go,' and that touched me. I really had to tussle with myself. I didn't want to let him down.

It was the same with Kéllé. 'I can't believe you're leaving me behind,' she said to me.

But all I knew was that I'd made up my mind and although this was a truly horrible moment, I had to see it through.

I said, 'Kéllé, please, don't do this to me. I have to go.'

She's a strong woman and, however much she wanted me to stay, I knew she'd be all right there without me, and she was. She even finished the show as the female runner-up.

Whatever anyone else felt about my staying or leaving, on that day at that moment I had to think about what was right for me. I had to be strong and fly home and fight for my relationship with Sheena.

* * * * *

In our three years together, Sheena and I did talk about marriage but, whether consciously or not, I guess it was something I was always trying to side step. I knew she wanted more commitment from me, but I was honestly scared. I already had one failed marriage behind me. What if this one went bad too? I didn't want getting married to spoil anything between us but, by avoiding the issue, somehow I seemed to force us into a position where we were pulling against each other. In the end, we broke apart. That's why I had to get out. That's why *Love Island* struck me as an ideal escape route.

I should have known that picking up life without Sheena wouldn't be that simple. The feelings I had were too deep. Too real. It was obvious in no time. The longer I spent away from her, the more I realised how much I wanted to be with her. I was in a paradise manufactured by a clutch of TV bosses, surrounded by some very beautiful women, but all I could think about was Sheena. She was in my head from the moment I woke up to the minute I closed my eyes again and fell asleep. I lasted in the show as long as I could but when my mind's made up, there's no shifting it. Thinking time was over. I had to get back and find a way for us to be together.

The first time we saw each other again properly was at my sister, Edele's, wedding. Even though we were split, Sheena was still very much a part of the family, so it was natural for her to be there. What wasn't natural was the silence between us. We didn't seem able to speak to each other the whole time. We were both involved in such a happy, family day, but we weren't together. And I was so miserable.

I had a lot of grovelling to do. I was the one who'd legged it to Fiji. I was the one who had to make it right. The one thing I was now more sure of than anything else was that Sheena was the woman I wanted to spend the rest of my life with – and I'd prove that to her by marrying her.

Eventually, I was able to break through the pain I'd caused her and she let me back in. But even then she began to get very frustrated when she thought I was still trying to put off setting a date. As a matter of fact she was absolutely right – but not because I didn't want to get married this time. I was having a ring specially made for her and it was taking time. And it hadn't been the easiest thing in the world trying to get her size without her working out what I was up to! When I proposed I wanted to be able to give her the ring and have everything perfect.

I was in pantomime while all this was going on, and Sheena came up with the idea that, when the show was over, we should go to Jamaica for a holiday. Her sister, Yvonne, was going out there with her husband, Ray, and I immediately thought, yes, that's where I can ask her to marry me.

Things still felt a little sticky between us but, two days before we were due to leave, I finally had the finished ring – although keeping it hidden turned out to be a problem in itself. I didn't know where would be the safest place to put it. As we headed for the airport, I had it tucked away in my pocket. I didn't want to put it in the suitcase because, if the suitcase got lost, that would be it, my dream of the perfect proposal destroyed by a mislaid bag. On the other hand, having it in my pocket wasn't good either because it would get picked up when I went through the metal detector. We got to the airport and I was seriously worried. I even wondered if I'd get away with going to a different security point to Sheena, but I guess that would just have looked weird. In the end, all I could do was slip the ring into the hand luggage and hope for the best. Fortunately, the bag wasn't opened up or searched. Brilliant, I thought. Phase one successfully completed.

As we made the 10-hour flight to Jamaica, I was very preoccupied. When should I ask the question? How should I go about it? I wanted to wait for exactly the right moment. That's how I spent the first four or five days of our holiday – waiting for exactly the right moment. I had the ring. Every morning when Sheena wasn't around, I'd take it out and look at it. I couldn't wait to ask her to marry me. I was just never quite sure when to do it.

One morning, we were driving along the coast in our rented 4 x 4 with Ray and Yvonne, when we met a guy called John who was in a Jeep with a museum emblem on the side. We got talking and discovered that this was a man who'd once been involved in the corporate world, but had got so tired of the constant rat race that he'd sold up and moved to Jamaica. He'd bought some land and now his life was all about art and searching out and buying artefacts for the museum he'd established on the island.

John was such an interesting character that we decided we'd like to take a look in the museum. He pointed out where it was – along a track on the edge of a mountain which went straight up. This wasn't a road, or a dirt track, or anything. It was boulders, pure rock, with just a hint of a trail where you could see that somebody did manage to get up there.

The girls took one look and thought, definitely no. But me, I said, 'It's okay, it'll be fine.' I was quite excited. So, we piled back into our 4 x 4 and started to climb up the steep incline.

It was when we were about half way up that I started to wonder what in the world I thought I was doing. The rocks were falling apart and breaking away underneath us. We'd slide back a little then lurch forward. I couldn't turn around to try and roll back down. I had to keep on going forwards. The girls were shouting and screaming by this time, convinced we weren't going to make it.

Eventually we got to a flat part, but a little further on, the rock face just went straight up again. This time, Ray and I thought it might be best to go on foot to see where it went. That didn't turn out to be such a good idea either. We'd hardly scrambled far when we heard the unwelcome noise of dogs barking.

We looked at each other.

'That doesn't sound too good,' I said.

It wasn't. All of a sudden, 12 aggressive-looking dogs leaped out in front of us.

We could see a house in the distance which we assumed must be John's, but it didn't look as if we stood a chance of getting to it. Very slowly, keeping a wary eye on the dog pack, we backed off to where the girls were. It was a pretty nasty moment.

We were starting to explain that we'd have to try and make our way back, when John appeared in his 4 x 4. He was absolutely astonished. He couldn't believe that we'd driven up the mountain. He had a big Toyota with huge, chunky tyres that made relatively short work of those boulders, but we'd made that trip in our little rented contraption. No one else ever drove up there. He was so excited we'd attempted it that some kind of connection formed between us. We were obviously complete raving lunatics like him! And with that, he invited us up to the house.

That house was unreal. John had hand-built it himself. He'd literally dug it out from under the rock face. You could see the pickaxe marks. There'd been no machinery, no massive bulldozers to do the job in a couple of days. Building the house and creating the roadway had taken this man three years.

I was so inspired by his spirit of determination, his instinct for survival, his strength of character, that my own energy was revved up to 100mph. That's when I knew I was going to do it. That's when I knew the moment was right to propose.

Sheena and I were staying in a resort called Jake's in Treasure Beach, which is a truly beautiful place. We had a three-bedroomed cottage so close to the sea that at night the waves beat on the bedroom wall. It was stunning.

We got back from our trip up the mountain and I went straightaway and took out the ring. Sheena was in the main sitting room.

I said to her, 'Come with me.'

She was in the middle of something and answered, 'I'm going to put something in the bedroom.'

I didn't say anything, but she told me afterwards that I just gave her one look that simply said, 'No. Come with me.'

She stopped in her tracks, put down whatever she had in her hands and followed me.

We went up to the roof terrace. The sun was just starting to slip down and touch the ocean. It was so peaceful, so serene. But I still didn't quite know what I was going to say. Until Sheena spoke again.

'Baby, this is the most romantic place I've ever been in my life.'

That was it. That was all I needed.

'Good,' I murmured.

Then I spun her around and got down on one knee. Only, when I opened my mouth I found I still couldn't ask her to marry me. All the emotion, all that feeling I had for her, came bubbling up and I couldn't get the words out. When I took the ring out of my pocket, we were both sobbing fit to break our hearts! As I slipped it on her finger, she managed to say yes, and I hadn't even asked the question.

When I eventually calmed down enough to speak, I just said, 'Marry me,' and fortunately Sheena hadn't had a re-think while I was crying my eyes out and she kindly said yes again.

In the heat and emotion of the moment, what I hadn't realised was that I'd actually put the ring on the wrong hand! Someone else had to point it out to me. I felt like a bit of a doughnut, but I didn't really care. To be honest, it wouldn't have mattered to me if I'd put it on one of her toes. I'd been waiting for just the right moment and when it came I grabbed it. It didn't happen quite like I'd imagined, but it was exactly the way I wanted it to be. Perfect.

CHAPTER 18

Living Proof

"THEN GOD FOUND ME. I WAS STANDING AT THE VERY
EDGE OF MY EXISTENCE WHEN HE TOOK HOLD OF MY
HAND AND SAVED ME."

I'm looking forward to the future. I can say that now and mean it. It's
not something I ever used to think about. I was always the super-cool
one, drifting by with no particular goals, taking what came along and
aimlessly wending my way through. Nothing would faze me. Somehow,
I'd find my own path, even though I never planned anything. I never
tried to be something I wasn't, was never obsessed with the idea of
fame and fortune or a glittering career. I wasn't a driven person in that
sense. I took one day at a time and was lucky enough to find that doors
opened for me in the most unexpected places without my having to go
around kicking them in. It's different now. I feel an excitement about
what's around the corner – the next opportunity, the latest challenge.
Inside me, there's a sense of expectancy. And I like that.

The offer to be on *Dream Team* was another one of life's little
surprises. Out of the blue, I was being asked if I wanted to do an acting

job. *Dream Team* wasn't like the other TV work I'd done. It wasn't a reality show. This was a football drama put out on Sky One with actors – real actors, not people like me. The series followed the ups and downs of the professional and private lives of everyone involved in the fictional Harchester United F.C., supposedly in the West Midlands, and the character offered to me was called Eli Knox. He was a big gambling tycoon who, on the toss of a coin, took a chance on buying the recently relegated club.

I didn't think about it too much when the offer came through. Looking back, I guess that's how I ended up involved in most things – by not thinking about them too much! The job sounded interesting, a different experience, but I have to admit that the idea of it did scare the hell out of me. I wasn't an actor. Not only that, but it was a real struggle for me to read and write. If I agreed, I'd be faced with having to try and fathom out scripts, having to learn all those words. What if I couldn't do it? It was another big risk. But, in my own lackadaisical way, I was a risk taker. I couldn't seem to help myself. So I said, 'Yeah, I'd love to do that.'

'Great news, Shane,' came the reply. 'We'll bike your script over to you tonight. You'll start filming in the morning.'

What?! That was all a bit quick, even for me. How in the world was I going to manage to decipher a script in barely more than a few hours, let alone learn the thing as well? But I'd said yes and I was committed. And, to tell the truth, I was absolutely petrified.

The script duly arrived via motorcycle courier and I stayed up till 3.00 or 4.00am working my way through it, trying to understand it and break it down to the best of my ability. I got myself as prepared as I could although, as so often in the past, I really hadn't a clue what I was doing. I guess I assumed that, somehow or other, I'd be able to blag my way through, just like I usually did.

I had to be at the studios at 7.00am so, without having had a wink of sleep, I left home an hour before and, on the way in the car, just went over and over my words, trying to memorise them and get them to stick in my head.

I didn't know anything about filming. I didn't realise that scenes aren't necessarily shot in the order they appear on the page. As far as I was concerned, my introductory appearances should have given me quite a slow, gentle introduction into the whole drama-making process, allowing me to build up reasonably comfortably to my big scene. That was where, as Eli Knox, I was going to have to face the entire football team to tell them that, because I was the new owner of the club, I now owned *them* – as individuals. I arrived that morning thinking, it'll be all right, you've got all day to get to that part. And I got the shock of my life when I was told that that was the scene of mine they wanted to shoot first.

We went for the first take. I walked as purposefully as I could onto the set to say what I had to say. I looked straight at the footballers. All 14 of those actors stared back at me expectantly. I opened my mouth and … nothing. Silence. My mind went totally blank and not a single word came out. Then, in that horrible quietness, with all eyes fixed on me, pinning me down, I heard, 'Cut. Let's go again.'

Go again? I hadn't been able to go the first time! The pressure was really on and I knew what everyone must have been thinking: Who is this Shane Lynch? He's never been to drama school. He's obviously never had an acting class in his life. Who does he think he is, waltzing in here, getting this role? We've had to fight for our jobs. He hasn't. It's all just landed in his lap.

I was sure I could see it in their eyes and I didn't like that. I had to find a way of breaking the ice.

'Look, lads,' I said, 'I've got to be honest with you, I'm petrified. I've never done anything like this in my life. I'm just asking you, please, to bear with me. If you have to go anywhere today and I hold you up I'm going to apologise now because this is the first acting job I've ever done.'

They were the best words I could have spoken – better than getting my script right first time. From that moment, the atmosphere seemed to change and all the guys were brilliant. Everyone in that room started to try and help me out, give me advice and tips on how to remember things and not lose concentration. I didn't know, but the second I forgot what I had to say, I could shout, 'Line!' and my line would come straight back at me from somebody who was sitting there with the script. Someone in the crew would always be following it as a scene was being filmed, so losing your lines wasn't a problem. You just had to listen for the prompt, stay in character and carry straight on.

From that tricky first day, my two episodes gradually grew into 28, and I ended up having a great time on that show. It was a brilliant experience for me.

I'd never planned to be an actor, any more than I'd planned to be a pop star but, oddly enough, *Dream Team* wasn't my first offer of an acting job. My agent, Dave, had already been in touch with me asking if I wanted to do pantomime.

To begin with, I laughed. 'Pantomime? Not really, no.'

I didn't know how to take him seriously. But then Dave explained it in financial terms – and I couldn't believe I could earn so much for a few weeks' hard graft. There was big money in it. So I changed my tune.

Dave also told me that pantomime would be a good way into the acting business for me. I was a known personality and that could offer another branch of work.

The way it turned out, before my first panto job came up, I had the opportunity to be in *Dream Team*, so I was able to try my hand at a serious role and then launch into some Christmas time clowning around. All financial gain aside, I found that I actually much preferred the seasonal mayhem to the dramatic stuff. I know a lot of people shun the idea of panto – it's great fun and the audiences love it, but I guess it's not the classiest or most theatrically artistic way to earn your living! But I've been offered roles over the last four years and been honoured to take part in three *Snow White and the Seven Dwarfs* and one *Cinderella*. Each season I get to work with new actors, and it's always very humbling to think that they've spent the year struggling to get jobs, yet here am I, the school kid who couldn't even read a book, being handed work because people know who I am.

I don't think of myself as a natural actor. I don't believe I'm going to Hollywood or anything like that. But you never know what's going to come your way and, for as long as I get the opportunities in panto, I fully intend to take them. It's hard work at Christmas and the schedule is pretty rigorous, but it has to be one of the best times of my year.

* * * * *

It was my friend, Ben Ofoedu, who first suggested that I should take the story of my journey to faith in Christ out to an audience. The idea scared the pants off me to begin with. *Me* talk about my life and how I came to know God? To be honest, I didn't feel that what had happened to me would be very interesting to people. I didn't think it would reach anyone. But Ben thought differently.

He set up a meeting with entertainer and author, Steve Legg, and a man called Dave Bemment who runs The Lighthouse Agency, a Christian artist organisation. Dave explained a bit more about how it would all work, how I could actually go out on the road sharing my experiences, and I suppose the more I thought about it, the more I began to feel that maybe I was wrong. Maybe I did have something to say and I should be getting out there and saying it.

My first 'gig' was at City Gates Church in Ilford, Essex. The speakers I'd seen standing up at the front in churches were proper preachers. When they got up and addressed the people gathered there, they were speaking a message. They were talking about God. They were teaching. So that's what I thought I needed to do. I didn't feel the story of how I found my way out of a truly dark time and became a Christian was interesting enough on its own. That first attempt at letting people know what had happened to me turned out to be more about me trying to deliver a good message than anything else.

It was like that a few times before I began to realise that actually, it wasn't my job to try and get up there and be a good preacher. I wasn't there to teach people. I was there to share my own personal experience of God and the changes He'd brought about in me and in my life. That's what people wanted to hear from me. That's what fed them and inspired them, not me spouting at them with some kind of make-believe authority. And the more I delved into my background, rooting out and telling the funny little anecdotes that make someone's story so personal, the more people began to connect with my life. The end result even started to become something quite powerful.

The format for each event is very relaxed, very informal. Steve Legg acts as the host, generally opening the evening with his own individual mix of comedy and magic, and then we sit down together and he interviews me. We have a chat; it's as simple as that. It has nothing to do with me preaching because I'm just there to tell my story – although the questions Steve asks me can be quite incisive, so I have to be very honest, very open about myself and the person I used to be.

I don't know what it is about getting up in front of people, but the time always races by. One minute it seems I'm psyching myself up, and the next, it's all over. And every time it's finished, I don't want to stop. Maybe I'm just one of those people it's not easy to shut up once they get going, but I always feel I could have said more, could have gone on longer. I never get tired of going over it. Being able to share the experiences I've had makes me feel incredible.

Then there's the way people respond. I open myself up to them and, afterwards, they come and open themselves up to me. They seem prepared to reveal the most intimate details of their lives, their relationships, the situations they've found themselves in. It's as if they're desperately searching for answers to their own difficulties in the solutions I've found to mine. And when they end up giving their lives to God, it's so thrilling, so touching.

I'm not a therapist. I don't really know how to answer a lot of the questions I get asked, but I can listen and I can explain how it was for me, and that helps people. For some of them, it might be the first time they've ever opened up to anyone, the first time they've been able to speak about difficulties in their lives and perhaps start to face up to them. Those are moments of real awakening, and I can't begin to describe what it's like to be involved in the beginnings of transition in someone's life. This is God's work that I'm doing with Steve. I'm so honoured to have that opportunity, so privileged. It's a part of my future plan now and I'm certainly going to go on with it.

* * * * *

And then, of course, there's Boyzone. We might have been split for quite a while, but it never really went away. A year and a half ago, I asked Ronan to come back, to re-form the band. I sent him a text saying, 'Please come back and let's do something. It'll be awesome.' Life was going really well for me and I was doing a lot of TV shows and personal appearances. But there was just something more I still wanted to do. I wanted to sort out the unfinished business I always felt there was with Boyzone and the press. As individuals, we had all broken out and pursued our own ventures of one sort or another, but there was always that collective face to us. We were still the lads from Boyzone, never seeming to establish ourselves that much as separate identities that the link wasn't always there.

Ronan replied to my text with, 'Okay, I'll look into it and see what I can do.' And, before I knew it, things started to gain a bit of momentum until they got serious enough for me to think that a Boyzone reunion could actually happen.

One of the biggest decisions we had to make was whether we should be considering our comeback with or without Louis Walsh. I felt very much that he should be involved, but that we needed to make sure we were all in agreement about everything. There was no room for wrangling in this. It was important that we all wanted the same things.

As a band, we then called a meeting with Louis to see how he felt and to work out whether he or we could find a way to push things forward. I was doing a personal appearance at a club in North Wales that weekend, so I took the ferry from Holyhead, jumped across the water and met up with the others at the Four Seasons Hotel in Dublin. There was a camera crew waiting when I arrived. It wasn't a news crew. We just wanted a record of our discussions, a kind of catalogue, I suppose, for our own benefit.

Everyone was very positive. There seemed little doubt that we'd be able to get a recording together, even go out on tour. We sat in that room and spoke about where we were as individuals, both professionally and personally, what we liked and didn't like from the past and the way Boyzone was controlled. It was clear that, if we were going to embark on this journey, we were all going to be involved in making the decisions more than we ever had been before. In those roller coaster years of the 1990s, when the band's success had escalated way beyond its tenuous beginnings trundling haphazardly around Ireland, I didn't really care what we were doing as long as we were doing something. This time around, it was going to be very, very different. We had an element of choice, a stake in the control – and we were going to make use of them.

But, in the end, this wasn't a project that was going to get off the ground quickly. After that initial contact, we spent the following six months phoning each other, talking it over, exploring the possibilities. The next time we got together for a meeting, it was with Polydor. Universal actually called us in and started discussing the new album they'd like us to release at some stage. The idea would be to revamp some of our well-known hits, with the possibility of recording a couple of new songs in amongst them to be released as singles, which sounded like a great idea. But, again, there was no immediate follow-up and everything went quiet. It seemed as if that opportunity all but disappeared.

By this time, my wedding to Sheena was getting close. Stephen Gately had already agreed to be my best man, but I'd also sent invitations to Ronan, Keith, Mikey and Louis. I had a feeling that this could be make or break. It was going to require a pretty extreme effort for them to get to the day because they all seemed to be scattered around the globe at the time. If by any chance all the lads and Louis Walsh turned up, I was fairly sure that meant they were dead serious about getting together for the new recording.

As it happened, every one of them appeared. It was brilliant. I was so excited, so looking forward to the moment when I could call Sheena 'my wife'.

We held the ceremony and celebrations at Kinnitty Castle, County Ofally in Ireland. It's a magnificent thirteenth century building set in the most beautiful grounds – everything we could have wished for in the fairytale wedding realm, and more besides. That must have been the one occasion when I had no qualms about standing up, centre stage, in front of my family and friends. I think I was the proudest man alive. We'd had a bit of a bumpy ride recently but now, here we both were, Sheena looking absolutely stunning in a perfectly fitting cream gown, its delicate skirt of lacy tiers cascading to the ground; me in an ivory coloured Marc Wallace suit offset dramatically by a deep purple shirt. It was my wedding, after all. I thought I should give the jeans and vest a rest for the day.

The lads had a whale of a time, and I took the opportunity to join them for a while to drink some Guinness, have a laugh and a joke. It was good to share a moment locked away in our own little corner. I guess that was when I knew for certain things were finally going to take off again for Boyzone.

A couple of weeks after I got back from honeymoon, I began phoning around to see how it was all moving. The record company said they still hadn't been able to find a new song for us, so I rang Louis. We'd been hanging around for long enough and now I just wanted to get the show on the road.

'Look, Louis,' I said, 'let's just announce a tour. What do you think?' Louis was more cautious. He said it was a big gamble to go out on tour with no high profile promotion going on, but I told him I was convinced we could do it. Our fans were still out there, without a doubt, and I strongly believed that if we announced a tour, they'd want to come and see us enough to go out and buy tickets. People were interested, I knew that. I was involved in a lot of different things and virtually everyone I bumped into was asking the same thing: when are you going back out on tour? Not 'if', but 'when'. True, the band had been apart for a few years, but we all knew we could still go out and deliver.

With murmurings about our reunion buzzing through the industry, unexpectedly we were offered the chance to appear on the live 2007 *Children In Need* night. *Children In Need* is the BBC's massive annual charity event raising awareness and much-needed funds for needy youngsters throughout the UK. It was such a great cause and we were delighted to take the opportunity to be a part of the live show. Not only that, but it forced us into a position where we had to move things forward. We now had something to aim for – a reason to get together and rehearse.

I suppose I never really stopped to think about what it would be like performing with the other lads again after all this time. There wasn't a moment when I questioned it: would it still work? Would we still gel together the way we used to? But if, somewhere, I did have any doubts, just a short while in the rehearsal room blew them clean away. It was as if time hadn't passed at all. Those eight years of being apart seemed to disappear and we were just the same five lads, laughing and joking, messing around with microphone stands, acting the fool. Somehow it was automatic. It was there. It was funny. But at the same time, there was freshness about it. It was like a new lease of life.

Halfway through that week, we got an offer for the tour from a promoter, John Gibbons.

'Here it is,' he said, 'do you want to go for it?'

You don't refuse something like that! We snatched it up, agreed to announce the tour on *Children In Need* and put the tickets on sale.

On the charity day itself, I was sitting in rehearsals at the BBC Television Centre in London with Sheena. She was going to be performing too, singing in the choir backing Westlife.

I remember leaning across and saying to her, 'Eight years ago, I would have been sitting here pretty drunk waiting to do a TV show like this.'

That was a moment of huge realisation for me. How far I'd come since those days, how much I'd changed. I virtually threw it all away back then. All I had was anger and disrespect and hatred towards just about everything and everyone. Now I could sit there stone cold sober. I could appreciate what was going on around me. I could soak up the excitement and the anticipation, because it was real. I wasn't drunk. I wasn't being false about anything. I was being myself – and it felt amazing.

The show itself, our first live TV appearance together for eight years, was more than a little nerve-racking. To begin with I felt fine. I wasn't too nervous. I spent some time in the dressing room, going through the routine, checking my clothes were right, looking at every last detail. This was a big night for us and I really did feel confident and comfortable with myself and what we were about to do – until two minutes before we had to walk out onto the stage.

It was our record company PA lady, Sam Wright, who came in and said it: 'When you've finished your medley, you need to walk across to Terry Wogan and Fearne Cotton and speak into the camera to the autocue.'

And that was it. It was like flicking a switch. My brain went into some kind of freeze mode and the song we'd been rehearsing shot right out of my head. Sam Wright had just told me I was going to have to read. On live TV. And I went blank. After all this time, I was still scared to death of an autocue, still thrown by the pressure of having to read something there and then, having to make sense of these strings of letters that were pretty well double Dutch to me.

From cool and collected, from 'no problem let's get on and do this gig', I dissolved into a mess. I was clutching a piece of paper with something written on it, trying to read it, trying to memorise it. I was so panic stricken, so absorbed in getting the words into my head for this interview afterwards that I almost forgot I was there to perform!

Suddenly, I heard us being announced. The music began, the audience erupted and there I was, out on stage. How I sang that medley of songs and got through the moves, I'll never know. With every step, the only thought that was in my head was, 'Autocue, autocue. Oh no, AUTOCUE!' It was a truly horrible moment but somehow I had to push myself through it.

Other than that sense of mind-scrambling terror, being involved in the *Children In Need* night was a sensational experience. The Boyzone tour dates were announced and, the next day, special VIP Saturday ticket sales opened. Then, the following Monday at about 10.30am, I got a phone call from Ronan. He was ecstatic. The first 200,000 tickets had already been sold – and that was 10 days before they were actually being released. It was the most astonishing response. Ever since we'd been throwing the reunion idea around, I knew deep down that we could do this, but I guess you wouldn't be human if there wasn't some faint shadow of a doubt niggling away at you somewhere, saying, 'What if no one wants to know?' But 200,000 tickets already? They wanted to know all right!

I'd like to think that money wasn't a major factor in Boyzone getting back together, but that's not actually very realistic. Whatever we're doing in life, money is important. We need it. And, from the point of view of the band, we obviously couldn't go out on tour without money being an issue. It's not just a matter of what the five of us are going to make out of it. There's the promoter, the manager, the arenas, the merchandise, the whole tour budget. Money is an issue because being in a band is a business and you have to get on and deal with it.

For someone like me as the man I am now, I can't believe I'm getting the chance to do this again. It's like some sort of time-travel dream, but it's coming true. I'm getting the opportunity to step back into the industry that led my life for seven years, only I'm stepping back as the person I am today, not yesterday's lost little kid who got swept along with the momentum of it all, not knowing how to steer or when to put the brakes on.

This time around we're all deeply involved in developing the show. It's a very hands-on project rather than us sitting back and letting it happen all around us. We didn't care so much about our own input when we first started out. Back then, it was more a case of, 'Okay, we've got two weeks of rehearsals so let's get in there and learn our moves.' The band and the dancers were picked for us. We just did as we were told. Now we're picking the whole team ourselves, the people who are right for us and who we feel comfortable with. We don't want to hang around on the outside. We want to be right there in it, making our own decisions, our own choices. We want to create something that's going to be perfect.

We each have our own project to work on, our own aspect of the show to bring together. Mine is the choreography – not that I'm choreographing the show, but I'm sorting out who we're going to work with, watching routines, sifting through what I like and don't like, then reporting back to the lads.

And Mark Plunkett is back with us. He's never been away in a sense because he's been working as Ronan's manager, but now he's looking after the five of us again. He's still the best tour manager in the world. When I think that he was the guy who managed to get us all up and out of our beds in the mornings all those years ago, I have nothing but admiration for the man. That must have been a task and a half. The thought of Boyzone today without Mark Plunkett isn't a thought worth having.

In amongst the work of putting the show together is the business of getting in shape for the performances. We all have personal trainers on hand to put us through our paces. This is a second chance for us and we want to be looking good and buzzing with energy. The gigs were good before, with a range of lighting and effects boosting everything that we did. But now we want them to be even better. We want to push some boundaries. We want to put on a show that's a real spectacle. We've all grown up and have so much more to offer. I don't want to stick with just the dance moves anymore. I want the opportunity to take the whole stage. I know some tricks now and some fire stunts from when I did *Cirque de Celebrité*, and I want to be able to use them.

I also have a real sense of excitement and expectation about being back on the road. There was a genuine camaraderie between us in the early years and I'm so looking forward to having that again. There were all those things that made being on stage together so special – stupid moments really like the little glances between us, the banter. But that was all part of what made you feel so alive when you were out there.

Then there was that team behind you, supporting you to its utmost – the live band, the dancers, the unbelievable parade of articulated lorries it took to deliver that £2,500,000 to £3,000,000 rig you were standing on as you reached out to thousands of screaming fans who just loved you to pieces. It's what dreams are made of. A virtually untouchable existence that so few get to embrace. Yet here I am, being given the chance to live it twice over. Only this time I'm older and I know I'm not going to be overwhelmed by it.

* * * * *

These days, I live a very simple life. I love everything I share with my wife, and I'm also happy just to spend time on my own. I can do that now because I've learned to like my own company and who I am. I don't need to be surrounded by things to find contentment. I walked that route and it didn't work.

Now I like going down to my yard. That's where my shed is, my little getaway. It's exactly like the porch back at my parents' house where I'd pass so much time as a small child with my toy cars and my made-up town. In my shed and my yard, I can tinker away with my cars and chainsaws, my JCB, my hammers and nails and screwdrivers. What I'm making, nobody knows. I don't think *I* even know. But what I've found is peace. That's my downtime.

A lot of my uptime is about making music and gigging. Irish folk music is what I've grown close to. It's ironic that I've spent the last 13 years of my life in the UK, but every year I get more Irish.

As if all that isn't enough, I still to get to drive the most amazing cars. Real thoroughbreds. It seems that every year I get a phone call from Porsche and they invite me to try out one of their 996s or 997s, or whatever brand new model they have out at the time. I even get to race in the Porsche Championships.

Dunlop have been a wonderful support to me, too, over the years. They ring up and ask if I'd like to come and race one of their cars, whatever they might be entering in a championship. It's such an incredible feeling being called up to join the team, being able to indulge that passion. I guess it's where the heart of me will always lie. Music is something I learned to love and I'm so grateful for that. But cars are something I was born to love. It's in my blood.

But the One I have to thank most for my extraordinary life is God. Without Him and without Jesus, I know I wouldn't be here anymore. I wouldn't have a life to live. I went on a journey to search for meaning and fulfilment, but I took a lot of wrong turns, bad turns that dragged me into real darkness. Then God found me. I was standing at the very edge of my existence when He took hold of my hand and saved me. I hear people ask me, 'Do you really believe that?' But it's more than belief. It's knowing the truth. That's not meant to sound like some old, hackneyed cliché. It's what my life is. My life with God.

Pure and simple.